Landscaping
with
Antique Roses

Landscaping
with
Antique Roses

Liz Druitt
G. Michael Shoup

The Taunton Press

Cover photo: Mike Shoup

First printing: February 1992
Printed in the United States of America

A FINE GARDENING Book

FINE GARDENING® is a trademark of The Taunton Press,
Inc., registered in the U.S. Patent and Trademark Office.

The Taunton Press, 63 South Main Street, Box 5506,
Newtown, CT 06470-5506

Library of Congress Cataloging-in-Publication Data

Druitt, Liz.
    Landscaping with antique roses / Liz Druitt and
G. Michael Shoup.
        p.   cm.
    Includes bibliographical references and index.
    "A Fine Gardening book" — T.p. verso.
    ISBN 0 942391-04-0
    1. Old roses. 2. Rose culture. 3. Landscape gardening.
I. Shoup, G. Michael. 11. Title
SB411.65.O55D78   1992
635.9'33372 — dc20
                                        91-30006
                                        CIP

We dedicate this book to Miss Pamela Ashworth Puryear, whose shared knowledge and passion drew each of us separately into the world of old roses.

Contents

Foreword

Our modern world is one of continual change, where old things give way to new with increasing speed. Too often, however, the new is not necessarily better than the old, especially where roses are concerned. Amid much fanfare, new cultivars are introduced each year and proclaimed to possess better attributes than their predecessors. Yet in a very short time these same roses lose their favored status and vanish downstream in the continuing flood of still newer introductions. Catalog descriptions notwithstanding, it eventually becomes clear that one thing many of these new roses lack is staying power. They don't have what it takes to go the distance with rose growers and exhibitors.

"I've tried growing roses, but they always die. I just can't grow them." When I hear this frequently repeated lament, I wish for an opportunity to take that person to visit some of the old-fashioned roses growing in a cemetery or vacant lot or along a roadside. These beauties flourish with little or no care, most certainly missing out on the daunting regimen of spraying, fertilizing and other ministrations prescribed for their modern counterparts. Perhaps after such a tour the hapless gardener would begin to see that there are other roses in the world besides modern ones. And that some of them might even be—dare I say it?—better.

When an old rose is found surviving, and often even thriving, in a neglected setting, it is likely that the rose possesses traits that make it well adapted to that area, perhaps better-than-average resistance to pests or environmental extremes. It is also likely that there once were many different varieties of roses grown there and that the rest of them died out because they lacked the ability to adapt. In effect, Mother Nature has had a hand in weeding out the ne'er-do-wells, and those that survive are the best she has to offer us for our own gardens today. If these survivors do well under abject neglect, just think how well they are likely to perform in your garden with only a minimum of care. What better roses could there be for someone who yearns to indulge a gardening passion without conflicting with a hectic work schedule?

If there is a secret to growing old roses successfully, it comes directly from this lesson taught by Mother Nature: Choose varieties appropriate for your area. Few rose books adequately emphasize this important point. Human nature being what it is, a glowing description or a gorgeous photograph will often dictate the choice of roses for a garden. I admit that I, too, have been seduced by such enthusiastic presentations. But mostly they have led to disappointment, and I have found it far better to follow the advice of the poet Alexander Pope: "Be not the first by whom the new are tried nor yet the last to lay the old aside."

The older roses are often called "heritage roses" nowadays, and it is indeed an apt term for some of them, since they have been passed down in families for several generations. More often than not, their original names have been lost, but these intrepid survivors exhibit a will to live that transcends names. It is we who need the names in order to talk about the roses and distinguish among them conveniently; all the roses need is a good place to grow and they will share their beauty with anyone willing to enjoy it. Only one person at a time can fall heir to great-grandpa's old pocket watch or grandma's brooch, but rooting cuttings of family heirloom roses gives many relatives a chance to share their ancestors' horticultural keepsakes. Spreading the plants around also ensures that the variety won't be lost in a sudden freeze or other disaster.

Filling your garden with appropriately chosen heritage roses will give you an interesting array of bloom types and growth habits, an exciting wealth of colors and fragrances, and fewer corpses after a calamitous winter. Whether the roses are grown as compact shrubs, swags, espaliers, pillars or freestanding fountains of bloom dense enough for birds to nest in, their diversity can be both astonishing and inspiring. Even the most jaded gardener is often moved to creative efforts when old roses are the subject.

Unfortunately, there is also a dark aspect to the world of heritage roses. Given the increasing redevelopment of older neighborhoods and the suburbanization of formerly rural areas, the old roses in such sites have little chance to survive on their own anymore. Unlike wild plants, most of them cannot persist indefinitely without some help from humans. No matter how resistant old roses might be to pests, diseases or climatic extremes, most cannot withstand being crowded out by fast-growing vegetation. And none can resist the onslaught of bulldozers and herbicides. Once every plant of a variety has been lost, that variety is gone forever. No amount of genetic engineering can resurrect it from extinction. Help is needed before that point is reached.

Fortunately, that help is on the way.

The Heritage Rose Foundation is a nonprofit corporation that had its origin in the realization that we can no longer take it for granted that our old roses will be preserved as they have in the past. Their future is entirely dependent on people who are willing to grow them and pass them on to future generations. The Foundation has as a primary goal the creation of gardens devoted to the permanent preservation of our surviving heritage roses. To meet this goal it needs sites in several areas of the country so that each rose variety can be grown at a location where it is well adapted and where its beauty can be displayed to best advantage. These gardens will also serve as germ-plasm repositories for tomorrow's rose breeders and reference collections for anyone interested in studying the relationships among varieties. It has been gratifying to see the amount of interest generated so far, but we have only made a beginning. Much, much more is needed.

It is my hope that this book will inspire its readers to enjoy their old rose heritage by growing a few plants firsthand and regarding them as a very special trust. Anyone who grows these roses is helping in some way to preserve them. I like to think of them as true horticultural treasures—an invaluable legacy that we have merely borrowed for a while from our grandchildren. It is both our pleasure and our responsibility to see that old roses are carried safely into the 21st century and beyond.

—Charles A. Walker, Jr.
President, Heritage Rose Foundation
Raleigh, North Carolina

Acknowledgments

Our combined experience of gardening with old roses spans, at this point, only about 16 years — not long enough to make us experts on the subject, only long enough to confirm our great enthusiasm. This book reflects our experience with these roses at the Antique Rose Emporium (our place of business) and in our own gardens at home. In order to get an expanded view of the way the roses we describe in this book behave in different microclimates, we have depended on information from heritage rose enthusiasts who garden with and collect old roses across the South and West and on both coasts. Without the help of visits to their gardens in the warm Zones (7 to 10) of the United States and access to their notes and slides, our scope would have been much more limited.

We are particularly grateful to the following people for their time, hospitality, generosity with pictures and information, and shared delight in the roses. Their help was invaluable, and any errors in this book are ours.

Our heartfelt thanks to: Mrs. Mary Anderson, Mrs. Russell M. Arundel, Glen M. Austin, Mrs. Cleo Barnwell, Dr. Robert E. Basye, William Bennett, Conrad Bering, Marion Brandes, John and Marie Butler, Carl and Lionelle Cato, John and Jeanne Crowley, Joyce Demits, S.J. Derby, Alison Duckworth, Rosie Dukes, Henry Flowers, Siegfried Hahn, Peter and Charlotte Haring, Peggy Heinsohn, Kathy Hendricks, Virginia Hopper, Suzanne Inman, Charles and Lephon Jeremias, Ruth Knopf, Deanna Krause, Mike Lowe, Greg Lowery, Malcolm Manners, Clair Martin III, Mary Rae Mattix, Louise Noisette Merrell, Inell Partin, Miss Pamela Ashworth Puryear, Tim Rhay, Phillip Robinson, Alan P. Romanczuk, William F. Safron, Jr., Stephen Scanniello, Margaret Sharpe, Paul Schmidt, Holly Shimizu, Doris C. Simpson, Randall M. Smith, George R. Stritikus, Conrad Tips, Susan Ursula, Mitzi Van Sant, Charles A. Walker, Jr., Helen Blake Watkins, Dr. William C. Welch, Ruth Westwood, Jane White, Miriam Wilkins, Elizabeth R. Winston and Joe Woodard.

And, above all, our deep gratitude to Jean Shoup and to the indispensable staff and crew of the Antique Rose Emporium.

Introduction

The beauty and hardiness of a rose called 'Mermaid' first got me hooked on antique roses nine years ago, and my fascination with and unbounded appreciation for them has been growing ever since. I didn't start out as a rose lover. To my thinking, roses were just one bush with a thousand different flowers—something for the specialist, and I was a generalist. Master's degree in horticulture in hand, I had started in the nursery business in 1976 as a grower of woody ornamentals for the landscape industry and retail centers here in central Texas. But I soon lost interest in the overused and, for this area, "exotic" plants I was working with (Ligustrum, Pittosporum, etc.) and began to look for plants native to Texas that might fill the same niche.

On our forays to hunt native plants, my staff (which numbered two at the time) and I also started finding everblooming roses surviving without any apparent care in rather desolate surroundings. This was an enigma to me, for I had never thought of roses as something that could endure the notorious extremes of the Texas climate without a gardener's care.

'Mermaid' opened my eyes. In 1982, while taking an unaccustomed route back to the nursery after a delivery, one of my co-workers chanced upon a huge rose covering a chain-link fence. He made an unauthorized "rustle," brought back flowers and cuttings, and urged me to go see it. It was surviving, indeed, performing spectacularly, in a completely neglected setting, and my first thought was that there must be a landscape niche for such a specimen. A rosarian identified it for me, but I could not find 'Mermaid' anywhere in commerce. Soon, it and the other survivors we stumbled across over the next couple of years became the foundation of the Antique Rose Emporium.

It wasn't until 1984 that we discovered that an organized group of Rose Rustlers existed in this part of Texas. (Interestingly enough, they were forming into a loose confederation of enthusiasts just about the time I first saw 'Mermaid'.) Joining the Rustlers opened up a whole world of new varieties. We went out on rustles, swapped "found" roses and talked a lot about what would and would not grow. I began to think of old roses in terms of classes and to expand our collection by seeking out more varieties in the classes I knew offered proven survivors.

At the nursery we gave our finds household names like "Old Gay Hill Red China" (for the town where we found it) or "Highway 290 Pink Buttons" (found on Highway 290) to help us remember where we found them. We got help from other rosarians, botanical gardens and literature in our struggle to identify the found roses. Many of them had once been in commerce, in some cases as many as 150 years ago, but only a few still were. As our collection grew, we created a catalog to publicize these great roses that survive in

Texas and provide an alternative to ordinary nursery shrubs. Those were our initial criteria: survival and usefulness. Then we realized that old roses are far more wonderful than that. They have a delightful fragrance, are resistant to pests and disease and exhibit a splendid diversity of form. Yes, and they flower, too. These roses fit to a T the niche I had originally had in mind for Texas native plants.

Public response to our offerings was growing so fast that it was decided to create a display garden to show off our collection in its best light and to try to get visitors hooked on the virtues of old roses. We started the display in 1985 with a cottage garden and a small formal planting. The garden has grown to cover three acres and includes perennial borders, an herb/rose garden, rock and water features and a multitude of vertical elements from tripods to swags to covered walks. We've combined Texas native plants with roses much as a pioneer gardener might have done here in the 1850s (but on a much larger scale).

Our goal has been to give credibility to these plants, and we find ourselves part of a recent upsurge of interest in antique roses. We have collected over 500 different roses, of which we market 250. The 15 acres of containerized roses in our nursery cannot keep up with demand, and we don't see any indication that it will slow down. Even large nurseries and commercial chains that previously sold only modern roses have begun to offer heirloom varieties (though their selection is quite limited).

Tastes change. Many of the rose classes that were eclipsed when the showy flowers of the Hybrid Tea were introduced are reasserting themselves. I have even heard it predicted that 30 years from now, only perhaps a dozen Hybrid Teas will still be on the market. I'm not sure the reduction will be so drastic, but change is certainly in the air. Just since 1983, I have seen antique roses that were once unknown become household words — at least among gardeners. I've watched the concerns of rose breeders change from a single-minded focus on the flower to seeing the whole plant. There is interest in breeding once again for fragrance, disease resistance and diversity of form. Indeed, some visionaries are breeding varieties that they hope will do what no rose has done before — provide everblooming groundcovers, cascade from hanging baskets and dispense with thorns and the need for spray programs. With this change in focus, I am beginning to glimpse the past in the future. Which brings me, finally, to the matter of how and why this book came about.

In 1986 Liz Druitt joined our staff as a gardener and soon advanced to become manager of the display garden. It quickly became evident that her skills as a writer could be put to good use. She expanded the information in the catalog until it became a valuable reference guide to antique roses, and her numerous articles on our roses have helped to popularize them with the gardening public. In addition, she began a monthly newsletter for our subscribers. Working together over the years, answering over and over again the same questions from customers and participants in our seminars, we realized that there was a shocking lack of information on gardening with old roses. We decided we had better combine my large portfolio of photos and years of experience as a grower with her knowledge of rose history and talent for writing to create a book that would answer these questions.

Many gardeners we talked to were facing the same intimidation I felt back when I didn't want to grow roses, and we had nowhere to send them for answers. The great majority of books on roses in general and old roses in particular certainly weren't written with our climate in mind, and none of them really made it clear how versatile these plants could be in the garden. We want our readers to understand that these are friendly plants, and we want to provide not only a view of the flower (the focus of so many other books) but also insight into how the rose performs in the garden. We base our descriptions and recommendations largely on our own experience in the somewhat harsh setting of Texas, but we've also done a lot of consulting with rosarians, growers and old rose enthusiasts in all areas of the United States where these roses grow. We hope this book will be a beginning—and one not limited to the South. A given variety may perform slightly differently for you than it does for us, depending on your climate and soil, but it won't be radically different, and you can count on it to do well as long as you're not outside its USDA Zone tolerance. Our descriptions of a variety's garden use will be useful everywhere, for that reflects the genetic character of that rose and it will not change from Zone to Zone.

We know from personal experience and from the letters and comments of many repeat customers that there is no way one can begin to appreciate the versatility of these roses until after a few seasons of working with them. Nothing we say here will substitute for the benefits of hands-on experience. But we hope to answer enough questions and generate enough enthusiasm to launch you into the world of old roses with confidence. Be aware, however, that these are captivating plants, and once taken with them you're never likely to be the same.

—*Mike Shoup*
Independence, Texas
February, 1992

1▪Designing the Garden

W e, the authors of this book, grow old roses in our own gardens. Old roses are true garden roses, which means that they perform well overall in the landscape, offering beauty in their habits of growth as well as in their flowers. They can be combined successfully with other sorts of plants to delightful effect and don't have to be grown separately and carefully protected. The difference we have found between old roses and modern roses is like the difference between a horse you love and ride and a horse you are training for the Derby. Old roses are not only beautiful but far more generally useful, and, as long as you choose varieties suitable to your climate, not very fussy in their requirements. The fact that they are easy to grow is a quality that we have learned to appreciate greatly.

It is difficult to go wrong when you plant an antique rose. We have seen roses planted in every conceivable spot in various landscapes, and we have never found ourselves saying, "Good Lord! Why there?" Roses go. They belong. And there are enough variations among them to match nearly every quirk of personal taste. There is almost nothing you can do in the garden with other plants that you can't also do with antique roses —the only exception being to grow them in heavy shade.

Creating a spectacular garden with antique roses is not difficult. Old roses offer beauty of form as well as flower, are disease resistant, require little care and are amazingly versatile. Pictured are 'Fortune's Double Yellow' on the chimney and 'Zéphirine Drouhin' on the fence. (Central Texas, late March)

Old roses comprise a very large group. The American Rose Society lists some 56 classes of roses in all, including the Grandifloras, Floribundas and Hybrid Teas with which most gardeners today are familiar. Of these, the Society has defined Old Garden Roses (with capital letters) as any varieties belonging to a class that was recognized to exist before 1867, the introduction date of the first Hybrid Tea. Thus, 'Rosette Delizy', which was introduced into commerce in 1922, is still an Old Garden Rose because it is a member of the Tea class, and Tea roses were widely grown before 1867.

We have learned not to be snobs about date or definition when we are choosing roses to grow for ourselves. Any rose, new or old, named or unknown, that thrives and performs in spite of our Texas heat, alkaline soil and sometimes irregular care is likely to win our affection. It is impossible for either of us to answer the frequently asked question of which rose is our favorite. That changes according to the day, the weather, the freshness of bloom and richness of scent at a given moment, the way the light hits the garden and which part of the garden we are looking at. There are so many kinds, all so different in flower, leaf, thorn, size, form and habit. How could we possibly ever choose just one?

The best we have been able to do is to narrow down the choice somewhat for our readers. With the idea that some gardeners will discover old roses for the first time through this book, we have tried to avoid presenting an overwhelming number of choices by limiting the discussion specifically to 80 excellent varieties in 12 classes (five of which we gather together under a general classification, "old European Roses"). All of these are Old Garden Roses in the full American Rose Society definition. Instead of trotting out the full title for every mention of them, however, we will generally refer to them in the text as "antique roses," "old roses," "old-fashioned roses" or simply as "roses."

Until quite recently, Old Garden Roses were difficult to find in commerce, having been supplanted by more modern developments like the Hybrid Teas, which present lovely flowers but are not useful landscape plants. The roses that our grandmothers and great-grandmothers grew, on the other hand, were genuine garden varieties, and included wild ramblers, charming pillar roses, tiny bushes for window boxes and big buxom shrubs for accenting a wide expanse of lawn. The flowers were widely varied, and their fragrances were often so individually potent that the older classes could be told apart by scent alone. In a study of the sense of smell whose results were published in *National Geographic* (October 1987), the scent of roses is listed as one of the most recognized fragrances in the world. How could we have forgotten that and changed our allegiance to roses that have no scent? How could gardeners have turned their backs on the varied forms of the old roses and embraced the stiff bush that produces the modern roses?

It's a question of fashion, really, and of familiarity. Each generation can be surprised and pleased by the things that were enjoyed by our grandparents but were uninteresting to our parents because they knew them too well. Sometimes it takes a little distance to re-appreciate a beauty that hasn't changed. This is as true for the garden as it is for painting styles or hem heights.

There was a time, for example, when rose lovers in general didn't much care for the high-centered flowers of the early Tea roses (parents of the Hybrid Teas), though they did appreciate their free and frequent bloom. Gardeners then were used to broad, flat flowers that opened wide and voluptuously gave out all their fragrance and beauty at once. The Teas were felt to be slow in reaching that "perfect" open state where they could be cupped in the hand and savored completely, and they were seen as stingy with their perfume while in the bud stage. Some growers recognized the potential of the new forms, however, and in a half-century tastes changed so that high-centered, slowly opening roses were all the rage.

Throughout the South, antique roses have survived in places such as this traditional swept-earth garden belonging to lifelong gardener Mrs. Addie Breedlove. None of her roses have "store-bought" names, and all are cherished. (Central Texas, April)

Not all of these antique roses flourished in perfect condition. Here in Texas, we have seen neglected old bushes, near leafless, whose flowers had shrunk, due to heat and drought, to quarter-sized miniatures of themselves. But the plants were there, and they were blooming, and with the first rains of autumn they filled out and formed full-sized buds again. It was this sort of positive behavior that led us to begin including old roses in our own gardens: the flowers bravely attempted in August and December, the foliage that came back after blackspot and grasshoppers had ravaged it, the plants that survived when we forgot to water them and flourished when we remembered. We planted them, we became fairly addicted to the incredible diversity of fragrance and the lush colors, and then we fell in love with their plastic quality in the landscape. We mean plastic in the sense of flexible, adaptable and versatile, which are qualities that many new roses just don't have.

With all of these virtues, plus the bonding of familiarity, it isn't surprising that those who did keep and value the old roses passed them around freely among friends and family members. When older roses had passed out of fashion and were no longer commercially available, it was almost entirely due to such private individuals that they were still planted and given a chance to survive.

As new varieties came into the market, out-of-style beauties were cast out of the gardens of those who could afford to change their minds about perfection. Roses are tough, though; particularly some of the older varieties that were around before much of a chemical support system was available. Banished from the gardens of the fashionable, these plants didn't just disappear like the Cheshire Cat, leaving only a smile and a memory behind. The strongest (and sweetest) were salvaged by hired gardeners for their own yards, or were kept on by sentimentalists or people out of touch with the whims of the world, or were carried off by emigrants who wanted something familiar to tie them to their old homes. Also, many old roses lingered in undisturbed sites: Roses that had once been planted along fences somehow survived after the fences had fallen down, and roses in cemeteries lingered in memory of the dead.

The warm areas of the South, as well as the areas of the East and West Coasts where the climate is between USDA Zones 7 and 10, have proven to be a fertile hunting ground for collectors of forgotten roses. Many varieties have recently been restored to commerce that survived only because they were shared among friends and family, often outliving not only their original planter but their own names. 'Granny's Rose', in all its many forms, is everywhere in this congenial climate. Some specimens have been more or less accurately re-identified through research in the old books, but even the varieties that remain foundlings have the full measure of human tradition and affection added to their very substantial basic garden value.

Landscape Design: An Overview

The key to integrating antique roses into your own garden is to stop, for the moment at least, thinking of them as "roses." That word usually brings to mind only the flower, or perhaps the stiff bush, of the Hybrid Tea. Think of them instead as plants that can provide a wide variety of forms, colors, densities and other features. The old roses have quite distinct personalities, and once you begin to know them, you will develop an instinct for where they belong in the landscape. As we grew familiar with the various classes of old roses, the word "rose" began to conjure a wide range of images in our minds, and we were soon planting them everywhere.

Landscaping a garden is similar to decorating the interior of a house. Both require advance preparation: painting, perhaps, in the one case, and most definitely soil improvement in the other. Then cherished possessions are arranged carefully so that the effect is both attractive and comfortable to use. This is not the work of a moment. A satisfying garden, like a well-decorated house, develops over time. It is an extension of the gardener's personality; a place to live with, a place to spend time in; something whose beauty can help support the soul against the worries of the outer world.

Time is an especially important element in the well-decorated garden because the plants that are the "furniture" go through great changes as it passes: growing, blooming and following the cycle of the seasons. It is only through the passage of time that you can really come to know the roses and other plants, see how they work together and how the garden as a whole pleases your taste. We have a good friend who has placed benches under rose arbors at opposite ends of her large garden; one to view the garden at its best in the morning light and the other to take advantage of the setting sun. "Most of the time I just sit there and enjoy," she says, "but I'm always noticing things that have changed on their own or that I want to change. If I didn't spend that time sitting and watching, I would miss all the action as the different combinations of plants mature through the year. I've learned more about what I like and what I really need in my garden by sitting on my benches than I have by digging and planting and studying the catalog pictures."

Our friend's observations have helped us to the conclusion that landscaping a garden is not a finite event, something you can do and be done with. It goes on all the time. You see a salmon-colored perennial that clashes with your pink China rose 'Old Blush' and decide to transplant one or the other, changing the whole personality of a bed and opening new possibilities for its design. Or you realize that a white climbing rose will carry the cool color of your white house farther out into the yard and provide visual relief from the summer heat, so you invest three or four years in training it to do just that.

There are many, many landscaping styles, and old roses will fit into most of them. We've noticed that many people don't know what they want in their gardens until they've seen something that takes their fancy (which is why we developed over three acres of display gardens at the Antique Rose Emporium). Others know precisely what they want, but are unsure how to achieve it.

It takes time for a landscape to develop. Antique roses will reward the gardener with flowers the first year, but many can take three years to reach a mature size. While you wait, a garden bench is the perfect place to sit and contemplate the changes. (Central Texas, March)

Especially when you are beginning with old roses, the simplest choice is often the most effective. Here, a single climbing rose (probably 'Madame Alfred Carrière') softens what would otherwise be a stark and uninviting entry. (Northern California, May)

It isn't our purpose to set fixed rules about how to design with old roses, but rather to give an idea of the wide range of niches these roses can fill. The rest is very much a question of personal taste. There are, however, some guidelines to bear in mind when you're thinking about creating a garden. These are elements of design to which professional landscapers have devoted extensive study. We can only touch upon them here, but they may help guide your imagination.

The main function of landscaping is to define space — open it, close it into rooms or corridors, frame it into pictures, trick the eye into thinking it larger, smaller, closer than it really is, and to do all this harmoniously. Many elements combine to make a good design, and we refer to some of the most important of them throughout this book: line, mass, balance, scale, association, density and texture.

Line is the outline of the spaces that make up a landscape. If you draw a picture of an individual plant or a plan of a garden layout, you will discover its line. It could be the arch of a willow, the curve of a path or the sweep of a hedge. Line draws the eye, and landscaping is about creating a picture that pleases the eye. Because they vary so widely in size and natural form, old roses can be used to create many different lines in the landscape, depending upon how they are trained, pruned or not pruned.

A pegged rose is a series of arched lines, a row of pillar roses is a series of vertical lines, yet each presents a certain collective **mass** as well, in the sense of the quantity of visual space each occupies. Mass in a garden can be achieved with an individual plant, a group of plants, a grove of trees, a stand of bamboo, a hedge of roses. Because density (see below) is also a component of mass, as the seasons change, so too will the balance of mass.

Given that each plant, group of plants, structure and outlined space within the garden has a certain visual weight, it is important that the weight in one part of the garden be in **balance** with the weight in another part. The balance does not have to be exactly equal to be pleasing. Vertical elements can balance each other or be balanced by horizontal elements, and vice versa. Something dense may need another element of equal density for balance, or it could be countered by something quite airy, but large. It is a matter of determining how much importance a given element has to the eye. A single plant of the tiny China rose 'Rouletii' could never balance the sprawl of a 'Mermaid' in full bloom, but a dense planting of 'Rouletii' probably could. Balance also changes as one walks through a garden, allowing plantings to display different aspects of interest.

When trying to bring a garden picture into balance, one of the elements to consider is **scale**. Plants in the landscape should have proportions that are in scale with whatever they are near—a structure, a tree, a pool or other plantings. A giant hedge, for example, would dwarf a cottage, and a low foundation planting could look foolish on a three-story house. We have heard a number of tales of woe from people who planted large climbing roses in small gardens without taking the question of scale into consideration.

When you're choosing the plants to put together within a given, defined space, there are additional design elements to consider. Deciding whether plants close to one another mix well leads you to the question of **association**. Do the plants contrast, do they blend together well or do they clash? The object is to avoid discord between individual plants and between landscape elements as a whole. For example, a specimen rose bush might not work well in close association with a specimen camellia because they can be too much alike to complement one another, whereas a pillar rose in the sun might be beautifully accented by a pillar of ivy in a nearby shaded area.

The **density** of individual plants influences the visual balance of the garden as well. Every plant (and structure) has visual density; some "feel" light, others seem heavy. Roses, like most deciduous plants, change throughout the year. They can look particularly massive in full bloom, less so when in leaf and quite airy in winter. In our gardens, different classes of roses are associated with different densities. The Tea roses, for example, are heavily foliaged and have much more visual weight than do the climbing Noisettes, which have a graceful feminine quality. Yet in terms of actual mass, the Noisettes are far larger plants.

The **texture** of a plant is the sum of all its visual characteristics—leaf size, density of foliage, the line of the branches, size of the flowers. It is the pattern of the plant, and like a pattern on cloth, it can clash with or complement other patterns. For example, a rose with delicate but very thorny branches like 'Fortune's Double Yellow' would make a nicely patterned picture next to a patch of bamboo or a glossy, fat magnolia tree, but would lose its special interest if combined with another thorny climber.

Especially for beginners with antique roses, there is one general design principle that we stress again and again: Remember that it is your own taste that you are pleasing, and the more time you spend getting to know that taste and observing your own garden, the happier you will be with the landscape you create. Start slowly and simply, and let the garden grow as your knowledge does.

Guidelines for Integrating Old Roses into the Garden

Incorporating antique roses into an existing garden or using them as elements in a new landscape is not difficult. As we said at the beginning of this chapter, roses go. That doesn't mean, however, that there aren't guidelines that will make it easier for you to get the results you want. This is true of cultural requirements as well as design requirements. We have adjusted our own garden plans year after year to correct some of the problems caused by our initial inexperience. Color combinations have been improved and refined; established plants have been relocated because we miscalculated their eventual size; trellises have been rebuilt because we misjudged the weight of a mature climber. Old roses are tough, and they have generally survived our mistakes, but it would have been nice to have avoided the mistakes in the first place.

Choosing planting sites:
Basic cultural requirements

We have learned from experience that the better start a rose plant has when first put in the ground, the healthier it will be and the more trouble-free pleasure it will give you. There are very few limits to the places an antique rose can be planted. If you walk around your property with the basic requirements in mind, you'll be surprised at how many options you've got. What follows is a general overview of the conditions that most old roses prefer. If you are worried about site problems specific to your area (hardpan, acid soil), contact the local Agricultural Extension agent and/or local rosarians for more detailed advice. The important point is that antique roses are easy to grow. Add them to flower beds, display them around the yard, use them as a privacy screen, drape them along your porch railings and enjoy them thoroughly.

How much sun? First and foremost, roses like a lot of sunshine and fresh air. This can mean anything from total burning exposure on a windswept hillside (many of our roses, especially the Chinas and Teas, thrive on that) to six or more hours of direct sun and some discernible air movement. Roses will not perform very well in heavy shade. They will tend to grow long, spindly canes with few leaves and fewer flowers, and they are more subject to attack by insects and diseases. Being trapped in oversheltered pockets of stagnant air also seems to weaken them, making them particularly subject to fungus problems. Choosing the right location in the beginning will prevent many potential problems.

East side, west side? There are differing opinions about the point of the compass most favorable to a rose garden. The prevailing idea is that planting on the sunny, protected south side will shelter the more tender roses, but we haven't found this to be automatically true. In a mild freeze, a protective southern exposure can be beneficial. In a hard freeze, roses that have already been exposed to the colder temperatures on the northern side may have hardened off gradually and thus will be less damaged. We have found that an eastern exposure is

For maximum health, antique roses need a site with six or more hours of full sun each day and rich, well-drained soil. The designers of this garden of old and modern roses at the Korbel Winery in Guerneville, California, were careful to plan plenty of room for the mature size of the Noisette climber 'Lamarque', which plays a strong role visually even when out of bloom. (Northern California, May)

particularly advantageous in that it allows the roses to have the benefit of sun all morning while protecting their flowers from the burning light of the Texas afternoon sun. In general, if your chosen spot has the necessary six or more hours of direct sunlight, your old roses will probably be able to cope with most weather situations (provided, of course, that you've chosen a variety suited to your Zone).

Soil quality   Another consideration is the condition of the soil. It doesn't matter whether it is acid or a little alkaline, as long as it is not too extreme in either direction. Antique roses have a pH preference of roughly 5 to 8. It also doesn't matter much whether you have dense clay or sandy soil, because the texture of the dirt can be improved as you prepare the area for planting (see pp. 74-75). Proper drainage is a much more important concern. Old roses are tough and can tolerate a wide range of conditions, but with the single exception of the 'Swamp Rose', *Rosa palustris*, they don't like to have their roots in soggy soil. Good drainage is critical to

the health of old roses. That waterlogged hollow at the bottom of your property can no doubt be improved with French drains and built-up beds, but you might want to leave it as a very last resort.

Evaluating the competition   Another factor to consider when choosing sites for your roses is possible root competition from large, established trees and shrubs. Aside from the shade problem, it's not a good idea to plant most young rose bushes under large trees because they will have a tough time fighting the massive root network for the nutrients they need to get established. Vigorous climbing roses

The key to landscaping with old roses is to see their inherent garden form in addition to their flowers. Left: The bush of Rosa eglanteria ('Eglantine') echoes the form of the hills behind it and provides a graceful accent. (Northern California, May) Above: The mature bush of R. moschata ('Musk Rose') has a chunky habit and beautiful foliage. When out of flower, it holds its own as well as any ornamental bush, and it captures every eye when in bloom. (Virginia, May)

can be an exception to this rule. If you can dig a large enough hole to let them spread out their roots without too much initial competition, they'll grow their canes through the branches and up to the light fairly quickly. If you feel that you really must plant bush roses very near a big tree, plant them on its south side for maximum sun and plan to give them extra water and nutrients to help balance what will be taken by the tree roots.

Planting near buildings and walls Roses make excellent foundation plantings and gorgeous hedges, but choose a site that has enough space to plant them at least 2 ft. away from any wall. For one thing, the concrete foundations of a house or garage draw water away from the surrounding soil, and this could

quickly stress the roses if they aren't given extra rations. But allowing adequate space is also a good idea because it enables the rose to develop a more balanced and stable root system and a more attractive bush. Even climbers should be planted at least 2 ft. from a foundation or wall. They are easily trained back against the building and will grow better with the reduced water stress. When planting close to a building you should also take into account the drip line from the roof (if there are no gutters) and avoid planting roses directly under its impact.

Sizing the rose to the site

A final reminder about scale: When you're deciding where to plant old roses, remember that they will grow. One of the most common mistakes people make with old roses is not sizing them properly for their designated site. Hybrid Teas, the roses most people are familiar with, are generally restrained in their growth habit. Old roses, on the other hand, range in size from 12 in. to over 40 ft. tall. Unless they are stunted for some reason, they will grow to the size their genes dictate, and trying to prune a 15-ft. climber so it fits on a small trellis will be frustrating for the gardener and counterproductive for the rose.

When deciding which rose to plant where, it's useful to know the rose's mature size. The Rose Use Chart (pp. 97-101) and the individual Encyclopedia entries (pp. 111-217) provide this information for the 80 varieties we discuss. A good nursery catalog should do so as well. If it says a bush will be 6 ft. by 6 ft., that means that eventually it will touch everything 3 ft. out from its base. Young roses can seem puny when first planted, and the tendency is to think that more are going to be needed to fill the space. But overplanting only ruins an otherwise effective design, and in two or three years you'll have to remove every other bush or dig out the climbers that ate the porch. We cannot even begin to count the number of times people have asked us how to move 'Mermaid'.

The plant form as a landscape element

Once you've determined which parts of your garden are culturally suited for old roses, the next step is to make them part of a successful design. And remember, the key is to see them not only as bearers of flowers, but also as plants in their own right. Even when not in flower, old roses provide line, mass, texture and density just as surely as any other garden plant. Old Garden Roses also provide a variety of sizes and forms that can be at home in almost every style of garden.

The genes of a rose dictate the form the plant has. If you fall in love with the flower of a particular variety, you should also like, or at least be willing to live with, its form. The landscape photographs in the Encyclopedia were chosen to give an idea of the differences in form for different classes and varieties.

Rose classes:
Different personalities in the garden

Each of the different Old Garden Rose classes has a distinct "personality," so if we're looking for a rose to fit a certain niche, we first decide which classes have suitable qualities and then we look within those classes at the varieties. The entries in our Encyclopedia are organized by class, and we go into detail there on their class characteristics and landscape strengths. We strongly suggest that you read through the Encyclopedia to get a thorough feeling for the classes before making final decisions about which antique roses to use in your own garden.

Species roses, widely varied in form, are those that grow in the wild, and they will bring this untamed quality to the garden. Never subjected to a breeding program, their beauty and grace are inherent and their spring display is overwhelming. Hybrid Multifloras are very near to the species roses in their capacity for display, and those that are closest to *R. multiflora* retain the wild rambling habit that can be so attractive.

China roses can be show-stoppers, but they are also the most reliable workhorses of the rose garden. Robust, leafy shrubs that produce flowers reliably over a long season, Chinas can be counted on to provide mass and color. Teas, on the other hand, can take center stage and will outshine nearly every other class with their spring and fall flower show. Similar to the Chinas in both size and shape, they are more stately in appearance, almost self-important.

The softly draping Noisettes are as feminine as the Chinas and Teas are masculine. They have a vine-like quality and provide a look of romance and fantasy— perhaps because they fairly drip with nodding flowers when in bloom. Many of the oldest once-blooming classes are encompassed by the designation "old European roses." These important roses are some of the most enticing when in bloom, and the classic can be lush and colorful in the garden. Any connoisseur of fragrance and history in roses will find them indispensable.

The Bourbons are a cut above even the Teas in weight and quality of bloom, and their otherwise rather ungainly canes make them ideal for pegging (see pp. 53-57) or use as an accent at the back of a border. Their flowers and scent make them worth the little extra trouble to integrate them into your design. Bother balanced by value is even more true of the Hybrid Perpetuals, the first class really to show the heavy hand of breeding for flower over form. These somewhat angular roses integrate well with modern roses in form and retain the most spectacular qualities of old rose flowers, so they can find a place in a broad range of garden styles.

Designing with color

The background of nearly every garden is an array of green. The ability to work with all the shades and textures of leaves and combine them with the shades and textures of flowers marks a successful gardener. There are rules about using color in the landscape (something white looks bigger than it is, something red looks closer than it is), and they can be found in several other books. We would rather not lay down rules, for we have too often seen the happy result of breaking them; but if you are just starting out with old roses, some guidelines might help.

The flowers of Old Garden Roses are most often in shades of pink, purple, crimson, cream, buff and white. There are reds as well, but the overtones are blue-magenta and they blend well with their cousins. Yellows are unusual, but there are a few. Definitely lacking are the orange and orange red tones so prevalent in Hybrid Teas. When combining old roses with other flowering plants, it's best to stay within the range of pastels. In our gardens, we have mixed the old roses with Texas natives and other perennials and annuals that flower in shades of blue, crimson, pink and white. Flowers with hard colors, we've found, don't really work well with most Old Garden Roses.

Ignoring the virtues of white flowers can also be a mistake. There seems to be a prejudice against white roses, and people reject them because they "want some color in the garden." Yet we have seen nothing more impressive than the way white roses can glow and take on a life of their own when the light begins to fade. In harsh sunlight, whites tend to wash out, as they can also do against a background of bright sky. But we are not usually out in our gardens in the heat of the day, and it is the pale roses that make the garden come alive at dusk when most other colors, especially the reds, fade into darkness.

Timing the bloom

The color in a garden of old roses is not static. Some varieties bloom only once a year, others bloom twice and still others may have blossoms as long as the weather stays warm enough. The Rose Use Chart (pp. 97-101) and the Encyclopedia entries indicate when and how often a given variety will bloom in the Zones listed, and you can use this information to create a garden where an antique rose will almost always be in flower.

Even if you plant only roses that bloom once a year, it is possible to have as many as two or three months of spectacular show. For us in Zone 8, some of the earliest roses are 'Lady Banks' Rose' (*R. banksiae banksiae*), 'Cherokee Rose' (*R. laevigata*) and 'Fortune's Double Yellow', which can flower in late February or early March. The latest to begin blooming are 'Prairie Rose' (*R. setigera*) and

The penstemons, dianthus and other perennials at our display gardens were chosen to complement the soft pastels of Old Garden Roses. The color, form and texture of every plant's leaves were also considered as part of the overall design, since both the roses and perennials are sometimes out of flower. (Central Texas, April)

'Veilchenblau', which wait until May, and the 'Musk Rose' (R. moschata), which flowers in late May or in June. By planning for the natural bloom times, you can create a wonderful interplay of color as roses come into and go out of flower. (A hard, late freeze can compress the bloom sequence in some years, holding back the early bloomers, although the mid-season to late varieties will flower on schedule.)

We have noticed a very strong public prejudice in favor of the remontant roses—those that bloom more often than once a year. People have come to think of rose plants as merely something to keep the rose flowers up off the ground, and so it is no surprise that there is a preference for varieties that appear to bloom more. The spring display of a once-blooming rose is something we look forward to all year. Yet we don't mind when it is over, for the display can be so intense that more would be too much of a good thing. When the once-blooming roses are resting they are still very much an integral part of the garden; their unique form maintains their "presence" and provides a backdrop for plants that are in flower.

Fragrance

Perhaps more so than with any other garden plant, roses are associated with fragrance, and old roses have it in abundance. People often request specific roses from us based solely on the memory of their fragrance. We've had customers open up and become our instant friends simply because we handed them a rose to smell. The response is more than just to the pleasure of the scent; it seems to reach deeply into human emotions.

The importance of fragrance to the rose itself is biological. Scent attracts the appropriate insects for pollination and ensures survival of the species. The all-encompassing term "rose scent" covers myriad individual variations in perfume. Each class, particularly of the older roses, seems to have a characteristic perfume that may vary amongst individual members but generally differentiates the members of one class from the members of another. The blurring and blending of perfumes occurs through crossbreeding, so the more mixed the rose's ancestry, the less easy it is to place it in a class by smell alone. It is quite possible to distinguish the sharp, fruity scent of the Chinas from the cool, dry fragrance of the Teas or the rich, lemony perfume of Damasks, but once you get into Hybrid Perpetuals, which are a blend of those classes and more, the fragrance is wonderful, but the distinctions are less clear. In addition to variations in scent, some varieties simply have a larger quantity of oils in their petals and therefore have more fragrance. The classic example is the semidouble varieties of Damask roses that are the basis of the rose-perfume industry.

Not everyone can smell every fragrance, and the perception of scent varies from person to person more than you might think. Of the two authors of this book, one finds the rich, flowery perfume of the Bourbon roses to be the epitome of olfactory delight and is little affected by the scent of Chinas. The other was initially seduced into the world of antique roses by the almost edible raspberry fragrance of the China rose 'Cramoisi Supérieur'.

Choosing roses on the basis of fragrance is a subjective decision based on the nuances of scent that are personally appealing, so planning a rose garden for scent is not the same as designing one for beauty of form, though amongst old roses the two qualities are frequently entangled. There are so many richly fragrant old roses in various forms that there's no reason they can't also be part of a successful visual design. Simply bear in mind that you must match the mature size of the plant with the size of its niche in the garden and plan to place the roses where you can best get the effect of their perfume — by a bench, along a walk, framing a door or window, over an arbor at the garden gate. The Rose Use Chart on pp. 97-101 and the Encyclopedia entries offer basic information on fragrance, but we suggest you smell the roses yourself, if possible, before you choose.

Seasonal changes

If you plan to use a very large number of antique roses in your garden, remember that in all but the warmest Zones these are deciduous plants. After a heavy freeze, your luxurious landscape may begin to look bare. Winter is not the time of greatest beauty in the rose world, but if you have planted with the underlying form of the rose in mind you will still have an interesting landscape. The naked rose canes, reduced to stark and essential lines, have an architectural quality that is both enduring and serene. We actually like the restful look of dormancy, and weaknesses or strengths in the design will show up while we are not distracted by color and texture. In contemplating the bones of the garden, we begin to reflect on what we may want to change.

In most Zones roses are deciduous, so a garden full of antique roses will not always be lush and green. This is our Zone 8 display garden after an unusually hard freeze. Two weeks earlier, everything was in leaf, with scattered flowers. Most landscapes will have more winter interest in the form of evergreens and large trees, but nonetheless, dormancy should be considered as an element of the garden's design. (Central Texas, January)

If you design with the bare-bones form of the rose in mind, it will be an interesting feature in the garden even in deep winter. This R. palustris ('Swamp Rose'), perhaps the most graceful of all roses, is even more exquisite after an ice storm than it is in full bloom. (Central Texas, December)

Some antique roses hold their leaves much longer than others and, in areas that don't freeze, they can even be evergreen. Here in the South, we are blessed with blooming Tea and China roses in December and January if the weather remains clement, but they are the first to be damaged by a freeze because they don't automatically go dormant. Hardier classes like the old European roses, Hybrid Multifloras and, to a degree, the Hybrid Perpetuals sense the coming of winter and drop their leaves and store their energy in the roots to prepare for the onslaught of severe cold. A few of the 80 varieties we discuss in the Encyclopedia will reward the gardener with some fall color before going bare, among them the 'Swamp Rose' (*R. palustris*), 'Prairie Rose' (*R. setigera*), 'Eglantine' (*R. eglanteria*) and 'Madame Plantier'. For the rest, fall color is an unpredictable factor, and we wouldn't recommend counting on it as a part of your garden design.

A more reliable fall and winter show is put on by those varieties that produce a colorful display of hips. Rose hips can vary greatly in size (from smaller than a pea to over 1 in. long), shape (round to urn-shaped to oval) and color (light orange through red to almost black). The Rose Use Chart (pp. 97-101) indicates whether a given variety forms enough hips to make them worth considering as part of your garden design. Chapter 4 contains information on how to ensure a good display of hips by not pruning away the spent autumn flowers (see p. 91).

Many antique roses produce a display of hips, which can provide garden color and interest in fall and winter. The hips vary in color and shape from variety to variety. At right are the softly prickly hips of R. cglanteria; *above are the unique hips of the 'Macartney Rose' (*R. bracteata*), an invasive parent of 'Mermaid' that was once used throughout Texas as fencing. (Central Texas, August)*

2 ■ Integrating Roses into the Landscape

We human beings have an instinct for beauty and are always trying to change our surroundings to suit our idea of it. One thing most of us agree upon is that hard lines and sharp angles are uncomfortable to look at. Inside our houses we drape curtains around rectangular windows and move furniture and pictures to draw the eye away from the basic boxy shape of most rooms. Outside in the garden, almost everyone makes some sort of effort to hide the abrupt angle where their house meets the earth, even if a foundation planting of evergreen shrubs is the limit of their creativity. (Texas rosarians Margaret Sharpe and Pam Puryear put it best when they coined the phrase "moustache landscaping" to describe this look.) Straight lines and angles can be beautiful, but there are very few of them in nature. They are easier for us to appreciate if they are broken with some kind of softening influence; interrupted with more natural, irregular forms.

Pillars spaced evenly along a path support climbers that create the effect of an enclosed walkway. The 8-ft. tall posts support 'Zéphirine Drouhin' (foreground), 'Sombreuil' (white), 'Souvenir de Madame Léonie Viennot' (creamy pink) and 'Ards Rover' (red). A single wire supporting extra-long canes goes from the top of each post to an arbor just out of view. (Central Texas, April)

Left: This is a classic "moustache" landscape, pleasant but one-dimensional. With a graceful, curved porch and impressive columns, this house is a natural candidate for more rewarding landscaping with old roses. Above: Just one well-placed blooming rose bush can make a big difference in the visual appeal of even a plain house. Few other specimen plants could do what the China rose 'Old Blush' does for this house nine or ten months a year. (Central Texas, April)

The older roses, roses that were selected for the form of the bush as well as for their fragrant flowers, are marvelously easy to use for this sort of basic improvement. Even one carefully chosen rose bush planted near the house or against a surrounding wall can make an amazing difference in the visual appeal of your property. One climbing rose trained to drape along a chain-link fence will change it over time from a barren, unattractive necessity into an acceptable support for luxurious beauty.

One reason old roses are such a benefit in the garden is that they are multidimensional, improving a location not only with their attractions of form but also through the color, shape and fragrance of their flowers. When you add a rose to a landscape you are adding a seductive element that will entice you not only to look at your garden but also to go out and be in it. The more roses you have, of course, the stronger the attraction.

A single rose, in this case the climber 'Tausendschön', can soften the sharp architectural angles of a building at the same time that it accents the beauty of chosen features, such as this door. (New York, June)

When you are cautiously entering the world of old roses and want to start with just a bush or two, there are several ways you can use them to get the most out of their fine qualities. If your main desire is to improve the appearance of your house, try to place the rose where it will fulfill that purpose, but also where you will pass close to it frequently. You don't want to crowd the rose into a cramped or shady space, because roses need sun and room for their roots to expand. You should also avoid planting under the drip line of the roof. These are the only real limitations.

A rose bush planted between the house and the sidewalk or at a corner that gets regular foot traffic will both decorate the house and let you appreciate the flowers at close range. The old Tea roses are ideal for this purpose. Their handsome vase-shaped form, abundant healthy foliage and minimal care requirements make them an excellent choice for a beginner with old roses. Also, they bloom for nine or ten months in our warm southern climate, giving a first-time rose grower maximum reward for minimum effort. The constantly blooming China roses, with their vigor and vivid crimson and pink flowers, are equally attractive and easy to grow. They also vary in size more than the Teas, so they can more easily be matched to a specific niche.

A transition from drabness to beauty: A young plant of 'Seven Sisters' begins to cover a chain-link fence. (Central Texas, April)

Bush roses are probably the easiest for a beginner to grow because they require no training, just the simple care and infrequent trimming described in Chapter 4. Climbing roses should not be seen as intimidating, however. They need a little more attention to keep them attractively trained, but it is not difficult to work with them, and they add a wonderful new dimension to the garden. Climbing roses are dealt with in detail later in this chapter, and we encourage gardeners who are interested in old roses to make use of them as much as possible. The repeat-blooming varieties such as climbing Chinas and Teas and Noisettes are remarkably effective even when only a single plant is used on a wall or fence.

Roses and Companions: Variations on the Perennial Border

After you have experimented for a while with one or two bushes of antique roses and learned to depend upon their beauty and easy care, you may want to expand your garden ideas. Old roses are not snobbish or delicate about their companions; they will grow happily alone, with other varieties of roses or with a great mixture of other plants. This leaves the possibilities for experiment wide open. You can add more roses to existing flower beds or design completely new plantings with roses as a focus. This is where your personal ideas and good taste become most important in creating your garden fantasies.

The luxurious English perennial border with roses and a multitude of other flowering plants mixed in a long, semiformal bed is a common fantasy of many gardeners. An entire border is too much garden for most yards, but the principles behind it can be applied to a variety of situations. Tall plants at the back, middle-height plants in the middle of the bed and low-growing plants in the front is the basic rule of thumb. This arrangement allows all the plants to be seen and provides a soft transition from the flat grass of a lawn to the taller mounds of flowers and foliage.

To create a bed of this sort, a rose bush (or several, if the space is large) can be used as the backbone or focal point of the planting, with a mixture of perennials of varying heights and complementary colors filling in around it. We find that the blues, pinks and reds of the salvias (*Salvia* spp.) go excellently with the soft, rich colors of antique roses, as do Shasta daisies (*Chrysanthemum maxima*), pale blue plumbago (*Plumbago auriculata*) and certain silver-grey plants like lamb's-ears (*Stachys byzantina*) and artemisia (*Artemisia arborescens*). Violets, strawberries and all sorts of herbs like thyme and rosemary make good old rose companions, and lilies and irises offer handsome foliage contrasts. In order not to be overwhelmed with choices, it's helpful to visit gardens in your area and talk to local nurserymen about what is available and what is practical and will grow well for you; then limit your choices to just a few of the best selections. Over time, you will develop your own opinion about what works and what doesn't, and there is no law against changing your mind and rearranging the whole bed as its possibilities become apparent.

We recommend starting fairly small, and placing your bed of roses and perennials as you would place a rose bush growing by itself. This kind of bed, with its natural mounding forms and rich colors, is just as effective as the specimen plant in softening overly stark lines and angles. There is a natural tendency to place a flower bed in the dead center of the yard, but this wastes a lot of its potential as a landscape accent. Fragrant roses and their companion plants are very pleasant to be around, and if you place them as carefully as you would arrange furniture in a room, you will not only improve the appearance of the various structures on your property (house, fence, shed, and so on), but also create new "living spaces" for yourself. Gently curving the edges of the bed helps to create a welcoming look and allows for the inclusion of seating arrangements. Benches of stone or rustic wood are easy to set up, or if your yard is a bit more formal, wrought iron may add the perfect finishing touch.

The important point is to plant your roses where you can easily interact with them. Old roses cry out to be looked at and to have their perfume inhaled and their colors appreciated. They can create a garden atmosphere of warmth and invitation that is difficult to resist.

Some reliable choices for a first old rose
'Old Blush'
'Duchesse de Brabant'
'Hermosa'
'Souvenir de la Malmaison'
'Cramoisi Supérieur'
'Marie van Houtte'
'Marquise Boccella'
"Maggie"

The Vertical Garden: Climbers and Their Supports

Once you have gotten seriously interested in antique roses, you cannot help but want to include a number of climbing varieties in your collection. Climbing roses can transform an uninspired landscape into something wonderful, yet the vertical is the most under-used element in the modern garden.

Climbing roses come in all sizes, and nearly every class of roses has some climbing members. Many of the wild, or species, roses are climbers because this trait helps them work their way up through trees for a share of the sun. The existence of rose prickles can be blamed on these enterprising specimens: Prickles are a much more effective tool for catching and holding among tree limbs than they are for protecting the plant against browsing animals. Since many species that grow in open areas and have a shrubbier form (such as *Rosa gallica*) also have prickles, there's a possibility that roses developed from a common climbing ancestor.

*The vertical line is often forgotten when designing a garden, yet it adds
a vital dimension. Climbing roses draw the eye upward and increase the
visual size of the garden. They also create the sensation of being
surrounded by flowers, in this case, by the flowers of 'Madame Alfred
Carriere'. (England, June)*

Whichever came first, the climber or the shrub, roses sport and mutate back and forth freely between the two forms. This has created such a diversity of available climbers that one can be found to enhance nearly any garden space. It also means that a little thought must go into the selection of a climber, as it is possible to choose one that is too large or too small to meet your needs. The Rose Use Chart on pp. 97-101 gives the relative sizes of the varieties we discuss. Beyond that, arranging a climbing rose in a designated space is a matter of training, limited only by your own creativity.

In 19th-century Victorian gardens, rose-covered pillars, tripods, gazebos, arbors and swags of rope or chain between posts were *de rigueur* features of the well-dressed landscape. The element of height had been discovered, or rediscovered, and it became an important consideration in garden design. The vertical element is important to us as well, and not just as a fashionable trend.

When roses are trained upward they carry the eye with them, expanding the dimensions of the garden into multiple levels and increasing the feeling of being sensually surrounded by flowers. By the use of climbing roses, any structure, from a functional house to purely decorative pillars and tripods, becomes a part of the garden. By the inclusion of these vertical structures, the garden becomes more and more an extension of your living space, an environment in which you actively wish to spend time, whether in entertaining or in solitary musing.

Once you have begun to grow climbing roses, it becomes hard to feel comfortable in a one-dimensional garden. The vertical has enormous impact, yet it is somehow familiar and satisfying, visually right. If you are bored in your landscape, if it feels dull and unoriginal, vertical expansion may be the missing ingredient. Even if you are a moderate and cautious gardener, you won't want to miss the opportunities for beauty that climbing roses provide. For a little investment of time and training, a climbing rose can give more satisfaction than almost any other plant in the landscape.

Fastening rose canes to their supports

Climbing roses need to be trained up on something in order to display themselves properly, so a discussion of climbers necessarily includes a discussion of rose supports. The simplest way to support a climbing rose is to drape it over or train it along an existing structure. (Chain-link fence, plebeian as it is, offers plenty of opportunity for training since there are so many points to which a rose can be tied.) On a fence, or any other support, you want to train the rose canes to each side as much as possible. When a cane lies horizontal, the change in nutrient flow and the more even distribution of sunlight cause new growth to appear at every bud joint instead of just on the end of the cane. Thus, the more nearly horizontal you get each cane, the more flowers you are likely to see.

We fasten our roses to their supports with low-visibility green plastic stretch-ties. It's easy to snap just the length you need from the roll, and the stretchiness means that the tie won't choke off and kill the rose cane as the cane grows. These ties tend to disintegrate after a year or two exposed to the weather, but by that time they've usually been replaced as we've groomed and retrained the rose, or the cane is so established in its position that a fastener is no longer needed. Other gardeners use other products—paper-covered twist-ties and natural raffia string are the most common—but these need to be monitored and loosened as the canes increase in thickness. String is usually tied fairly loosely because it has to be cut to be replaced. Tying string in a figure eight, with the crossed portion between the cane and the structure, will help keep the surface of the cane from chafing as it moves in the wind.

The simplest way to support a climbing rose is to drape it over a fence, tying the canes in place. Here, 'Fortuniana' is combined with a red climber to echo the colors of the house trim and give a decorative look to the picket fence. (Central Texas, April)

Fastening canes to openwork

It may seem simpler just to weave rose canes through a fence or trellis than to go to the bother of fastening them with ties. This can certainly be done to great visual effect on any kind of support as long as it has sufficient openings. There are several drawbacks, however, one of which is that you must have great patience. The canes have to be bent carefully so they won't break; canes that are too young and succulent or too stiff with cold will snap right off. Also, most roses are thorny, and they are guaranteed to sink a fair number of thorns into you before the training is over. Roses don't have clinging tendrils or invasive rootlets, but their thorns (or more properly, prickles) were probably developed to help them catch and hold in the branches of trees as they flung themselves upward in search of vital sunlight. These thorns will catch and hold on everything in sight, and you are likely to be irritable and slightly bloody if you try to do fine weaving, even if you wear sensible gloves.

Another drawback to weaving a rose in and out of tight spaces is that if a cane dies and you have to unweave it to get the brittle and unattractive dead wood out, you will curse yourself for having been so artistic. It is easier to tie the longest canes against one side or the other of the support and work the shorter lateral canes very loosely through them. Flowers will poke through both sides anyway, so you won't lose the effect either way.

Fastening canes to solid surfaces

If you have a solid surface such as a brick wall, chimney or wooden privacy fence, the training methods to get the rose up and properly displayed are slightly different. We find U-shaped fencing staples invaluable as tie-off points that can be driven into any wooden surface. They can also be hammered into the crevices between bricks or stones and mortar. This is probably not good for the mortar, but the effect with the rose is very pleasing. These tie-off points are invisible under the foliage. We have trained 'Fortune's Double Yellow' this way on a stone building at our display gardens, and it looks as if it is growing quite naturally up the wall (see the photo on p. 4).

Climbing roses such as this Noisette, 'Madame Alfred Carrière', can be used to express personal style. This sturdy trellis at the Governor's Mansion in Austin, Texas, is one option of training. (Central Texas, March)

Trellising on walls

It is a natural step to move from decorating fences and walls in the garden to decorating the actual walls of your house with roses, but there are two things to bear in mind if you decide to do so. First, a painted wall will provide a color contrast with the flowers of the rose, and, second, the wall will eventually have to be repainted. Instead of fastening the climbing rose directly to a painted wall, it's a good idea to put up a trellis of some kind to support it, either leaving room between the trellis and wall for the paintbrush or planning to take the rose down periodically.

The lightweight, fan-shaped trellises sold in most garden stores are not a good choice for old roses. Any vigorous old climbing rose will overwhelm them in the first season of growth, for a mature climber is a very weighty affair. The simplest and quickest trellis to put up and take down is made of wire, as shown in the drawing at right. To make such a trellis, drive an X made of two pieces of concrete reinforcing bar (rebar) securely into the ground about halfway between the spot where the rose will be planted and the foundation of the wall. (Remember that the rose should be at least 2 ft. from the foundation and not under the drip line.) Twist 8 to 12 long strands of heavy flexible wire at one end around the waist of the X, fan them out evenly and then secure them with nails or eyebolts to sturdy wood (the fascia, rafters or top plate) at the top of the wall. Even though the wires act as a support for

A Wire Trellis for Climbing Roses

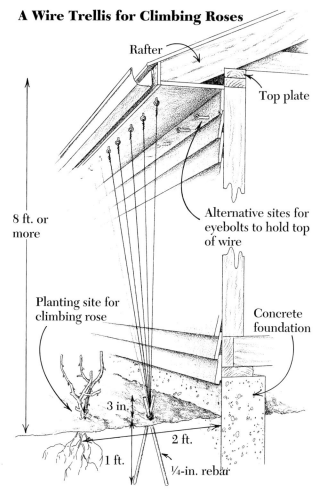

To make a simple, fan-shaped wire trellis, wrap one end of 8 to 12 strands of 12-gauge wire securely around the waist of the rebar X and attach the other end of each strand to one of the eyebolts (or nails) you have spaced out evenly along the top line of the trellis. The eyebolts should be securely fastened to sturdy wood at the top of the wall.

These climbing roses are trained on fan-shaped wire trellises that not only display them, but also create "walls" for the arbor, which will be solidly covered with flowers by April. (Central Texas, February)

The two climbing 'Old Blush' roses on sturdy wooden trellises at the Admiral Nimitz Museum in Fredericksburg, Texas, are only one year old. (Central Texas, March)

the climber and don't take much actual weight, they need to be securely fastened top and bottom. They should also be at least 2 in. out from the wall so that there will be air movement and room to work when training the canes onto the wires. The width of the fan will depend on the space available and on your own sense of proportion. Wire trellises can be used in many situations; they aren't elegant, but the wire is nearly invisible under the rose foliage most of the time, and they are very easy to dismantle.

Many other kinds of trellises can also be used against a wall, as long as they are sturdily built. Wrought iron is ideal, since it is indestructible yet often delicate and graceful looking. A simple rectangular trellis of 2x2 lumber is easy to construct and can make a

handsome support. We recommend treating any wood that you use with a preservative recommended by your nursery. Many preservatives can harm plants, as can lumber you purchase that is already treated.

Freestanding trellises
Any trellis strong enough to hold up a climbing antique rose is probably strong enough to stand on its own, which leads into a whole new area of garden design. If the long canes of a climber are trained along the horizontal members of a trellis, with shorter canes and laterals woven up and down through them, the covering of foliage and flowers should be very thick. This flowering wall can be used to screen an area, form a picture on its own or divide a garden so that it acquires secret places and surprises. If you make sure to provide for the plant's basic cultural needs, there is no reason this kind of structure can't be used in many places where other plantings or structures are more

traditional. A rose wall to shade a patio, or one to stop the eye at the end of the garden, or even to disguise a carport are all possibilities—and a gazebo is really little more than four walls of trellis meant to create a room of roses.

Pillars and their variations

In the words of G.A. Stevens in *Climbing Roses*, "A pillar is a post, and a pillar rose is a rose tied up to a post." Nothing could be clearer, or less romantic sounding. In actuality, pillar roses are a beautiful feature in any garden. They are an excuse to use a climber as a focal point, just as one would use a specimen rose. These blooming columns can be used singly to give height and color to a small garden or a specific garden area. They can also be used in rows to lead the eye along a path and suggest a division of space without actually blocking the view. Pillar roses can be set into a large flower border as part of the backdrop or tallest layer, but they are even nicer if used where they can be seen up close and the flowers, so conveniently placed for smelling, can be properly appreciated.

Roses suitable for pillars are usually climbers in the 8-ft. to 12-ft. range, though that depends, of course, on the height of the post itself, which in turn will depend on the size of your garden and the type of spectacle you want to create. As with trellises, posts to support roses need to be quite sturdy and rot-proof, and they need to be set securely into the ground so that they won't lean. The canes can be trained up the post in a spiral, like a barber's pole, or braided around it by wrapping the first cane clockwise, the second counterclockwise, and so on. Either way is attractive, and each has the desired effect of bending the canes somewhat toward the horizontal so that the foliage and flowers will cover the post thickly from bottom to top. At strategic points the canes can be fastened to fencing staples driven into the post.

Once the basic concept of pillars is understood, there are many worthy variations on this theme. The simple method of training can be used to turn any post, from a sunny porch column to a tall lamp pole, into a rose pillar. Long-caned climbers can be used

Trained on a trellis at the end of a porch, the found Bourbon rose "Maggie" screens the side yard from view and creates new spaces within the garden. (Central Texas, April)

Wrapping rose canes at an angle increases their flowering potential. This climber has been braided up a cedar post by wrapping some canes clockwise, others counterclockwise. (Central Texas, February)

The Noisette rose 'Jeanne d'Arc' (on the right) can make an attractive pillar. For a fairly slow grower, this method of training puts the flowers in a strategic position to be enjoyed without bending. (Central Texas, April)

specifically as pillar roses so that they will reach the top of a post and cascade out in an umbrella of flowers. Three posts can be fastened together into a tripod, with a separate climber for each leg or with one hugely vigorous variety like 'Fortuniana' submerging the whole thing. Posts can be joined at the top by lengths of chain or heavy rope, and climbing roses trained up into pillars and then draped or loosely braided (to keep from becoming top-heavy) along these swags. This was a Victorian favorite and is a visual delight.

Pillars joined at the top by flat or arched rigid supports are another beautiful feature. One alone will frame a gate or entryway, while a series of pillars makes an enticing arbor. Be sure to make the arches high and wide enough for comfortable passage, however. We had an unfortunate incident occur when a low-slung climbing rose snagged the toupee from the head of a gentleman walking beneath it. He didn't seem to mind much, but we were terribly embarrassed by our lack of foresight.

The only drawback to training climbing roses on pillars is that once every second or third year the whole plant will have to be taken down for grooming and removal of dead and unproductive wood from the interior. If this is not done, at least in our warm climate where climbing roses do not die back much in winter, the plant will build up thickly, cutting off light and air to the canes on the inside and increasing the possibility of disease. In general, however, climbing roses are remarkably healthy, and the older varieties in particular thrive and perform with no more than standard care.

It is so tempting to add climbing roses immediately to a garden that we need to repeat our statement that a good garden takes time. You need time to plan rose supports and to choose varieties that are both pleasing to your personal taste and of the proper scale for your garden design. Also, climbing roses take longer than bushy varieties to reach full-blooming maturity because they have to build up so much mass in addition to forming flowers. It often takes three years before an everblooming climbing rose can properly claim that name.

Climbers must be trained if they are to give a formal display, with the new growth worked into the overall pattern at least once or twice a year as it ripens, and you need to be sure that you do not take on a larger project than you will enjoy maintaining. All these points need to be taken into consideration, but a few years from now, when you are reclining on the bench under your fragrant arbor and gazing admiringly over your rich and multi-layered garden of flowering trellises and blooming pillars, you'll be very glad, after all, that you took the necessary time.

Some reliable choices for climbing roses
A large number of the roses in our Encyclopedia are suitable for use as climbers. None of them is especially difficult to work with, but some of the easiest for beginners are:
   R. banksiae banksiae ('Lady Banks' Rose')
   'Rêve d'Or'
   'Old Blush, Climbing'
   'Zéphirine Drouhin'
   'Sombreuil'

An arch of roses, like this Noisette 'Lamarque', makes a beautiful frame through which to see a garden picture. (Central Texas, March)

Here, 'Archduke Charles' planted in a double, staggered row 20 ft. long creates a hedge. It hides the foundations of the porch and provides an attractive backdrop for the colorful, low-growing perennials. (Central Texas, April)

The Horizontal Line:
Hedging and Edging with Roses

As Victor Hugo wrote in *Les Misérables,* "the beautiful is as useful as the useful, perhaps more so." In the case of antique roses, this is remarkably apt, for they are nothing if not beautiful and yet they can be turned to nearly any purpose in landscape design. One such application is the replacement of the ordinary green hedge.

Hedges have a number of simple purposes. They can screen something from view, such as a propane tank or the neighbor's yard. They can be used as foundation plantings to disguise the blunt point of contact between a building and the ground. They can be used to delineate a path, a fence or a wall, in which case they perform the function of both softening a strong visual line and calling attention to its best points. They can substitute for a fence, either to form a barrier or to frame a space, giving the visual cue that the picture ends there and you are not to look any further.

The one flaw in hedging with roses is that, in most Zones, roses are dormant and leafless for two or more months of the year. The great advantage, however, is that much of the rest of the year, if remontant varieties are used, rose hedges will be colorfully decorated with beautiful, scented flowers.

Types of hedges
There are two basic types of hedges: formal and informal. Informal hedges can be made up of any grouping of roses if the varieties included have at least a few traits (such as size or growth habit) in common. One of our neighbors once purchased a number of roses grafted onto rootstock. The desired varieties eventually died, but the rootstock, a vigorous climber, continued to thrive. As suckers and long, thorny canes appeared in her garden to give notice of yet another surviving rootstock rose, our neighbor dug them out and transplanted them to a long berm at the back of her property. Mixed with

other outcast roses that were too big for her garden, the resultant hedge is large, loosely formed and, she says, "sort of accidental but cheap, and perfectly glorious in the spring."

A large, informal hedge requires very little shaping and just needs the basics of feeding, watering and removing the occasional dead cane. Neat, formal hedges will need clipping every six to eight weeks. This keeps them in bloom and relatively uniform in size. Since roses, even the old ones, have remarkably tangled bloodlines, it's a good idea for a beginner to choose one variety for a formal hedge rather than mixing different bushes. There are myriad subtle differences in form, leaf shape, flower size and number of petals, exact time of bloom and even the color of the new growth that make a hedge of mixed varieties charming, but certainly less uniform than a row of all one sort. Once you get to know the roses, however, it is possible to find several varieties in some classes that are near-twins, differing only in their flowers. Mixing these roses in a pattern can give the overall uniformity of the hedge a little extra flair.

Planting formal hedges
Roses for hedges should be planted just as you would plant any other antique rose (details are provided in Chapter 4), giving due consideration to soil and sunlight, the drip line and the distance from the foundation. The spacing for individual bushes depends on the effect you wish to achieve with your hedge. If you want a solid, unbroken line, most Chinas and Teas can be spaced between 2 ft. and 3 ft. apart. As they mature, the bushes will merge together nicely. If the size of the structure warrants an especially thick hedge, the bushes can be planted in two staggered rows with about 3 ft. of space between each bush in each direction. If you've chosen varieties from classes other than Chinas and Teas, check to see what the mature size of the bush will be to determine how close to space them.

'Seven Sisters' serves double duty here. Trained thickly on a pillar, the rose frames the view into and out of the house entryway and also acts as a privacy barrier by screening the windows. (Central Texas, April)

Pruning formal hedges

After the first year's growth, it is good to prune the whole hedge hard, removing about one-half the total growth. After that, production of both foliage and flowers is increased by light pruning on a regular basis about six to eight weeks apart, or after each flush of blooms. We trim our everblooming rose hedges with the shears twice a year, in early spring and early fall, clipping the bushes back about one-third so that they are uniform in size and height. At the most, no more than one-third of the bush should be cut off after the first year, particularly in the case of Tea roses, which don't respond well to hard pruning. Only every second or third spring do we go

into the hedges with hand pruners, cutting out any dead wood and opening up the interior of each bush for air circulation. Teas and Chinas are remarkably healthy plants and don't seem to be afflicted with any special problems, even given our disregard for what would be considered normal pruning practices.

Choosing varieties for informal hedges

When the object of planting a hedge is to form a screen or barrier, the roses should not only be planted close together (no farther apart than their minimum width at maturity) but chosen specifically for vigorous growth. A low screen can be designed with almost any of the moderately sized bushy roses, but to cut off the view of, say, the neighbor's yard, requires plants that will reach 6 ft. or more in height. Some of the sturdier climbers and species roses perform beautifully in this situation. Hybrid Multifloras like 'Russelliana' and 'Trier' are a good start, as are the fragrant *Rosa eglanteria* ('Eglantine') and other species roses like 'Fortuniana' and *R. laevigata*, the 'Cherokee Rose'. In the July/August 1990 issue of Bev Dobson's *Rose Letter*, Texan Conrad Tips writes about a truck farm on the outskirts of Houston that had "thick hedges, fully 10 or 12 feet tall, of *R. laevigata*, quite a sight in bloom." Few of our yards need quite that much protection and privacy, but it gives an idea of the willingness of the genus *Rosa* to meet any requirements.

A large hedge can be allowed to grow a little wild, if space allows, or be kept in some semblance of order by an annual clipping right after the spring bloom. It's worth reiterating that you must make sure you size the roses that you plant to your garden space. Otherwise you might end up with a large, unruly planting rather than the mannerly barrier you intended.

Choosing varieties for foundation plantings

For foundation plantings to cover up the base of your house, you will want to choose from very bushy everblooming varieties such as Chinas and Teas. Many roses in these two classes range naturally between 4 ft. and 6 ft. high and can be kept pruned to 3 ft. or 4 ft. high if necessary. They also tend to be very leafy and nearly as wide as they are high, both good qualities for hedge plants.

Species roses such as this R. banksiae banksiae ('Lady Banks' Rose') make excellent barriers if one has the room for them. Here, perhaps 25 plants have been allowed to naturalize and cover some 400 ft. of embankment along a highway. (Northern California, May)

Accenting line

There are situations in which it is more desirable to accent the existing line of an attractive structure, such as a wall of handsome stone. In this case, the suggestion that we made on p. 24 about enhancing and interrupting a strong line with the use of a single rose bush can be expanded.

A series of bushes at wide intervals functions just as well as a more closely planted hedge to soften any bluntness, but allows the beauty of the background to show clearly through. Almost any varieties of rose bushes can be used in this sort of planting. Once the uniformity of the hedge is discarded, the individual roses can be of all different classes, including some each of the Bourbons, Hybrid Perpetuals, species, old European roses, Noisettes and Hybrid Multifloras. If the line of planting is long enough, it will always give a horizontal impression even if the roses are widely varied in form, color and season of bloom.

Creating borders

On the more restrained end of the scale is the idea of using a line of roses as the frame or "edge" for a specific garden picture. Mid-sized rose bushes can be used this way to divide the garden from surrounding land, and here once again, the Chinas and Teas come into their own. Plants of a roughly uniform size, whether they are all the same variety or a mixture of compatible varieties, form a very graceful stop for the eye and increase the interest in the space they define. We don't mean that you must surround your garden with a rose hedge to get this effect, though of course you may if you like the idea. A simple line of roses at the most significant point, whether planted in a straight row or curved along to fit the edge of a property, will make the necessary impression of a complete garden frame.

Even the smallest varieties of antique roses can be pressed into service to make this sort of edging. The little Chinas like 'Rouletii', 'Le Vésuve' or 'Hermosa' can be used charmingly to finish out a larger bed of mixed roses and perennials. Planted on 12-in. to 16-in. centers, such roses can enclose an herb garden or surround a bird bath to great effect, calling

This combination of 'Mrs. B.R. Cant', 'Safrano', 'Bon Silène' and 'Perle des Jardins', all Teas, works well as a formal hedge because the plants are all similar in size and habit. (Central Texas, December)

Because the surrounding landscape is on a large scale, these full-grown bushes of 'Autumn Damask' create a clear line with a hedge-like effect even though they are planted 30 ft. apart. (Northern California, May)

attention to these particularly attractive features within the garden at large. Chinas don't mind about pruning one way or another, so small hedges or edgings of China varieties can be clipped back to the required size as often as necessary– after every bloom cycle if you like, or twice a year as with other everblooming hedge roses, if that is enough.

Some reliable roses for hedges

Rose hedges are a very valuable tool in garden design, and the beauty and fragrance of their flowers redoubles their worth. We include here a very short list of "hedgeable" roses in different heights, just as a starting point.

For 2-ft. to 4-ft. hedges:
    'Rouletii'
    'Hermosa'
    "Pam's Pink"
    'Le Vésuve'

In a mixed planting of Old Garden Roses at the Confederate Cemetery in Lynchburg, Virginia, the roses enhance the strong line of the wall without masking its beauty. (Virginia, May)

This 18-in. tall sundial is edged with a possible seedling of the small China rose 'Rouletii' (study-named "Highway 290 Pink Buttons"). The rose edging has the same function as the dwarf yaupon (Ilex vomitoria 'Nana') hedge that borders the beds around it —to define and contain a small area. (Central Texas, June)

For 4-ft. to 6-ft. hedges:
  'Marie van Houtte
  'Madame Antoine Rebe'
  'Old Blush'
  'Jean Bach Sisley'
For 6-ft. to 8-ft. hedges, or larger:
  R. eglanteria ('Eglantine')
  'Russelliana'
  'Trier'
  'Champneys' Pink Cluster'

'Veilchenblau' and 'Lady Banks' Rose' have been allowed to grow together in an informal fashion at the back of a garden surrounded by woods. (Virginia, May)

Roses by Woods and Water: The Natural Look

A naturalized area does not have to be unplanned or unkempt. Rather, it is a strategic way to create a garden, or an area within a garden, where there is a lack of tension and a feeling that the design is in harmony with nature.

One of the delightful qualities of many of the old roses is their self-sufficiency. Many varieties have shown that they don't need human care by their habit of surviving long after their original caretakers have moved away or died. Not every old rose is this tough in every situation, but by far the majority of varieties discussed in this book can be naturalized wherever the climate and planting conditions meet their needs. This sort of independence can put a crimp in a nurturing gardener's ego, but it is a

landscaper's dream. It allows old roses to be used at a distance from cultivated areas, enhancing or shaping a vista and blending with the existing features, such as trees or sloping hillsides. Here in Texas, it allows us to grow roses on barbed-wire pasture fences, enlivening their ever-present monotony. The very rose that started the Antique Rose Emporium, in fact, was a plant of the species hybrid 'Mermaid', naturalized on a wire pasture fence in rocky Central Texas and blooming freely under the scorching August sun.

Varieties for naturalizing

Species roses and Hybrid Multifloras like 'Seven Sisters' and 'Trier' are probably the best choices for completely wild plantings that will get little or no care, because they can thrive without it once they have reached a reasonable maturity—say, two or three years old. All naturalized roses will have a better chance of carefree survival if they are well planted (see Chapter 4) and get plenty of water for at least the first year.

If you are going to use roses in semi-civilized surroundings as a transition between a garden and an uncleared area of brush or thicket, any of a large number of the sturdier climbers will do. They will be happy to fling themselves haphazardly into small trees and drape gracefully over unkempt bushes and rough fences. In this type of setting, you will probably want to make at least an annual effort to clean out any dead wood and keep the roses looking somewhat groomed.

By letting roses grow into trees you can get a very graceful effect, as with this **R. multiflora carnea.** *The trick is to choose a tree with an open form, like this Texas redbud, that will let sunlight filter through to the rose. (Central Texas, April)*

The wildlife factor

Naturalized plantings of roses offer benefits above and beyond their intrinsic beauty. They are a safe home for all sorts of birds, many of which nest in them. Small fauna such as lizards and beneficial insects will thrive in the protection of the rose thickets and improve the whole environment of the garden by preying on unwanted pests. Many varieties, especially the species roses, offer a display of colorful foliage and hips in fall and winter. The hips will keep birds interested during the dormant season, bringing a feeling of life and activity to that part of the winter garden. There is no real reason to spray a naturalized rose with any chemical or fertilizer, so a healthy microenvironment can be created within it.

There are two points that gardeners who want to plant roses away from maintained areas need to take into account. One of these is that the birds will at some time make deposits of whatever seeds they have been eating. Most of the time this is not a problem, but sometimes undesirable plants can get a start this way in the fertile soil under the roses. We know a County Extension Agent who swears vigorously that a bird's goal in life is to spread hackberry seedlings everywhere it perches. An occasional check for nuisance plants will keep them from ruining the picture you hoped to create with your roses.

The second possible problem with unguarded roses is that horses, deer and cattle find them irresistibly edible. The thorns are no deterrent at all: In fact, the only rose that deer are reputed to avoid is the thornless 'Lady Banks' Rose'. Deer repellents work in some situations, but there is really no reliable way to protect roses planted outside a fence. Keep this in mind when you are choosing a planting site. Most wild browsing animals won't come into a regularly inhabited yard, but we did hear of one exception. One of our clients complained bitterly because he had fenced his yard on only three sides, since the

R. banksiae lutea ('Yellow Lady Banks' Rose') appears to light up this huge tree at Western Hills Nursery. In good conditions, banksias can grow over 12 ft. a year. (Northern California, May)

fourth bordered a lake. He had thought his garden was safe, he said, until the morning he came outside to find most of his roses gnawed to nubs and the guilty beaver swimming away with an entire uprooted bush between its teeth. Most settled areas are not quite this much at nature's mercy, however, and there are many safe and excellent sites for naturalizing roses.

Naturalized roses and water features

An area of the garden in which roses can be used to give a natural aspect to what is usually a man-made feature is near a pool or pond. Water is intensely attractive to most of us, and a water feature in the garden draws the eye like a magnet. When brought into balance with the surrounding landscape through the graceful, flowing accent of a rose, it becomes a garden ornament without peer.

A small body of still water is the perfect mirror for the grace and loveliness of certain old roses. The naturally arching varieties like 'Russelliana', R. palustris ('Swamp Rose') and 'Madame Plantier' (or even some of the more open and free-form varieties like 'Honorine de Brabant', 'Blush Noisette' and some of the Damask roses) have flowing lines that seem to belong close to water. Roses with single or semidouble flowers also seem to belong there by virtue of their clean simplicity.

A water setting is perfect for R. palustris, the 'Swamp Rose'. The only rose that doesn't mind wet feet, it can be planted right at water's edge, where the natural elegance of its form is accented. (Central Texas, May)

Only the 'Swamp Rose' is at home planted with its roots actually in the water, but other roses will have no trouble a little higher up the bank of a pond or in a bed close to the edge of an artificial pool. Large climbers like *R. multiflora carnea* can be planted quite a few feet from the water and allowed to mound up on themselves and spill out until some of their long canes hang right over the surface to shed petals on its reflective calm.

Water makes an excellent backdrop for rose plantings because of the complementary lighting it provides. On sunny days sparks of light are caught in every ripple, while at other times the water surface will be dark and leaden. This means that rose flowers of every color will have their moment of peak visibility and intensity when seen against this changeable background.

The only time that roses and water don't mix is when there is some kind of spray or fountain involved. The constant moisture in the air and on the leaves provides an environment in which fungus diseases thrive. With this single exception, there is no more appropriate or naturally beautiful combination than antique roses and water.

Some reliable varieties for naturalizing
R. multiflora carnea
R. banksiae banksiae ('Lady Banks' Rose')
'Mermaid'
R. laevigata ('Cherokee Rose')
'Trier'
'Seven Sisters'

Some reliable varieties for use by water
R. palustris ('Swamp Rose')
'Russelliana'
'Jeanne d'Arc'
'Mutabilis'
'Nastarana'
'Madame Plantier'
'Blush Noisette'

This 'Blush Noisette' is thriving by a water feature at our display gardens. It is planted in well-drained soil 2 ft. above the water level so its roots don't get too wet. (Central Texas, October)

The colors of 'Clotilde Soupert' and 'Hermosa' complement each other nicely in this unusual stacked arrangement of container-planted roses. (Central Texas, April)

Roses in Containers

There are many excellent reasons to grow a rose garden in pots—especially as our population and mobility increase, giving us smaller spaces to live in and less time to stay in each place. Container gardening is potentially the most creative and universally available way to garden; the rules for doing it well are not complex, but they merely need to be adhered to fairly strictly.

The virtues of a container garden

If you live in a "no dirt" situation such as an apartment or condominium, a few antique roses in containers on a sunny balcony can put an easy, fragrant garden where none existed before. Roses in pots can personalize and beautify a rented yard and can be moved with you from place to place.

Containers make a garden portable and therefore possible. The only requirement that must be met by the garden site is that the roses get adequate sunshine, six or more hours a day.

One advantage of a mobile garden is that it can always put its best face forward. You can rearrange pots to feature whichever rose is in finest bloom—something that is impossible to do with roses fixed in the ground. You can even bring blooming roses inside the house for short periods of time. They don't like any low-light situation for long, but they make wonderful and fragrant decorations for dinner parties and special events. They will need to be sent outdoors for sun as soon as possible, however, or they will gradually lose condition. For gardeners in the North, everblooming varieties of tender roses can be grown successfully only in containers so that they can be moved inside for protection when the temperature begins to drop.

The marriage of rose and container: Form, color and space

In creating any kind of container garden, you are dealing with the principles of form, color and space. Form involves the shape of the chosen container and the new shape it makes when combined with the growth habit of a specific rose. Many variables are possible. You may decide that an erect, narrow bush like the Hybrid Perpetual 'Marquise Boccella' looks best in a tall, narrow urn, mimicking and accenting a particularly fine vertical line of your house. Or you may prefer the same rose in a rounded, bulbous pot that visually stops and anchors the plant instead of stretching it out.

Color involves the contrasts between the container, flowers and green foliage, as well as the contrast of all three with the chosen background of sky, walls, fences or other plants. Pink roses, for example, can be grown in orange clay pots, but they will look more attractive in almost any other color of container. Grey weathered wood, cream-colored clay, blue glaze would all be lovely—even black plastic would be an improvement. Red roses, on the other hand, look great in orange pots but are hard to see against any dark wall or with dark green foliage in the background. White flowers show beautifully against most backgrounds, but vanish against a pale sky. Many color choices are purely subjective, but it helps to know that white roses are not a good choice if you're going to pot them up on a high balcony and try to see them against the clouds, whereas they are of high value in front of an ivy-covered wall.

Judging requirements of space takes an extra effort of imagination, because the rose will change in size as it matures. This is a much more important consideration for planting in a container than it is in the open garden, where many boundaries are assumed rather than physically tangible. You need to consider the dimensions of your container, the eventual size of the variety of rose you have chosen and whether you plan to step it up gradually into larger pots or, if appropriate, keep it pruned to fit the pot in which it was first planted.

The rounded, closed shape of this container contrasts well with the airy form of 'Cramoisi Supérieur'. Eventually, this China rose will outgrow the small container, so a compact arrangement like this would have to be renewed every couple of years unless a more dwarf variety were chosen. (Central Texas, October)

Most questions of form, color and space can be answered by daydreaming as you wander through pottery stores, garden centers and your own yard. You may want to use a measuring tape to get at least a rough idea of the relative sizes of things. Most stores will not give out swatches of pots, but occasionally a nursery will be willing to let you have a flower from a rose you like so that you can test it for color against your house paint and various possible containers. Ask before picking, though!

When starting a container garden, it is important to remember that you are not limited to pots sold in stores. Absolutely anything can be a container for roses if it is big enough (5 gal. or larger) and can be properly drained. Navasota historian and rosarian Pamela Puryear reports that her great-grandmother recycled large enameled chamber pots for this use, planting them with young rose bushes whenever they got a few rust holes in their bottoms. "Not in good taste, perhaps," she comments, "but quite functional." Another friend of ours in California is using a weathered wooden rowboat as a planter. Beached artistically on rocks in the garden, it now houses two small crimson China roses and a large apricot Tea, accented with herbs and perennials. The effect is much nicer than a cement squirrel as a garden accent, and the boat is large enough that the roses will never have to be transplanted.

The roses in their pots function here as an architectural element. The white flowers are a lovely contrast to the peach brick and soften the lines of the entryway; their simplicity complements the formality of their setting. (Georgia, May)

Situating the containers in the garden

Once you've chosen the rose and the pot, you have to decide where to place the potted rose so that it is in balance, in terms of relative size, with the other features in its vicinity.

Each planted container is actually two garden elements at once, an architectural (or structural) feature and a growing plant. In arranging containers to please your eye, you must take into account not only the isolated beauty of each rose but also the effect of its placement in the surrounding area. Containers of roses can be set out on a patio or deck or arranged up a set of stairs to bring the intimacy of the garden closer to the house and to create a transition zone between artificial and natural features. Or they can be grouped around a swimming pool to make it seem less like a sterile bathtub of chlorinated water and more like a beautiful wild pond (sans mud). Roses in containers can even be used in the garden itself as specimens, or be set into a niche in a flower bed. When confined and elevated in a container, a rose is set apart from the garden plants in the ground, and it becomes an immediate focal point, an attraction that draws the eye to a specific area.

Planting roses in containers

Preparing a container for planting is simpler than preparing a bed in the ground because there is no digging to do, only mixing. We use a potting mixture that is two-thirds highly decomposed pine bark (a rich, lightweight organic material) and one-third builder's (sharp) sand. To this we add gypsum and dolomitic lime (½ lb. of each per cubic ft. of soil mix) and a timed-release fertilizer that will carry the necessary micronutrients as well as nitrogen, phosphorus and potassium. This mixture drains well, holds the right amount of water and nutrients and doesn't compact around the roots of the rose. We have found this to be an excellent mixture, but any combination that is at least half organic material to half soil will work well, if you add a little compost to give a better nutrient base. If you are buying a soil mix rather than making it yourself, read the label to be sure it has the necessary proportions of these ingredients. In addition, as with a bed prepared in the ground, it doesn't hurt to let a prepared

This 'Green Rose' in full bloom has been set on the steps of a pergola at the Korbel Winery gardens to draw visitors' attention to its unusual flowers. The orange terra-cotta pot enhances the color of this rose, and the all-green plant is an excellent backdrop for the bright colors of the pansies and perennials. (Northern California, May)

container sit for a few months before planting so that the various elements have time to blend and ripen—though we never seem to have that kind of patience ourselves.

Once the soil is prepared, the rose can be planted as if it were going into the ground. Be sure to soak the soil mix thoroughly before planting so that it will be evenly moist when the roots go in. Instructions for

planting both bare-root and container-grown roses are provided in Chapter 4. We like to plant roses into their new containers so that the final soil level is just a little below the rim, because we know that it will settle over time. When it has settled several inches, we add more planting medium.

Watering and fertilizing

Water is very important for roses growing in containers, and they should never be allowed to dry out completely. If the container is properly drained, you really can't water it too often, and if it is not well drained, you shouldn't be planting roses in it. A little work with a power drill can make the necessary adjustment. While a rose is just getting established, daily watering may be called for, especially if you plant it in the heat of the summer. Our roses in 5-gal. containers get watered every day, whereas those in half barrels can go for as long as a week without a soaking.

Fertilization is a little different for container-grown roses because they are in a closed system that cannot exchange chemicals with or draw nutrients from surrounding soil. We often put a half cup of blood and bone meal under the roots when we pot up a new rose, but a 0-10-10 chemical fertilizer will supply the same stock of slowly released phosphorus and potash. In addition to working balanced, timed-release fertilizer into the soil mix before planting, we also add it (as per label instructions) on the surface of the soil periodically after that. (Release time varies from 3 to 18 months, depending on the product.) This saves us having to guess the precise requirements of each potted rose and avoids the risk of overfertilizing and burning the roots.

If a rose is not as lush and green and blooming as we'd like, an occasional application of a nonburning foliar feed or fish emulsion will help supply the extra nitrogen that gets leached out of the soil mix through watering. We prefer the organic boost of fish emulsion, but we have to admit that its stench, even when "de-scented," can be a powerful attractant for cats and other pets, so this is one occasion where the nonorganic solution may be the most sensible.

Pruning containerized roses

As Old Garden Roses in containers mature, they require the same sort of minimal pruning as the same varieties in the ground (refer to Chapter 4 for details), with one exception. If a rose is going to be kept in a pot for a very long time, it may eventually be necessary to turn it out and shake away the soil, exposing the roots. Carefully clip off about one-third of the root system and replant the rose in fresh soil. It is also important to prune the plant back by about one-third at the same time to balance the root loss. Pruning keeps the rose vigorous and prevents it from getting rootbound. In a reasonably large pot you may not need to do this more than once every two or three years, and in something as large as a half barrel, you can do the same job by cultivating with a shovel or garden fork, just as you would in the garden proper.

Choosing varieties for containers

As far as we can tell, any rose will grow in a container. Roses are relatively shallow-rooted plants, so even a climbing variety can be grown in a space at least 2 ft. wide by 2 ft. deep. You may want to avoid the most vigorous varieties, and even a mannerly climber might be rather top-heavy (though a sturdy trellis can be used to steady it). We have seen 4-ft. square bushes grown in big wooden tubs and smaller roses in window boxes. We have even seen climbing roses in planters on the patio roof of a tall building, trailing long canes and clustered flowers down the walls and past the upper-story windows. Antique roses perform beautifully in pots, and the added element of mobility only increases their already wide range of decorative talents.

Some reliable varieties for small containers

Almost any variety can be grown in a large container such as a half barrel, but these varieties will be happy in small (5-gal.) containers:

'Hermosa'
'Stanwell Perpetual'
'Kronprincessin Viktoria'
'Rosette Delizy'
'Green Rose'

An ungainly rose in its natural state, 'Madame Isaac Pereire' bursts with bloom when pegged. This rose, at the corner of a bed between two walkways, is a focal point at our display gardens. 'Madame Isaac Pereire' will gradually come into full and glorious bloom, with the buds opening at the tips of the canes first and in the center of the plant last. (Central Texas, April)

Pegged Roses

Pegged roses create a unique effect in the garden that cannot be achieved any other way. They form wonderful, lush mounds of flowers that are controlled rather than free and wild like a naturalized climber, yet have no distinct edges. They seem to begin and end in the soil that nurtures them, arching neatly to a central point of union. Pegged roses provide startling amounts of flowers because pulling the canes down in order to peg them changes the flow of nutrients and promotes flowering at every bud joint along the whole cane, greatly increasing the bloom potential of the rose bush.

Having praised the technique, we must also admit that pegging is an odd thing to do to a rose. It's the sort of thing you do when you've already mastered the simpler levels of gardening and are casting about for a new way to entertain yourself. Pegged roses require more maintenance than do roses trained in any other fashion, and even with the most complete care, they can still appear unkempt during their summer growth spurt. They also take up a lot of space and are so unusual looking that they draw the eyes of all passers-by, including people who may irritate you by asking why your roses are growing down on the ground.

A sumptuous bed of pegged Hybrid Perpetual roses displays the form at its most attractive. Unpegged, these same plants would have only about half as many flowers and would be twice as tall, so they would have to be relegated to the back of the bed. (Northern Texas, May)

Varieties for pegging

Roses suitable for pegging are those that have long, flexible canes in the 5-ft. to 7-ft. range. Many Bourbon and Hybrid Perpetual roses are perfect in this way, whereas vigorous climbers are not appropriate because they so quickly grow out of the chosen form. Roses that are too leggy to be compact bushes but not really tall enough to be climbers are ideal. We've provided a list of suitable varieties on p. 57, but it is not meant to be limiting. We are still experimenting with likely candidates, and you should feel free to experiment in your own garden.

Pegged roses in the garden

Pegged roses work well as a focal point in the garden design. They stand out as a centerpiece, a sculpture made of roses. They draw an immense amount of attention not only because of their amazing wealth of bloom, but also because they are doing something a rose doesn't naturally do. One or more neatly arranged pegged roses can fill an entire bed where an eye-catching display is wanted. They can also be used to border any fairly large garden feature, such as a pool or, in the case of our display gardens, a windmill. It is important to recognize that pegged roses take up a lot of space and that proper proportions need to be kept in mind. It would look odd, for example, to surround a bird bath with roses that stretched out 7 ft. across. With a good-

The mounded shape and pastel colors of this pegged 'Madame Ernest Calvat' are repeated in the mounds of Louisiana phlox at our display gardens. (Central Texas, April)

sized pond, however, pegged roses can be particularly lovely, as they don't obstruct the view and the expanse of water balances nicely with the expanse of flowers.

For the same reason of proportion, most pegged roses fit into a mixed flower border only when it is a fairly large one, taking a place near the front or middle to show off their form and wealth of bloom. This type of training increases the number of garden niches that roses can fill by presenting them as a sort of mounding groundcover. It also gives some of the

taller Bourbons and Hybrid Perpetuals, whose magnificent flowers are truly their strong point, a chance to move from the back of the border into the limelight.

There is an excellent niche for pegged roses on slopes or banks where they can be trained to enhance the irregular shape of the earth with their soft, flowing lines. On sloping ground, the arched form of a pegged rose turns into a cascade of flowers spilling across a soft carpet of green.

In winter and early spring the spiderlike form of pegged roses shows up clearly. A low bank is an ideal setting for pegged roses, because the slight angle enhances the cascading effect of the arched branches. (Washington, D.C., February)

The winter nakedness of pegged roses seems less unnerving when their arched forms are blended in as architectural "bones" to maintain interest in a seasonally changing border. Underplanting pegged roses with early-blooming bulbs also helps to carry the roses gracefully through their dormancy. In our Zone, the foliage on the bulbs develops as the foliage on the roses thins out, and the blooms on the bulbs will be nearly over before they are overshadowed by the new growth of the roses.

One final word on deciding where to put your pegged roses. They'll be less work if grown in a fairly well-established bed. This is not because they require any better soil than roses trained in other ways, but simply because they can be nasty to weed, and an established bed is more likely to be weed-free. You will have to reach through the thorny canes to get at the weeds, and it can't be done comfortably unless the plants are spaced at least a human body-width apart. It's much simpler to start with a relatively weed-free location.

How to peg a rose

A rose is pegged by fastening down the canes of a suitable variety at or near the ends with 8-in. to 10-in. long metal hooks or U-shaped staples. The peg needs to be long enough to stay fixed in loose garden soil while keeping the rose cane under control, and it needs to be rust-proof for reuse. The canes can be arranged in any pattern that their degree of flexibility will permit: arched high and evenly spaced like spokes in a wheel, or pulled nearly level with the ground and swept all to one side to fit the configuration of a long, pointed bed. We have even trained half the canes of one bush up a pillar and pegged the others in a fan shape at its base. The shape of the space and your own ingenuity can dictate how you shape each rose.

Except at the tips, the canes of pegged roses need to be kept at least a few inches above ground level to allow for air movement and to enable you to work around them when you weed, mulch and fertilize. Our pegged roses have their tips fastened securely to the dirt, but sometimes this causes them to root at that point and send up distracting long shoots as they form new plants. (This is what happens in the propagation method called layering, described in Chapter 3.) We get extra plants this way, which is nice, but it does tend to spoil the formal look a pegged rose should have. We have found that scraping off the last few leaf buds with a thumbnail will discourage this habit somewhat. Removing these buds will also keep the tip of the cane from sprouting untidy new little branches—an especially likely occurrence if you have had to prune the cane to make it fit your space. If you want to avoid suckers, the most effective way to do this is to make sure the cane tips don't touch the ground. Using two pegging hooks at separate places on each cane will help reduce the tension on the tip so it can be pegged more loosely. We have also found that some roses, particularly the Hybrid Perpetuals in our garden, have a tendency to die back at the tips if they are fastened right to the soil. Raising the ends of the canes off the ground a little seems to keep this from happening so often.

Pruning and grooming pegged roses

Choosing which canes to keep and train for pegging and which to prune away is not difficult. Those canes that fit the space and bend the way you want them to are obviously the "keepers." Canes that are too angular or refuse to bend gracefully can be cut away at their base with sharp hand shears. Try not to leave a stub as it will spoil the graceful lines of the trained rose.

Pegged roses require grooming several times a year to remove any unsightly dead twigs and any canes that are awkward or unattractive. Newly grown canes need to be pegged down, and the existing canes will have to be thinned out to make room for them. Any cane tips that have accidentally rooted need to be dug up and clipped off cleanly.

This maintenance can be done at almost any time during the spring or fall. It is not crucial to work on pegged roses at a specific time of year, since your reason for pruning is not to stimulate new growth at the tips (as is the case with remontant bush roses) but to keep the plant shaped. Because common sense dictates that it's easier to work around the interior of a pegged rose and to make decisions about which canes to use when the leaves and flowers are not in the way, we generally fuss with our pegged roses just as they begin to come out of dormancy in spring (about mid-February) and during the warm days after the first fall frost. The only limitations here are that the canes must be warm enough to be flexible (they may snap in cold weather) and that the new canes must have matured past the stage when they are so tender that they break easily.

During the middle of the summer, there is a period that seems unavoidable when a pegged rose puts up long, succulent new shoots that must be left alone to harden. At this time it would be nice to be able to throw a blanket over the bed so as not to be questioned about the wild shoots waving about in the center of each carefully trained plant. Midsummer and midwinter (when the naked canes look like huge spiders) are when it is hardest to explain why you have pegged your roses. For the rest of the year, while they are giving their stunning performances, it is usually only necessary to explain how you have persuaded them to produce so many flowers.

Some reliable varieties for pegging

'Madame Isaac Pereire'
'Madame Ernest Calvat'
'Honorine de Brabant'
"Maggie"
'Paul Neyron'
'American Beauty'
'Frau Karl Druschki'
'Madame Plantier'
'Cardinal de Richelieu'
'Celsiana'

3 ▪ Rustling, Propagating, Purchasing

Before you can begin to garden with antique roses, you must of course acquire antique roses. Old roses are not as difficult to come by today as they were even three or four years ago, since the number of commercial sources has increased as the popularity of old roses has grown. Even so, you can't always pick up the rose you want at the corner nursery.

The alternative to purchasing roses through an established nursery is to get your old roses by finding existing plants and propagating them, usually by taking cuttings. Buying old roses has the advantage of being more certain and less time-consuming, but collecting them in the field is cheaper and more adventurous. We have been searching for old rose varieties for several years, often on forays organized by the Texas Rose Rustlers, a group of enthusiasts who gather annually to collect old roses. We have found that roses acquired in the field have an extra spice to them, a lingering trace from the thrill of the hunt, so we will concentrate first on how to find and propagate old roses on your own. (If you're interested in finding local rose rustlers, consult the list of rose associations on pp. 220-221.)

Taking cuttings is one of the most successful ways to propagate antique roses.

Discovering and collecting old roses is particularly pleasurable when shared with other enthusiasts. Here, the Texas Rose Rustlers are in action at an old cemetery in Victoria, Texas.

The Art of Rustling: Finding Old Roses to Propagate

One of the best places to search for surviving rose specimens is in long-established communities, especially in the backwater streets of older towns. Many interesting older plants are still being grown in less affluent neighborhoods where most people garden for the love of it rather than to keep up with fluctuating trends in landscape design. For these gardeners, if a plant performs well, doesn't require a lot of expensive upkeep and is easy to share with friends, it has a good chance of remaining a favorite. And, of course, the more a rose is propagated and planted, the better the chance that some specimen of it will survive local disasters.

Another likely place to run across very old rose bushes is in a cemetery—not a perpetual-care cemetery, but one where all the headstones are different and interesting snippets of personal information can be found in the inscriptions. We collected a nice pink Tea rose from in front of a stone dated 1893 that read: "Here lies our beloved Mother/Safe in the Angels' arms."

Identifying old roses

It is possible to recognize antique rose bushes with a fair degree of success once you know what you're looking for. The modern Hybrid Tea is such a distinctive plant, with its leggy, angular canes and large, glossy leaves, that after a while you can tell when a rose plant is not a Hybrid Tea. In general, if it doesn't look like a modern rose and you are in the right area for old roses, there is good reason to stop and look more closely. If the rose is in bloom, it is often possible to make a diagnosis by the old-fashioned flower form, soft color, smaller blossoms with lighter weight petals, or heavy scent.

If the rose is not in bloom, the general form of the bush can offer clues. Teas, Chinas and some Bourbons tend to be very bushy and have many branches with plenty of foliage (if they have been getting adequate water). Old European roses and Hybrid Perpetuals may present themselves as clumps consisting of many prickly canes and rather roughly textured leaves. Gallicas, the old European roses most likely to be found in the South, are distinctive in that they are usually only 3 ft. to 4 ft. in height. Noisettes, Hybrid Multifloras and some species roses are often found climbing on fences, trees and other

The presence of a graft union often indicates that a "found" rose plant may not be very old. The place where the rose scion was grafted onto the rootstock shows as a bulge at the base of the canes.

supports with a lushness and wild abandon that modern climbers rarely offer. Browsing through literature on old roses can help narrow down the possibilities. (We provide a short list of recommended books on pp. 222-224.) It doesn't really matter what the identity of the rose is, however, if you like the looks of it and want if for your garden.

The clue of the graft union

If you suspect that a certain bush is an antique rose but are not sure, check the base of the plant for signs of a graft union, visible as a large knot with changes in the bark where the top of the plant has been worked onto a rootstock. Finding this graft doesn't mean that the bush is not an old variety, since several nurseries sell old roses in grafted form. It does mean that the actual bush you are looking at is probably not all that old.

Grafted roses, though initially vigorous, tend not to have as long a life span as roses that are growing on their own roots. Whether this is because the sturdy rootstock tends to overpower the weaker top or because of other, subtler reasons of biological incompatibility, we can't say. We do know that, except in some areas of California, we have never found a truly old rose bush growing on anything but its own roots, and we believe this to be the experience of most old-rose collectors. We have even seen instances where a vigorous modern rose, such as 'Peace', outwitted its propagators and overcame the longevity problem by putting down its own roots and letting the foreign rootstock decay under it. It may be that many tough old roses that were initially grafted (a practice that dates back more than a hundred years) have done the same thing. At any rate, a mature rose bush that is on its own roots and thriving is almost always worth collecting simply because it has proven itself as a well-adapted survivor.

Propagating Antique Roses

Once you have found a rose and identified it as desirable, the next step is to propagate it so that you will have a plant of it in your own garden. By propagating old rose plants not only do you get handsome, hardy plants for your own use, but you are also preserving the actual genetic material of a historic variety. As Charles Walker, Jr., Director of the Heritage Rose Foundation, has pointed out, we don't all have the chance to save snow leopards or snail darters, but even a city gardener can rescue a valuable and perhaps rare old rose and keep it from being lost to the gene pool. Also, in the course of hunting for interesting old plants, you're likely to come into contact with fascinating people who have a wealth of plant lore they'll be happy to share with you. They will usually share cuttings from their roses, as well, but we would like to stress that it is important for "rustlers" to ask permission first.

Layering

The two most successful methods for home propagation of antique roses are layering and taking softwood cuttings. The first method is easier and more foolproof, though it doesn't offer the opportunity to create quite as many new plants at one time. Early spring or mid-fall (February/March or October/November for us) are the best times to try this technique because that is when the plants are most actively growing and day and night temperatures are most favorable for rooting.

The simple art of layering is shown in the drawing on the facing page. Choose a live, flexible rose cane and gently bend it down to form an elbow 8 in. to 10 in. from the tip. Make a slight nick (not too deep or the cane will break) on the bottom of the elbow and bury this portion of the cane 6 in. or 8 in. under the soil so that the foliage at the tip is still exposed to the open air. (Sometimes it is necessary to place a rock or

brick on top of the buried portion to prevent the cane from springing back up.) The small nick in the cane stops some of the nutrient flow at that point and promotes root growth there, while the rest of the living cane carries on as usual.

After the layered cane has been in place for about six weeks, give the tip a gentle tug. If there is some resistance, it is likely that roots have formed and that you have a new little rose bush ready to be cut off from the parent and placed wherever you like in your garden. If the weather is too hot or too cold for transplanting, layered canes can be left in place until a more appropriate time. (For ease of transplanting, you can layer directly into a pot, but you will have to monitor the cane carefully so that it doesn't dry out.)

Taking cuttings

Layering is the most practical propagation method if the parent bush is owned by someone you know or is easy to get to and not in danger of being destroyed. If, on the other hand, you are away from home, likely never to see the plant again, or are concerned that it might be bulldozed in six weeks' time, it is preferable to take cuttings. Also, although a given bush may have only a few canes suitable for layering, you can take a fairly large number of small cuttings without threatening its survival or ruining its appearance.

Once again, remember to ask permission first. Most gardeners are thrilled to share, but they will have to live with the result after you have clipped on their roses to your satisfaction. In truth, giving and taking cuttings is a process of sharing beauty that frequently brings out the best in everyone involved—though one of our local rose rustlers recommends keeping the car engine running just in case.

The most promising cuttings come from healthy, leafy canes that have a season's growth but are not too large and tough. This means they should be at least two months old (no longer soft and tender) but not so old that they've gotten woody. We look for firm, green canes about as thick as a pencil. Again, early spring and mid-fall are the best times to try this process, and of the two, fall is the more favorable. Using a sharp knife or sharp clippers (so as not to mangle the cuttings), first nip off the soft tip of the cane and any flowers, then cut it into 4-in. to 5-in. lengths, each piece with at least two and preferably three leaf nodes. Cuttings are much more likely to root if they have leaves to provide a support system while the roots are growing, so avoid bare sections of the cane. The more cuttings you take, the better your chances of success.

A new plant of 'Madame Plantier' has been created using the propagation technique known as layering. This plant was layered in February, and the photo was taken in November of the same year, by which time a very strong root system had developed.

Propagation by Layering

Cut here before digging up the new, rooted plant approximately eight weeks after layering.

2 in.

Roots will emerge here.

6 in. to 8 in.

1. Bend a long, flexible cane 8 in. to 10 in. from the tip and nick it no more than one-third of the way through.

2. Bury the cane 6 in. to 8 in. below ground level.

3. Leave about 2 in. of the cane's tip exposed above ground.

4. Weight down the cane with a rock or brick. This helps to keep the soil moist as well as holding the cane in place.

Transporting cuttings

Once you have got your rose cuttings, they need to be packaged for travel back to your garden. Many experienced rose collectors like to drop them into a bucket containing willow water, a root-promoting liquid that can be made by soaking short pieces of willow in a bucket of water for a day or two. Although it is true that willow water contains hormones that stimulate root growth, we don't use it for two reasons. First, we've found that roses root quite easily without it if cuttings are taken in the proper seasons. Willow water and commercial rooting hormones can make some difference to the success rate, but not that much, and they add an extra step to a simple process. Second, it is not a good idea to keep cuttings very wet. Instead of trying to preserve their capillary action as you would with cut flowers, it is best to let the cut ends seal themselves (callus over) so that the nutrients in each cutting are locked in and remain available while the plant is trying to strike roots.

Our method for transporting cuttings is to put small bunches of no more than 10 or 20 cuttings into a plastic bag containing a moist paper towel (and a label stating the location of the parent plant and its name, if known). The slight moisture keeps the leaves fresh but lets the process of callusing begin on the ends. Cuttings can even be sent through the mail this way. If you're in a hurry and without supplies, a damp newspaper wrapped around the cuttings will keep them fresh for several days.

Cultural requirements for rooting cuttings

Under the right conditions, rose cuttings root easily. Traditionally, some pioneer gardeners just stuck the fall prunings in the ground around the parent rose bush, stamped them in firmly and left them to sink or swim with a pretty fair success rate. We know several gardeners who still root their cuttings this way, and we have met others who learned from their mothers to cover each slip of a rose with a fruit jar and let it root out in this miniature greenhouse. Both of these methods show that common sense is often the equal of hard science, since cuttings do need to be set out in moist (not wet), well-drained soil in bright shade so that their leaves can get enough light and water to feed the plant until roots form, but where they will not get too stressed. The soft, partly shaded soil under an established rose bush provides the perfect conditions, and the ideal way to promote rooting is to create a closed environment such as a greenhouse (or fruit jar) where the humidity is maintained at a constant level. (A pebble or small stick should be slipped under the edge to vent the jar on hot days and prevent the babies from boiling.) You'll get the best results at times of year when night temperatures are between about 50°F and 60°F and the days are not over 90°F.

In sum, as long as you have loose, moist soil (good potting soil mixed half and half with perlite works fine, too), bright shade and constant (but not extreme) humidity, a good percentage of your cuttings will strike root. You can get these elements together in greenhouses with automatic mist systems (which is what we use as commercial propagators), in containers tented with plastic bags, with the fruit-jar technique (plastic milk jugs also work well with a little doctoring) or even in separate containers tented with plastic baggies. There are no restrictive rules as long as the basic needs are met.

Sticking cuttings

Before placing the cuttings in the ground or container that you have prepared, carefully strip off the bottommost set of leaves from each one, leaving the exposed leaf node intact. This leaf node will be under the soil and is an alternate spot for roots to form if they don't grow from the base of the cutting. If the bottom leaves are not removed, they can decay under the soil and promote disease. After exposing the bottom leaf node, stick the cuttings into the moist soil and firm it gently around them. Don't strip the top leaves from the cuttings! They are needed to feed the plant until roots form.

Once the cuttings are "stuck," they'll need little attention other than regular checking to make sure they don't get too hot, too dry or too wet. Excess water, the worst enemy, suffocates the developing roots and causes fungal diseases that can rot them.

To propagate roses from cuttings, first take 4-in. to 5-in. lengths of healthy cane. Each cutting should have at least two leaf nodes. Strip the bottom leaf from each cutting and keep the others. Stick the cuttings into the planting medium in a flat or pot (or under the parent bush), and keep them evenly moist, but not wet, until ready to transplant in six to eight weeks or more.

Protected from excess heat, moisture and dryness, this well-rooted cutting has already sent up a small side shoot in the eight weeks since it was started in September.

This transition stage is easiest for the gardener if the rose plants have been grown in pots from the beginning. If they began life in flats or greenhouse beds, you may wish to transplant them into pots first so you can acclimate them to their final garden site. When they have had a week or two to recover from the shock of being uprooted and moved, you can plant them in the garden. It will not hurt to let the new plants develop for a longer time before planting them out, as long as they have enough room in their container for the roots to continue growing without restriction. Follow the directions in Chapter 4 for planting your new roses, and be careful not to fertilize them for the first month after planting — they need time to get established before being pushed to perform.

Don't expect 100% success. Even the pros rarely get perfect results, but rose cuttings do root well, and you should have some positive results with almost any variety that performs well in your area. Chinas and Teas are the classes that root most easily in our climate; Hybrid Perpetuals and old European roses are the most difficult. Other classes range the spectrum in between.

Choosing Nursery Stock

The do-it-yourself methods of acquiring old roses are extremely satisfying but somewhat time-consuming. These methods don't fill up the garden quickly, and the effort they require may not be to every gardener's taste. There are a number of reliable nurseries that now specialize in Old Garden Roses (we provide a list on pp. 218-219). Most of these offer plants only by mail order, although a few also have retail facilities where roses in containers are sold.

Transplanting rooted cuttings

After about six weeks, tug gently on the tops of the cuttings. If they offer some resistance instead of sliding right out of the soil, chances are that you now have rooted plants ready to set out in the garden. If you have rooted them outdoors under a rose bush, they will be adequately hardened off and ready to be placed in their final location. If you have grown them under jars or in the greenhouse, they will need a few days in the open air, in partial sun, to get used to their new environment.

Size is not a criterion for judging a healthy antique rose. Both these plants were grown from cuttings "stuck" at the same time and rooted under identical conditions. Both are equally healthy. The plant on the left is the diminutive China rose 'Rouletii'; on the right is the Damask rose 'Ispahan'.

Commercial propagation techniques: Grafted vs. own-root

Many nurseries that offer old roses propagate as we do by rooting cuttings. This technique produces the roses on their own roots. Other nurseries use techniques that are more sophisticated than the home gardener may care to attempt. An example is propagation by tissue culture. This neat, scientific method requires only a small amount of cellular material to start new rose plants in test tubes in a nutrient solution. Entire plants with roots, leaves and even blossoms are formed in the test tubes by the time the roses are ready to be moved to containers with soil. Like roses produced from cuttings, tissue-culture roses are also "own-root" plants. This relatively new method still has some quirks, but it offers interesting applications for the future. The process takes up very little growing space, and being able to start many new plants from such small amounts of tissue means that endangered roses could be more quickly propagated and saved — sort of like rose rustling at a cellular level.

A much more common commercial technique is grafting, which involves joining a bud or scion of one rose variety to the vigorous rootstock of another. This is the way most modern roses are grown because it allows for rapid production. Grafting produces a plant that will usually perform vigorously for the first few years, but may then slow down or even fail. In our experience, it is rare to find a grafted rose more than 15 or 20 years old. It appears that the top dies out and the rootstock takes over, perhaps because of lack of care, an incompatible graft or a freeze that has killed it to the bud union. Roses on their own roots may grow more slowly for the first year or two, but their long-term performance is outstanding.

Evaluating nursery stock

Determining whether an antique rose plant from the nursery is healthy and vigorous can be confusing, not only because of the different ways in which old roses are propagated, but also because there is so much variety of form and behavior among the different classes. Overall plant size is not a criterion for judging a healthy antique rose. In the first year, for example, many Tea roses may grow quite slowly, whereas the Chinas reach their mature size more quickly and some species roses are downright uncontrollable. A one-year-old plant of 'Mermaid' might have thumb-thick canes that have to be pruned back from a length of 6 ft. in order to fit into a shipping box. An equally healthy, well-grown specimen of the Bourbon 'Souvenir de la Malmaison' at the same age might have reached only 8 in. in height with canes just ¼ in. in diameter. If you are used to large Hybrid Tea plants and your first old rose startles you by its different appearance, have faith and give it a chance in your garden before you abandon it. You may be surprised by the vigor of even the tiniest specimens.

If you have ordered bare-root roses through the mail, they should arrive looking fresh and unwithered, with green, vital branches and a proportionately sized root system. Again, overall size is not an issue. The only real reasons to be dissatisfied with a mail-order rose are if the plant seems overly dry, has shriveled stems, is moldy or fails within a brief time after planting. If this is the case, most nurseries will accept responsibility and send a replacement as soon as possible.

Buying bare-root roses: Successful timing

Be aware that nurseries in different climates have to adjust both their growing season and shipping season to their own Zone. This means that the availability of plants can vary widely, as will the amount of time you may have to wait for your order to be filled. We recommend reading each nursery's catalog carefully for this sort of detail and for suggestions on planting and caring for their products. Generally, unless they are shipped planted in containers, mail-order plants will arrive sometime during the nursery's dormant season, which may not be the same as yours. You may need to take protective measures to help your new roses adapt to the change in Zones. (We give details on pp. 80-82.)

In the South, it would be ideal to receive roses for planting in the fall, since our ground never freezes and the plants can spend all winter rooting out and getting established. It's difficult to procure mail-order roses in that season, however, because of the dormancy requirement, so fall is the time we visit the retail nurseries and purchase old roses that are being grown in containers.

Buying container-grown roses

Roses in containers can be bought and planted or repotted any time of the year with successful results. Fall through very early spring is prime time for planting in Zones 7 to 10, but there is no reason not to plant container roses in August if you are willing to give them extra water.

When choosing container plants, look for young specimens that are actively growing rather than large plants of the same variety that have obviously been in the pot a long time and may have a less active root system. We cannot stress strongly enough that health, not size, is the measure of quality when choosing old roses. A buyer looking at a species rose spilling out of its container may not like the looks of a puny little Tea rose that is only 12 in. tall at the same age, but the two varieties simply have different growth habits. Both will flourish and both are so tough that they'll probably be around for your grandchildren to enjoy.

One critical thing to remember about buying roses in containers is that they will need to be watered frequently until you can get them planted. The size of the container makes a difference, of course, and plants that have been grown in containers from the beginning will be under less stress than those that have been dug out of the field and then potted shortly before being offered for sale. It won't hurt to water a rose growing in a 2-gal. (or smaller) container every day, just to be safe. You can't overwater a plant in a well-drained container, and it's far better to water daily and protect your investment than to risk having the plant dry out and be damaged or killed. Of course, if you have transplanted your rose into a very large pot or half barrel, you may have to water only every four or five days. In our experience, however, even the largest containers benefit from a twice-weekly watering during the dog days of our Texas summer.

Rose mosaic viruses in nursery stock

Before we leave the topic of nurseries, there is one last subject to mention. There is a group of viruses, commonly called rose mosaic viruses, that can weaken the plants they infect and may limit their performance and shorten their life span. This type of virus sometimes shows up as an interesting mosaic pattern of yellow and green on the leaves of an infected rose. Sometimes there are no symptoms at all, except for general debility or an increased vulnerability to stressful conditions. The virus is passed on when infected tissue comes in contact with

Rose mosaic viruses can mottle rose leaves with yellow and green in various patterns. An infected plant may or may not show the telltale pattern, and it is impossible to predict whether the viruses will cause only imperceptible damage or seriously weaken their host.

a wounded area of clean tissue, which happens during the grafting procedure. Cuttings taken from an infected plant will probably have rose mosaic virus even if they are growing on their own roots.

Rose mosaic viruses can be destroyed by treating the material to be propagated (usually budwood for grafting) with heat over a period of time. A number of rose growers, both of old and modern varieties, are now involved in a program to eliminate rose mosaic from their stock, and we have noted those nurseries that sell virus-free roses under "Sources for Antique Roses" on pp. 218-219. It is worth asking at each nursery whether the roses you purchase can be certified virus-free. You will get better plants if they are, and if they're not, your request may motivate the owner to join the eradication program.

As long as you are satisfied with its performance, there's no reason to throw a rose out of your garden just because it is infected with rose mosaic virus; just don't propagate that plant. The disease cannot be transmitted by mechanical means, such as pruning shears or insects, so there is no risk to your other roses.

Rose mosaic viruses are a problem mainly in the United States rose industry. British growers also graft onto rootstocks, but they use primarily *Rosa canina* rootstock, which they grow from seed, and the viruses are not transmissible by seed. We hope that in another decade rose mosaic will be a bad memory instead of an active problem.

Growing Your Own Roses from Seed

All the propagation methods so far described (layering, cuttings, grafting and tissue culture) are ways to reproduce the exact genetic double of a given plant. When you grow a rose that has been produced by one of these methods, you are growing only one part of the bush. Other portions of the same bush may still linger by the pathway to some ruined plantation manor, on the grave of a child a hundred years dead or in the garden of a Chinese farmer. Genetically, these are all the same rose, though climate and soil variations may cause slight changes in appearance. There are only two ways to have new varieties of roses that have never before existed: One is to happen by chance upon a new genetic "sport" of a known variety and propagate it, and the other is to start from seed.

Growing from seed is different from other methods of propagation in that it involves two parents and thus two separate sets of genes. There is no way to know what the progeny will look like—any more than you can tell whether a human baby will favor the mother, the father or Great-Aunt Harriet. If you know both parents and the principles of genetics, you can make an educated guess, of course, and this is exactly what rose breeders do. From their educated guesses come each year's new rose introductions, as well as a lot more plants that end up on the compost heap. Even though breeders may work in a controlled environment, making sure that only the correct pollen fertilizes the chosen ovum, they still can't be sure of the results until they see the blooming plant. There are simply too many factors involved.

Breeding roses from seed is not difficult as long as you are patient and aren't particular about the results. Only species roses reproduce themselves exactly when grown from seed (that is part of the definition of a species rose), so if you are trying to grow seeds from any other class of rose, it's hit or miss what you'll get. Seeds are formed in roses just as they are in apples, which are close relatives. The blossom is fertilized, the petals drop, and the calyx swells and ripens into a hip, or fruit, with the seeds inside it. Once the hip has turned color (most are shades of red or orange) it can be assumed to be mature and ready to harvest. This will usually be in late summer—August or September for us. Formation of hips depends upon not cutting off spent blossoms, so you will have to allow your broodmares to look a little scraggly for a while. Not all roses will make hips, as some are not very fertile. Experience will teach you which are willing breeders, but we can recommend starting your experiments with 'Old Blush', a marvelously promiscuous China rose.

When you have collected the hips, split them open and remove the hairy seeds. Rose seeds can be dried and saved in an envelope (neatly labeled with parent and date) for quite a while, but in order to sprout they need moisture and a period of chilling. The least technical way to start rose seeds is to put them in jars containing premoistened (damp, not wet) milled sphagnum moss. Then cover them loosely so that they get some ventilation but don't dry out, and leave them in the refrigerator until they show signs of activity. This can take anywhere from a few weeks to a few years, depending on variety. You don't want to leave them in the refrigerator after they've begun to sprout, so you have to keep an eye on them. Don't let the refrigerated seeds dry out and above all don't forget to label them because it will be very difficult to remember which is what after a few months. (There are more scientific ways to proceed, involving stratification to soften the seed coat and very precise handling of materials and temperatures so that the results are more controllable. If you get seriously interested, it is worth doing some research.)

These are mature rose hips, picked in October. One has been split to reveal the ripe seeds.

Once a few seeds from one lot have started to sprout, you can assume that all of that same variety are ready to grow and plant them in a seed flat or into separate well-drained pots. Those seeds that have already sprouted can be potted separately, since you know they're going to grow, and this saves moving them from the flat to pots later on. The growing medium should be very fine and light (potting soil mixed half and half with perlite, or a mixture of two parts decomposed leaf mold to one part milled sphagnum and one part peat moss) and should be moistened thoroughly before planting the seeds.

Press the seeds gently into the damp mixture and cover them lightly to the depth of ¼ in. with more of the premoistened material. When the planting is finished, gently water the flat and/or pots and set in a

cool (50°F to 70°F) place out of direct sunlight. A garage often works well, though we do know of one bachelor who uses his unheated spare bedroom. After a week, most of the seedlings that are going to sprout (not all the seeds will be fertile) should have pushed through and will be ready to pot up individually and grow to garden size in a bright, sheltered area such as a greenhouse or coldframe.

When the first flowers appear, you'll have the joy of knowing that you're the only person in the world to have that particular new variety. Whether it turns out to be a superior plant or not, the proud feeling you'll have makes it worth going through the weeks of fuss at least once in your gardening life.

4 ◼ Planting, Protecting, Pruning

Gardening with antique roses does not demand a high level of skill. It requires instead that a gardener have common sense and no great addiction to rules. Every yard is a microclimate whose slight variations in soil, temperature and light can make roses perform differently than they do in the yard next door. What works for one gardener may not yield the same results for another, but Old Garden Roses have a wide range of tolerance for varied conditions so there is plenty of room to make mistakes and learn from them without fearing disaster.

We go into some detail in this chapter about preparing rose beds, planting techniques, protection from temperature extremes, pests and diseases, and the fine points of pruning. If our methods work for you, well and good. If not, feel free to adapt the basic information to fit your own experience and your garden's needs. "Rules," as G.A. Stevens writes in *Climbing Roses*, "are laid down for infants and beginners. The artist, be he poet, painter or gardener, is great only when he learns how to break them to advantage or to make new ones for himself alone."

'Old Blush' displays both flowers and hips at the same time. By not pruning off the last flush of flowers, you can encourage a fine fall and winter display of hips on those varieties that reliably produce them.

Getting Ready for Planting

While you are waiting for your old roses either to root, sprout or arrive in the mail, it's a good idea to evaluate the places you plan to put them. Chapter 1 deals in detail with the basic site requirements for a healthy rose. As we stated there, roses like a lot of sunshine (six or more hours a day) and fresh air, and they will not do well in heavy shade or in pockets where stagnant, moist air gets trapped. They're happiest without competition from the roots of large, established plants and trees, and they prefer soil with a pH range of 5 to 8 that has good drainage.

Preparing the soil

To a gardener, good soil is more precious than rubies. It is created naturally over a long period of time by vegetation that dies, decays and disintegrates into rich humus. It is alive with microorganisms and full of nutrients, with a texture that is thick enough to hold roots firmly but never so dense that it will block drainage. Good soil is usually dark in color and has a fertile, earthy fragrance that makes one want to dig into it immediately, preferably with bare hands. Karel Capek describes this reaction beautifully in *The Gardener's Year:*

> I find that the real gardener is not a man who cultivates flowers; he is a man who cultivates the soil....If he came into the Garden of Eden he would sniff excitedly and say: "Good Lord, what humus!" I think that he would forget to eat the fruit of the tree of knowledge of good and evil; he would rather look round to see how he could manage to take away from the Lord some barrow-loads of the paradisaic soil. Or he would discover that the tree of knowledge of good and evil has not round it a nice dishlike bed, and he would begin to mess about with the soil, innocent of what is hanging over his head. "Where are you, Adam?" the Lord would say. "In a moment," the gardener would shout over his shoulder; "I am busy now." And he would go on making his little bed.

Good soil is, quite literally, at the root of successful gardening, but unless you are very, very lucky, it is not something that you are going to find in your yard. Most of the vital top layer of soil is usually scraped off by bulldozers when a house lot is leveled for building. Anything left is often depleted of nutrients by the landscape plantings that are installed. Since tall grass, weeds and drifts of leaves are unfashionable, well-kept yards never have a chance to rebuild the precious layers of humus that were stripped away. Of course, some areas are so rocky or sandy that there wasn't any topsoil to lose, but this just adds force to our basic premise: If you want good soil, you will have to make it.

Do Old Garden Roses absolutely have to have good soil in order to grow? Not necessarily. You can plant the roses in gummy clay, stomp them in firmly, water and expect some results. Several little old ladies in our area do exactly that, and little old ladies are not to be taken lightly. If you want great roses, however, and want them to be long-lived, healthy and low-maintenance, then you really must start with the soil.

Making good soil is not difficult. All you need is organic material, a shovel and time. If you have reasonable soil to begin with (rather than solid clay, rock or sand), you can mix two-thirds of the soil with one-third organic material (by volume). Let the mixture take a month or two to ripen and then go ahead and plant. By organic material we mean well-decomposed manures, finely ground leaf or bark mulch, kitchen compost or anything of that nature. It is important that the material be decomposed to the point that it is dark, crumbly and earthy-smelling. If much of it is still pretty recognizable as bark chips or cucumber parings, it will continue to decompose after you've worked it into the ground. Since the process of decomposition can create enough heat to burn tender roots and also uses up nitrogen, material that is not thoroughly digested is not an ideal soil amendment unless you are willing to wait an extra few months for it to finish stabilizing before you plant.

There are many reference books that explain how to compost at home, using everything from kitchen scraps to shredded newspapers. You can also purchase composted manures and pine or fir bark at most retail garden centers. It is important to take the claim "composted" with a grain of salt when you make such a purchase, because much of the time the material is not sufficiently decomposed. You can either finish the process yourself by making a compost pile or go ahead and work it into the rose bed and let nature take care of it over time.

Adding decomposed organic material helps your existing soil in two critical ways. First, it improves the texture. Organic matter is not as easily compressed as is plain dirt, and the tiny openings between particles remain available to hold the air, water and nutrients necessary to support plant growth. If you have sandy soil that lets water and nutrients leach through too quickly, mixing in organic material as one-third or even one-half of the planting medium will greatly improve your gardening success. If you have heavy clay, adding one-third organic material will improve drainage and allow the root system of your rose to spread outward easily instead of struggling to grow. Clay holds nutrients well, and roses prefer it to all other soils; but a really tight clay can stunt their growth unless it is amended.

The second benefit of working organic material into the existing soil is that it acts as a sort of stimulating yeast. Good compost is alive with microorganisms, such as bacteria and mycorrhizal fungi, as well as with larger creatures like earthworms. These organisms process the nutrients in the soil and make them available to the roots of plants. The main purpose of allowing a prepared bed to rest and ripen for a month or two is to let the vitality of the compost infiltrate the more sterile existing soil. The longer you can bear to wait before planting, the richer and more nutritious your created soil will be.

If you live in an area with notoriously bad soil, you may want to ask the advice of the local Agricultural Extension agent about the benefits of adding amendments besides the organic material. Highly alkaline soils can be improved with iron sulfate or ground sulfur, while soil that is too acid can be tempered by adding ground limestone. Working agricultural gypsum into the planting area will slowly improve the texture of a dense clay soil.

Roses will get their best start if planted in a prepared bed that has been allowed to mellow for a few months. The soil in this large bed was amended with decomposed pine bark and sharp sand. The increased volume raised the bed above the original ground level and improved its drainage.

Preparing raised beds

Raising the proposed bed above ground level is another way to improve the planting area for your roses. This is excellent for drainage and especially beneficial in heavy clay soils. If you dig a hole down into clay, it doesn't matter how much rich compost you add, you still will have created a sort of bathtub that will hold plenty of water for the rose to sit in and rot. Raising the bed 6 in. to 12 in. above ground level (or even higher, since raised beds settle about 20% the first year) ensures safe drainage and a healthier rose.

To create a raised bed, just keep the soil that is already there and work your chosen organic material into it. Increasing the volume by one-third in this way ensures that the resultant mixture will be mounded up higher than ground level. If you have shoveled off the top layer of grass and weeds before preparing the bed, you may find yourself short of soil. Good topsoil (probably scraped from someone else's building lot) can be purchased to make up the difference. You can leave the bed unedged or frame it with old railroad ties, bricks or whatever you like, depending on the style of your garden. If you use railroad ties, beware of any that have been treated recently with creosote. As a rule of thumb, avoid lumber freshly treated with any preservative. Some of these products can wreak havoc in the garden if they leach into the soil.

If you are gardening in a very rocky area, you may not want to dig into the ground at all. Roses are relatively shallow-rooted, so building up a "planter" that is 18 in. to 24 in. deep will accommodate all but the largest varieties. If you have to make soil from scratch for this, the perfect mixture is one-third topsoil, one-third organic material and one-third builder's (sharp) sand. This is also a good mixture for potted roses, with a little agricultural gypsum thrown in to help keep the soil from compacting over time.

One final factor to consider is the size of the bed. This will depend on your level of energy: Bigger is better, but more of a chore. If you are planting a group of rose bushes or a hedge, try to extend the prepared soil for 2 ft. on each side of the crown of the bush. The absolute minimum for a single specimen is one-third wider than the rootball.

Planting Old Roses

Once you have prepared the soil and allowed it to ripen, you can plant at will. If you have purchased roses in containers, they will be ready to go into the ground immediately. The simple steps for planting them are shown in the drawing at right.

Planting Container-Grown Roses

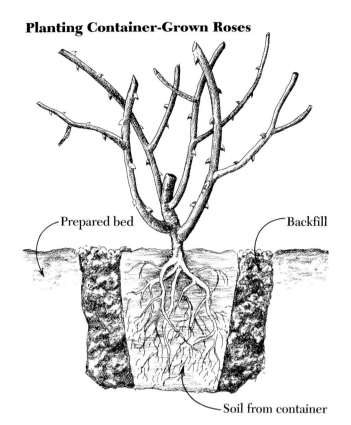

Prepared bed • Backfill • Soil from container

1. Dig a hole in the prepared bed slightly larger than the rose's container and equally deep.

2. Gently remove the rose from the container (try to avoid pulling on the plant itself) and place it in the hole.

3. Adjust for height so that when the hole is filled, the soil around the crown will be at the same level as it was in the container.

4. Fill in around the rootball.

5. Water thoroughly.

Dig a hole a little larger than the container and deep enough so that the rose will be at the same level in the ground that it was in the container. Slide the rose, rootball and all, gently out of its container and settle it into the hole. Pressing on the bottom of the container will usually loosen the rootball enough to slide it out easily. Pulling on the top of the plant too hard can damage it. The soil in which the rose was planted should stay in a mass with the roots. If most of it crumbles and falls off, you may want to treat the bush like a bare-root rose. When the rose is in the hole, scrape the loose soil back around it and work your shovel gently around the sides of the rootball so that the soil settles and major air pockets are

This healthy container-grown rose was removed from the pot at the nursery and shipped bare-root during the dormant season. When you receive a bare-root rose in the mail, remove it from the packaging immediately, clip off any damaged roots and canes, and soak the roots in water for up to 24 hours. Then plant the rose in the ground or in a pot.

eliminated. Water the newly planted rose thoroughly. If the soil around it subsides too far, add more until it is once again at the same level as was the soil in the container.

If you have ordered roses through the mail and received them bare-root, they will need a little more attention. They should be taken from the shipping box immediately and checked for signs of injury. Trim off damaged canes or roots with sharp shears just below the point of injury, then soak the roots in a bucket of water for anywhere from 1 hour to 24 hours, but not any longer or they'll get waterlogged.

If you can't plant bare-root roses in the ground immediately, bury them at about a 45° angle in moist earth, sand or compost, leaving only the branch tips exposed. This is called "heeling in," and it keeps the plants from becoming dehydrated and protects them from heat and cold. Make sure you bury them in a location protected from severe freezing temperatures. A cellar or shed is good. An alternative is to plant the roses directly into containers and keep them in a bright but sheltered area until planting conditions are right. Watered regularly, roses can be kept in containers (5-gal. size or larger) almost indefinitely.

Planting Bare-Root Roses

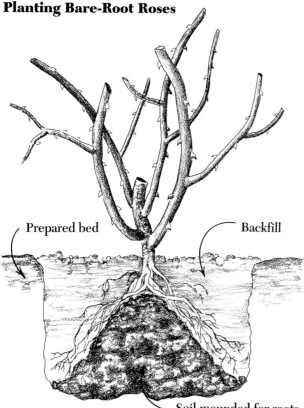

Prepared bed

Backfill

Soil mounded for roots

1. Dig a hole in the prepared bed large enough to accommodate the natural spread of the plant's roots.

2. Spread the roots evenly over soil you've mounded up in the bottom of the hole.

3. Carefully fill the hole with soil, tamping gently to eliminate air pockets. The final soil level should be where the crown shows a color change just above the roots.

4. Water thoroughly.

The technique for planting a bare-root rose is shown in the drawing above. Simply dig a hole in your prepared bed large enough to accommodate the natural spread of the roots. Like container-grown roses, bare-root roses should be planted at the same level at which they were previously growing. This can usually be determined by the soil staining on the crown or stem. (If you have purchased grafted roses

and would prefer them on their own roots, plant the crown of the bush at least 2 in. below the soil. This will encourage new roots belonging to the desired variety to form at the crown and take over the duties of the grafted rootstock.) Make a small mound of soil in the middle of the hole and spread the roots over it; this helps eliminate the problem of large air pockets remaining under the roots. Shovel the rest of the soil back over the roots, firm it down and water thoroughly. After that, container-grown roses and bare-root roses can be treated exactly the same.

Do not fertilize newly planted roses until they have had some time to root out and start a new flush of growth, perhaps four to six weeks after planting. It is all right to add about one-half cup of bone meal to the soil in the bottom of each hole; the phosphate in bone meal will help promote strong root growth and is released quite slowly. Applying a more balanced fertilizer too early, however, would push the rose to grow and bloom on top before the roots are well established, thus weakening the plant. The only additional care a newly planted rose will need is frequent and thorough watering for a few weeks, ideally once every three or four days to keep it from getting stressed.

Transplanting mature roses

The question of how to transplant a mature rose bush from one site to another comes up fairly often. It's always sad when a long-established old rose has to be moved, but if you are leaving town, or your grandmother's house is about to be sold to nongardening strangers or the site is being bulldozed for a parking lot there is little choice. If you can, try to take cuttings before digging up the plant. This will increase your chances of preserving it if some unfortunate accident should keep the original bush from surviving the move.

It's preferable to transplant in the winter while the plant is dormant, but that's not always possible. Just remember that you are putting the plant under tremendous stress by digging it up, and treat it as considerately as you can. Dig out the largest root ball you can manage, trying to keep the soil intact around the roots. Cut back the top of the plant until it is the same approximate size as the root mass, so that the remaining roots won't exhaust themselves trying to feed the entire original bush. (You can cut the top back first if it is in the way.) Don't let the roots dry out while the bush is being moved. If it is to be a long journey, wrap the rootball in damp burlap or newspaper. When you've got the rose planted in its new location, water it immediately and thoroughly. Continue to water it at frequent intervals: perhaps daily for the first week, and then every three or four days until the plant begins to show signs of recovery and active growth. If you cut the top back, keep the roots from drying out while moving and nurse the plant well with good soil and plenty of water at the new site, you should be able to transplant any rose at almost any season with success. Your rescued rose may not recover its original glory for a year or two, but if it was worth saving it will be worth waiting for.

Watering and Feeding Your Roses

Once your roses are planted and have settled in, taking care of them is not difficult. In our climate, roses like a good, deep soaking every seven to ten days, especially during dry spells. This kind of watering will encourage the roots to grow deeper into the ground and develops a sturdier and somewhat more drought-tolerant bush than one that is treated to more frequent, lighter sprinklings. If you can't afford an irrigation system that will take over the chore for you, simply letting a hose run for a few hours at a very slow trickle or drip will work fine.

Ideally, roses should be watered early in the morning so that their foliage will dry out quickly, but we've found by experience that old roses tolerate imperfect care. We do, however, recommend that you avoid daily wetting with a lawn sprinkler and watering in the heat of the day, when droplets of water can cause salts to build up on the leaves and can concentrate the sunlight enough to burn the foliage.

Roses also like fertilizer on a regular basis. They are known among horticulturists as "gross feeders." An established rose can be fed about once a month from early spring through early fall with any commercial rose food or balanced chemical fertilizer. We like to recommend alternating or replacing applications of chemical fertilizers with organic fertilizers such as fish emulsion, bat guano or manure tea (made from aged manure soaked in water). These organic products are particularly easy to use because they will not burn the roots if too much is applied and they help support the living micronutrients in the soil. All chemical fertilizers should be applied strictly according to the instructions on the label. More is generally not better! Almost every gardener has burned a plant to death by overenthusiastic fertilizing.

One critical thing to remember when applying fertilizers is to water heavily at the same time so that the ingredients will be dissolved properly. Fertilizer needs to be in solution for rose roots to be able to absorb it, and a thorough flushing with water will limit the chance of chemical burn. Unless your chosen fertilizer is specifically labeled as a foliar food, any traces of it should be washed off the leaves of the rose to prevent burns on the foliage.

It is up to you to decide which fertilizers you feel most comfortable using. We have heard everything from lawn food to hair clippings recommended, and one book even suggests planting a dead donkey under the rose bed. We do not personally have enough fanaticism to dig that big a hole, so we haven't resorted to the donkey. We also avoid systemic fertilizer/pesticides, that is, those that are put into the ground and then taken up by the root system. Systemics seem to be too strong for many of the antique roses and can cause some foliage mutation. Anything else will probably work fine, as long as you apply it according to the instructions.

Mulching and Cultivation

Mulching and cultivation are important elements of rose care. A 3-in. layer of mulch (such as bark chips, pine needles or leaves) not only helps protect rose roots from heat and cold, but will also continue to improve the soil as it decomposes into humus and gets worked into the bed. Unless you have very good soil already, the mulch layer seems to disappear rather fast, so you will probably want to replenish the mulch at regular intervals. We generally apply mulch every three months (at the change of each season), and we try to cultivate the beds freshly each time before we apply it. A bed that is regularly mulched and spaded will have almost unending vitality. In fact, a long-established bed in which the roses are no longer performing well can be revitalized by working it thoroughly with a shovel or garden fork. The incidental breakage of some roots is more than balanced by the benefits from improved aeration and drainage and renewed levels of micronutrients. To us, this demonstrates that the care and feeding of the soil is at least as important as the care and feeding of the roses themselves.

Protecting Roses from Extremes of Heat and Cold

Little, if any, cold protection is needed for antique roses in Zones 7 through 10, particularly if they are on their own roots (although a few of our roses are hardy only to Zone 8). The ground in these Zones never freezes deeply, so that even if the top of a bush is damaged in a sudden cold snap, there is usually plenty of vitality stored in the roots to fuel a quick comeback. One danger in the sunny South is that winters can be too warm, so that an unexpected hard freeze may catch a rose in a stage of active growth instead of settled dormancy. Even if a rose is on its own roots and not in danger of being killed off and replaced by the more vigorous rootstock, it is nonetheless distressing to lose the growth of several years. This rarely happens, but it doesn't hurt to take a few precautions, particularly with the more tender of the everblooming varieties.

The most important thing to do when a freeze is expected is to water your roses thoroughly. A well-watered plant is under less stress from dehydrating winds, and the water in the ground acts as an insulating barrier against the cold air. We saw proof of this one year when the above-ground portions of our most exposed roses were completely coated with ice after a sleet storm but came through the experience undamaged. At the same time, some of the more sheltered plants, which had no icy coating, showed withering at the ends of the canes from the temperature drop.

Another protective action is to mulch heavily around the bushes with bark chips, leaves, hay or whatever is handy. A 3-in. layer of mulch increases the insulation over the roots, keeps the soil temperature more stable and helps prevent water from evaporating too rapidly. In preparation for a really severe cold snap, it helps to mound the soil and/or mulch up to a depth of at least 6 in. over the crown of the rose. This mound should be raked back when the temperature begins to rise to prevent the rose roots from getting warm enough to break dormancy dangerously early.

It is more difficult to protect the tops of rose plants than it is to protect their roots. Usually, we make no effort to do this, trusting that Mother Nature knows what she's doing and that a rose said to be hardy to Zone 7 will indeed be so. If you have a less trusting nature and want to take extra steps, there are several things you can do. Loose brush or straw piled around the plants looks messy but does help protect them. Cylinders of tar paper can be stapled together quickly, placed around small or newly planted bushes and filled with mulch. We have sometimes even wrapped our pillar roses in thin sheets of insulating foam and then covered that with a layer of plastic in order to shelter their artistically arranged canes during a period of extreme cold. We have friends who regularly do this for their bushes. It's a lot of work, though, especially if you are trying to wrap plastic neatly around a thorny rose in a strong wind, and the benefits are worth the trouble only if the rose is very tender.

A layer of mulch will do wonders. It protects roots from the effects of heat and cold, smothers weeds and enriches the soil as it decomposes.

Wrapping a tender pillar rose may save a valuable plant from being cut back by an unusually hard freeze. The covering must be removed as soon as the weather warms up again or the rose may either cook or break dormancy too early.

Our main difficulty with covering the whole plant to protect it from the cold is that the weather here grows warm again so quickly. Seldom does a freeze last more than a few days, and when it is over you have to pull away the brush or unwrap the roses; otherwise they can boil in the sun or, worse yet, come out of dormancy inside their warm nest and become doubly vulnerable to the next freeze. In our unstable Zone, there is no easy solution (such as burying the roses in a trench for the winter as is done

in cold Zones) that we can apply once and be finished with for the season. For this reason, we prefer to depend on natural hardiness to see the roses through the winter.

If you live outside the recommended hardiness Zone for a rose you have a particular yen to grow, there is always the solution of growing it in a container. The cold-sensitive Chinas and Teas do very nicely in big pots and are quite successful in the North if they can be moved into a greenhouse or sheltered area for the duration of cold weather. Even climbers can be handled this way if the pot is large enough. Just remember that you'll have to move the container, so before you commit yourself to this plan you may want to obtain a rolling platform, or at least be sure you'll have additional labor on hand when needed.

Northern gardeners may be startled to learn that we find protection from the worst of the summer heat to be just as necessary as protection from the cold. When the daytime temperatures stay over 90°F and the nights are in the 80s, roses (and other plants) go into what is essentially another period of dormancy. They cease active growth and do little, if any, blooming. They often shed some leaves to cut down on water loss. If they are water stressed during this period, it can really affect the quality and quantity of fall flowers, so it is worth paying a little extra attention to your roses in hot weather.

Once again, a thorough watering is the main key to success. If the roots are well soaked every week or 10 days, you will be rewarded with better summer foliage, fewer overall disease problems and better fall bloom. In addition, a 3-in. layer of mulch is just as effective an insulator against heat as it is against cold and provides the added benefit of smothering weeds.

The only other practices to remember for extremes of both hot and cold weather are the "don'ts": Don't prune until after the last major freeze or after the worst of the heat (see p. 86 for details). That way you won't stimulate the tender new growth that is most easily damaged. If you spray, don't spray in the heat of the day. Wait until evening so the sun won't cause the oils in the spray to burn the leaves. Above all, don't worry. The old roses that have survived this long are the tough ones, not the high-tech ones. If you do your part with water and mulch, they'll do their part by living and thriving.

Pests and Diseases: To Spray or Not to Spray?

We are interested in rose health for several reasons. Most obviously, an insect-infested and disease-covered rose is less attractive than a healthy one. Spraying toxic chemicals, however, is an unpleasant and expensive chore, and, in addition, the trend in both agriculture and the ornamental plant business is away from relying on chemicals as a cure-all. This is important information to bear in mind, because it means that in 10 years' time many of the rose sprays available today may no longer be on the market. For these reasons, we strongly recommend good gardening practices (preparing the soil, proper watering, etc.) as an alternative to chemical support.

There is good evidence that the "heavy artillery" approach may be counterproductive. For example, the George E. Owen Municipal Rose Garden in Eugene, Oregon, has been using Integrated Pest Management (IPM) techniques on both modern and antique roses for the past several years. IPM practice does use chemicals, but only minimal quantities and only after trying less-toxic alternatives. The garden in Eugene has completely phased out both the use of fungicides and preventive spraying for insects, saving both time and money. Best of all, growth and flowering have been described as "spectacular" since IPM practices were implemented.

It is easier for us to do without chemicals because we deal with old roses, most of which have a better resistance to disease and pests than do modern varieties. We do not mean to imply that old roses are always disease and pest free. But they are very tough, and even if they are stricken with blackspot or mildew and lose a whole set of leaves, they usually recover in a season instead of growing weak and dying. This means that a gardener who grows old roses has the option of either treating problems as they arise or taking a wait-and-see approach.

The major task in dealing with insect and disease problems is to re-adjust our thinking on what is acceptable. Roses are living plants and are part of the natural world. They are meant to support some parasites, and they are also meant to self-select for

A rose's resistance to pests and disease can vary by variety. The low hedge in the foreground (a found rose that may be related to **Rosa wichuraiana**) *fell victim to a spider-mite infestation that had no apparent effect on the Tea and Polyantha bushes behind it. Damaged as it looks in this photo, the hedge was fully recovered in several weeks and bloomed on schedule.*

varieties that will withstand adverse conditions. This is what antique roses have done through the useful combination of time and neglect, and this is why they need less artificial protection.

The roses we grow in our own gardens show some signs of blackspot and mildew every spring and fall, when warm days and cool nights combine with high humidity to encourage fungal diseases. The petals on some of their flowers are marked now and then by sucking insects such as aphids and thrips. But we have learned by experience that our roses will not be killed or crippled or even stop blooming when these attacks occur. They may not be perfect specimens, but they are essentially healthy, and they grow and bloom vigorously. They support a population of aphid-eating ladybugs and mantises, birds nest in them safely, and we can make rose-petal jam with no worries.

Occasionally there will be a severe outbreak of disease in response to weather conditions, or in preparation for a major public event at the display garden, we may find our tolerance for blemishes greatly reduced. At such times we do resort to using a fungicide on specific plants that show a high level of blackspot or mildew. We are fortunate in having no Japanese beetles and very little spider-mite trouble, so we are trying to phase out insecticides completely in order to maintain the population of beneficial insects. We've also found that a high pressure hosing with plain water, especially on the underside of the leaves, can keep pest populations at a tolerable level.

Three common seasonal rose problems are (from top to bottom) powdery mildew, blackspot and rust. It is not always necessary to spray for these diseases; many old roses are highly resistant, and those that are somewhat susceptible may recover quickly. If you have an antique rose that is chronically affected by one of these diseases, it may be that that variety is simply unsuited to your climate or planted in a poor location.

The only way to determine what is necessary to meet your own needs is to spend time observing your garden. We walk through our gardens daily, just looking at the plants, seeing how they're doing and what they might need. Nothing can replace observation as a tool for maintaining healthy plants, and you will recover some of the time spent whenever you find that you don't need to spray after all. You will also become more intimate with the habits and cycles of your roses and more aware of all their beauties.

"Planting healthy" at the outset is the most low-cost, low-effort way to prevent severe disease and insect attack. A plant that is not overly stressed by environmental factors will be less susceptible to problems and swifter to recover from them. But if you do spray, please heed these warnings. First, be very careful of the time of application of any spray, including the soap-based "organic" varieties. If you spray your roses during the heat of the day, the oils and soaps can break down the natural protective coating on the leaves and make them vulnerable to severe burns from a hot sun. Early morning or early evening is fairly safe (evening is preferable). Old roses don't need, and sometimes can't tolerate, the heavy-artillery approach to spraying. And as we've seen damage in response to systemic pesticides as well, we are firm in recommending a minimalist approach. Treat only the problems you've got, and don't panic at the sight of a spotty leaf or damaged bud. Your rose will not die even if you neglect to treat it at all.

Aphids on a Tea rose. There are many non-chemical methods of controlling these pests before they build up to a serious infestation. Applications of beneficial insects or a strong spraying with water will both help.

If you are growing old roses with the idea of exhibiting them in total perfection at a show, or if you have old roses mixed in with Hybrid Teas that are on a strict spray program, you'll have to work out by observation the ratio between the positive and negative effects of spraying. You can also ask local rose-society members for their suggestions.

Pruning Antique Roses

Roses are shrubs in the truest sense of the word, which means that if a goat chews on a rose, it grows back fuller and bushier than it was before. The majority of the older roses seem to share this admirable trait. With the exception of some of the old European varieties and some of the Hybrid Perpetuals, there is little or no dieback on canes that have been pruned, so the precision clipping required by Hybrid Teas is simply not necessary. We are fairly sure that a goat doesn't check to be sure that he is biting on a neat angle slightly above an outward-facing bud or leaf node before he browses, so we don't worry either.

Why prune?

There are three important reasons to prune a rose bush, even though pruning is not a procedure that is required to keep the plant alive. First, bush-type roses in particular will benefit from the stimulation of being cut back, and they will respond by covering themselves thickly with lush new growth and a multitude of flowers. Second, the general appearance of the plant is improved by an annual or twice-yearly grooming to clean out dead and broken branches and to help the natural form of the plant display itself. Last, and by no means least, pruning is a form of preventive health care. Removing weak, dead and damaged canes eliminates tissue that is a target for disease and insect problems and allows the rose to focus its nutrients and energy on healthy, productive growth. Thinning out the interior growth allows air to flow through the plant more freely, keeping the leaves drier and the risk of disease lower.

When to prune remontant vs. once-blooming roses

There are three factors affecting when and how a rose is pruned. The first is growth habit. Bush-type roses are not the same as climbing roses in structure, and common sense dictates that they be groomed differently. The second is the plant's pattern of flowering, that is, whether it is once-blooming or remontant. The third is the season of the year and the ambient temperature.

Roses that give their all in a single massive display in the spring must not be pruned until after they have bloomed, whereas repeat bloomers are generally pruned six or seven weeks before the first spring bloom and can be pruned again for a lush display in the fall. The time to prune differs because once-blooming roses bear flowers on canes that have fully matured and gone through a winter, while repeat bloomers flower on the new growth of the season (about six weeks after that growth has begun). If a rose that blooms only once is pruned too early, much of the spring display will be lost to the shears.

The time of the year that you prune is important because pruning stimulates roses to put out tender new growth, which is easily damaged by heat and cold. We wait to prune our remontant roses until after the last hard freeze of the year. This is mid-February for us in Zone 8, but will be in late January for frost-free Zones, in early March for Zone 7 and even later for colder areas. Pruning too early not only removes the protective canopy of existing canes, but also encourages new shoots, and a rose that is actively growing is at increased risk in a hard freeze because its nutrient and carbohydrate supply is up in the canes instead of safely stored in the roots. As we explained on pp. 80-81 when talking about cold protection, under identical weather conditions, a dormant plant may be undamaged, whereas a plant in full growth can be killed. In Zones where there are many warm, sunny winter days, it can be difficult to resist the temptation to go out into the garden and start cleaning up the roses, but don't do it. You'll only have to do it again after the last freeze, and you may hurt your plants badly in the process.

Another bad time to prune is during the dog days of summer, when temperatures are extremely high. Stimulating new growth in the stress of heat and drought can be as crippling as midwinter pruning. If you wait until the worst of the heat has passed, the roses will respond much better. We strongly recommend an early fall pruning in addition to the spring pruning for remontant bush roses. The cool temperatures of fall seem to encourage the largest and most brilliant flowers, and the impetus of a good pruning ensures a plentiful display of these beauties six weeks later. For us in Zone 8 it is hard to choose between the April/May show and the one in October/November.

How to prune

In her book *My Roses and How I Grew Them*, written in 1900, Helen Milman describes perfectly how to approach the task of pruning roses by hand: "First cut out all the dead wood; then weak wood—that is, poor, thin-looking twigs. And when this is done just meditate a while on the shape of your plant, and make up your mind what to take and what to leave."

If you know when to prune and know the habits of the type of rose you're pruning, then Milman's directions are really all you'll ever need. We discussed some of the techniques of pruning in Chapter 2 when we looked at how to fit roses into a particular landscape niche. Here, we take a more general look at the theory of pruning, with a particular eye to how the various classes we cover behave under the clippers.

Pruning Old Garden Roses

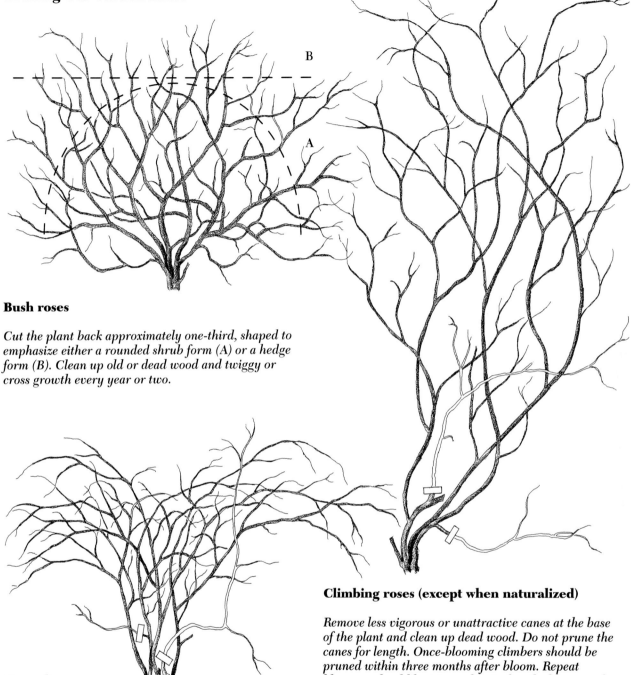

Bush roses

Cut the plant back approximately one-third, shaped to emphasize either a rounded shrub form (A) or a hedge form (B). Clean up old or dead wood and twiggy or cross growth every year or two.

Cascading roses

Fan to emphasize the grace of reclining branches. Remove any branches that don't fit the visual pattern and any dead wood.

Climbing roses (except when naturalized)

Remove less vigorous or unattractive canes at the base of the plant and clean up dead wood. Do not prune the canes for length. Once-blooming climbers should be pruned within three months after bloom. Repeat bloomers should be trimmed just after the bloom cycle to encourage heavy flowering throughout the year. Prune just before the plant comes out of dormancy in spring (early February in Zone 8) and before the fall growth (early September in Zone 8).

Above: This bed of Tea roses was clipped lightly with hedge shears in late February, and all the dead and weak growth was removed from the center of each plant with hand pruners. Right: The same bed photographed from the same angle in mid-April. The Teas responded to the pruning by covering themselves in flowers and new growth.

Pruning very bushy roses: Chinas and Teas

The easiest roses to prune are those that have a naturally bushy form with lots of internal branching. Most of the China and Tea roses are in this category. They can be painstakingly shaped using a pair of sharp hand pruners, but we have found that giving them an all-over haircut with sharp hedge shears is very efficient and takes the least amount of time. It is liberating to realize that you can go after some of your roses with a sharp weapon and pay them back for a million thorn scratches, especially since they not only will not suffer but will respond with enthusiasm. But don't get carried away and hack the bush to pieces. Removal of about one-third of the total bush is the maximum that we would recommend. Old roses don't need to be pruned hard to grow well. In fact, Tea roses will sulk if pruned too much (more than one-third), and besides, the more bush you have, the more flowers you get. If you like, you can go back over the bush after shearing it and tidy up any dead bits or weak growth in the interior with hand pruners. This is not aesthetically necessary for the very bushy varieties, because the new growth will cover all signs of pruning in just a week or two, but it does help maintain good health.

Left: The natural grace of a 'Swamp Rose', unpruned, is masked by a too-thick mass of canes. Above: After the bush is thinned out by cutting away selected canes at their base, the good bones of Rosa palustris show clearly.

Pruning less-dense bushes: Old European roses and others Roses that have a bush form that is not as well-branched as the Teas and Chinas, such as those with longer individual canes that tend either to grow in a loose, upright fashion or to cascade outward like a fountain, respond best to more thoughtful pruning than can be achieved with the hedge shears. Some old European roses and certain individual specimens like 'Russelliana' or the 'Swamp Rose' have this more arching habit, and they should be cut with an eye to exposing their beauty of form. They will usually look best if you simply thin them instead of cutting them back. Removing any canes at the base that spoil the graceful line, plus any dead material, will encourage the rose to grow in a fountain shape rather than as a chunky bush.

Pruning climbing roses Preserving the line is a major consideration when you are dealing with climbing roses, no matter how you have them trained. Climbers don't require pruning in order to bloom attractively, and they have a different habit of growth than do bush roses. If their canes are shortened at all, climbers respond in confusion by throwing out both new long canes and bushy growth at the same time, and soon they look more like a rose gone mad than a thing of beauty. All climbing roses require is removal of weak and dead wood, and the occasional thinning out of shorter canes that distract the eye from the basic form. Other than that, if a cane is doing something you don't like (such as smacking your car when you enter the driveway), feel free to cut it off. Try, however, to cut it at the base or at a natural branching point so that its loss is unnoticeable and so you don't leave an unsightly stub that will grow unattractive, long, witchy fingers.

In pruning climbers, don't assume that all the older canes should be discarded and the new ones kept. Climbing roses can produce flowers on the same cane for many years. As long as all the canes seem healthy, choose those that are most attractive and easiest to work with and cut away the extras cleanly at the base.

If your roses are trained more formally (neatly braided up a pillar, for example), you will want to take them down completely about every third year, depending on the variety's growth, and thin out weak or unproductive canes along with the dead wood. Thinning out the canes keeps the plant healthier by allowing better air movement, and it keeps the shape balanced.

Not pruning naturalized climbers   If you are using climbing roses in a naturalized landscape where they are seen at some distance, then you don't need to prune them at all. We recommend an annual effort to remove whatever dead wood may have accumulated, just for the sake of health and vigor, but even that is not required. Species roses in particular, such as 'Lady Banks' Rose' or 'Fortuniana', will happily fling themselves up trees and over obstacles and take care of their own basic needs with no help.

Just as a reminder, species roses and some of the other Old Garden Roses bloom only once a year and should not be pruned in the spring before they bloom. If they need to be pruned at all, wait until after they have bloomed and the flowers are fading before you tidy them up. Once-blooming roses won't give a good display if you have to keep cutting them back at the wrong time, so be sure to plant them in an area where their natural size is appropriate and won't cause problems.

Ensuring a display of hips

It is worth mentioning one other reason not to prune your roses. If spent flowers are allowed to stay on the bush, many types of roses will form hips (the rose fruit). Rose hips are quite varied and interesting. They come in different sizes and shapes and usually ripen in the fall, adding delightful color to the rose plant well into the winter. Hips are edible and can be used for jelly or tea or even rose-hip soup if you don't spray your roses with pesticides. The fruits of the rose are high in vitamin C and taste like a cross between apples and the tablets of vitamin C with rose hips that you can buy at the drugstore. Branches of rose hips make a fine addition to fall arrangements of cut flowers. Some roses, like the China rose 'Old Blush', are considerate enough to have flowers and hips at the same time, so you can enjoy them together. The Rose Use Chart on pp. 97-101 indicates whether or not a given variety forms enough hips for a good show.

If you decide to keep the hips, the only thing you have to do is leave the last crop of flowers on the bush. We have so many roses that we rarely bother to "deadhead" spent flowers, but many gardeners like to clip them off for neatness and to encourage a slightly heavier blooming. This doesn't affect basic pruning instructions for remontant roses: just leave them alone after their fall display. It does mean that you might want to avoid any clipping on the once-blooming roses, particularly the species varieties, except to remove dead or unsightly growth.

The decision to let your roses form hips is not only good for adding an extra visual dimension to your garden, it is also a wonderful excuse for doing the least work necessary. We don't think roses should require much work, so we are all for leaving spent flowers on the bush. When you clip the roses again in the spring, you can cut off all the (by now) dried hips and let the cycle of growth and bloom start all over again.

5 ▪ Encyclopedia of Selected Old Garden Roses

This Encyclopedia provides detailed information to help you determine which antique roses will fit your needs and which will grow best for you. It includes the most recent USDA Zone Map (p. 96) and a Rose Use Chart (pp. 97-101) for cross-referencing the roses we discuss. We have limited ourselves to 80 roses because we feel that this number provides quite enough variety to create an exquisite garden of any size.

Using the Encyclopedia

The Encyclopedia begins with a brief background of rose history and breeding to create a framework for the detailed class and variety descriptions that follow. Twelve classes of Old Garden Roses are represented (five of them under the heading "Old European Roses"). They are presented in order of their development, beginning with the species roses and their hybrids and ending with the almost modern Hybrid Perpetuals. Under each class heading, the varieties are listed in order of their date of introduction into commerce. The entry for each variety describes its history, appearance and particular charm and gives suggestions

The Noisette rose 'Alister Stella Gray'.

for using it in the garden. A close-up photograph of the flower accompanies each description, and most entries have a photograph of the rose in a garden setting as well, to give an idea of relative size and form. Those roses that have no landscape photo are cross-referenced to a variety that is nearly identical in garden form.

A word about quotation marks

We have followed the accepted practice of putting the official name of each rose, as sanctioned by *Modern Roses 9*, in single quotes (e.g., 'Mermaid'). The Latin names of species roses and their hybrids are in italics *(Rosa palustris)*, but the common names of those roses ('Swamp Rose') are in single quotes, as are previously accepted or alternate names. Double quotation marks indicate the study name of a found rose, such as "Maggie". Rose classes are capitalized, though the word "rose" is not part of the class name. Therefore, the class designation is Moss rose, but 'Moss Rose' is a previously common variety name for 'Centifolia Muscosa'.

The quick reference line

At the end of each variety description is a line designed to provide quick reference to the rose's character. A typical entry might read: Zone 7 / 3 ft. to 4 ft. high / 2 ft. to 3 ft. wide / very fragrant / light pink / remontant.

The Rose Use Chart

The same information found in the quick reference line, and more, is provided in the Rose Use Chart on pp. 97-101. The chart is arranged so that the varieties can be cross-referenced quickly if you are searching for a particular set of characteristics, say, a remontant white climber hardy to Zone 6.

Index to symbols in the Rose Use Chart

Zone hardiness   The Zone number assigned to each variety represents the coldest USDA Zone in which that rose will reliably survive. A variety rated for Zone 7, for example, might suffer severe freeze damage in Zone 6 and below. Certain roses, such as some of the old European varieties, are quite cold tolerant but may not do as well in the warmest Zones. If heat tolerance is a problem, the information is included in the discussion of that variety.

Our estimate of the Zone hardiness of a given variety is based on our own experience, on data collected from other experts and the rose literature and on the wealth of information provided by our customers in the mail-order business. If a rose does not perform well in a given Zone, our customers often write to tell us so.

Zone numbers are based on the most recent USDA Plant Hardiness Zone Map (see p. 96).

Size   Sizes are given for mature specimens and reflect our own experience with the variety in question. Some varieties may exceed the listed size, depending upon climate, location, richness of soil and other factors. Bush varieties are listed by height and width, climbers by height (i.e., length of canes) only.

Fragrance   Fragrance is so subjective that it is difficult to categorize. We have indicated only the intensity of fragrance in each variety, rather than attempting to key out its relative quality.
SF = slight fragrance or none at all
F = fragrant
VF = very fragrant

Hips   The color and shape of rose hips vary from class to class, with the species roses showing the most variation within one class. A variety designated "H" in the chart is one that reliably gives a good show of hips in the fall. "Few" means that there are enough hips to notice, though not a great show. This does not mean that the other varieties do not produce hips, just that they aren't usually present in significant numbers.

Garden form   Garden form is given for the most common usage of each variety in the landscape. Some varieties have more flexibility than others; further possibilities are suggested in the individual descriptions. Bush varieties that have a climbing sport are not indicated in the Rose Use Chart, but individual descriptions will note this information.

>   smB = small bush
>   B = bush
>   lgB = large bush
>   C = climber
>   C/B = can be trained as either a climber or bush

Color   The color abbreviations are those used in *Modern Roses 9*, the current standard for classifying roses. Our own perception of a color may differ slightly, since soil and climate can affect the color, number of petals and even flower size of many roses. The photographs provide an additional guide.

>   ab = apricot blend
>   mb = mauve blend
>   ob = orange blend
>   pb = pink blend
>   rb = red blend
>   yb = yellow blend
>   m = mauve
>   dp = deep pink
>   lp = light pink
>   mp = medium pink
>   dr = dark red
>   mr = medium red
>   o-r = orange-red
>   r = russet
>   dy = deep yellow
>   my = medium yellow
>   w = white

Frequency of bloom
>   RR = reliable repeat
>   R = remontant
>   SR = slightly remontant
>   O = once-blooming

"RR" indicates those roses like Teas and Chinas that bloom approximately every six weeks for us. The "R" designation is for those varieties that bloom heavily only in the spring and in the fall, though they may have scattered flowers throughout the growing season. An "SR" rose can be counted on to bloom well in spring, but may repeat only inconsistently for us in the fall. Your experience may be different. The once-blooming roses ("O") give their full display only once a year, generally in early to late spring.

Time of bloom   Because of their response to seasonal changes, different varieties of roses begin blooming at different times of the year. The order of bloom is usually constant, that is, 'Veilchenblau' will almost always bloom later than 'Apothecary's Rose'. Unexpected stress, such as a late hard freeze, however, may delay some of the early starters and thus reduce the amount of time between their first flowers and those of the mid-spring to summer roses.

>   E = early spring
>   EM = early to mid-spring
>   M = mid-spring
>   MS = mid-spring to summer
>   S = summer

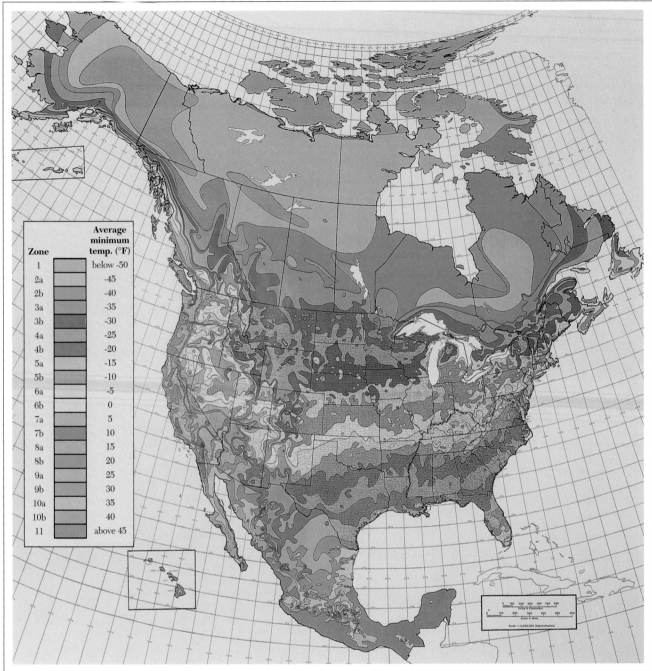

Zone	Average minimum temp. (°F)
1	below -50
2a	-45
2b	-40
3a	-35
3b	-30
4a	-25
4b	-20
5a	-15
5b	-10
6a	-5
6b	0
7a	5
7b	10
8a	15
8b	20
9a	25
9b	30
10a	35
10b	40
11	above 45

USDA Plant Hardiness Zone Map

Agricultural Research Service, USDA

Rose Use Chart

	Coldest USDA Zone Tolerated	Height Range (ft.)	Width Range (ft.)	Fragrance	Hips	Garden Form	Color	Frequency of Bloom	Time of Bloom	Page
Species Roses										
Rosa moschata 'Musk Rose'	6	4–6	3–4	VF	H	B	w	R	S	111
R. eglanteria 'Eglantine'	4	7–12	5–8	VF	H	lgB	lp	O	E	113
R. laevigata 'Cherokee Rose'	7	>15		F	H	C	w	O	E	114
R. banksiae banksiae 'Lady Banks' Rose'	8	>20		VF		C	w	O	E	115
R. roxburghii 'Chestnut Rose'	6	5–7	4–5	SF	H	B	mp	SR	MS	116
R. palustris scandens 'Swamp Rose'	4	4–6	4–6	SF		B	mp	O	MS	117
'Harison's Yellow'	4	4–6	3–5	F	H	B	dy	O	EM	119
'Stanwell Perpetual'	3	3–5	3–5	VF		B	w	RR	E	120
'Fortune's Double Yellow'	8	>12		VF		C	yb	O	E	121
'Fortuniana'	7	>20		VF		C	w	O	E	122
'Mermaid'	7	>20		F		C	my	R	EM	123
R. setigera serena 'Prairie Rose'	3	>8		SF		C	mp	O	S	124

Key

Fragrance
SF = slight fragrance
F = fragrant
VF = very fragrant

Hips
H = good fall show
few = enough to notice

Garden Form
smB = small bush
B = bush
lgB = large bush
C = climber
C/B = trained as either a climber or bush

Color
ab = apricot blend
mb = mauve blend
ob = orange blend
pb = pink blend
rb = red blend
yb = yellow blend
m = mauve
dp = deep pink
lp = light pink
mp = medium pink
dr = dark red
mr = medium red
o-r = orange-red
r = russet
dy = deep yellow
my = medium yellow
w = white

Frequency of Bloom
RR = reliable repeat
R = remontant
SR = slightly remontant
O = once-blooming

Time of Bloom
E = early spring
EM = early to mid-spring
M = mid-spring
MS = mid-spring to summer
S = summer

	Coldest USDA Zone Tolerated	Height Range (ft.)	Width Range (ft.)	Fragrance	Hips	Garden Form	Color	Frequency of Bloom	Time of Bloom	Page
Old European Roses										
'Apothecary's Rose'	3	2–5	2–4	VF	H	B	dp	O	E	128
'Cardinal de Richelieu'	4	3–5	2–4	VF		B	m	O	M	129
'York and Lancaster'	3	3–5	3–5	VF	H	B	pb	O	M	130
'Celsiana'	3	4–6	2–4	VF	H	B	lp	O	M	131
'Ispahan'	3	5–7	2–4	VF		B	mp	O	EM	132
'Autumn Damask'	4	3–5	2–4	VF	H	B	mp	R	M	133
'Madame Plantier'	4	4–6	6–8	VF		B	w	O	M	134
'Celestial'	3	4–6	3–4	VF	few	B	lp	O	MS	135
'Fantin-Latour'	3	4–6	3–5	VF		B	lp	O	M	136
'Crested Moss'	4	3–5	2–4	VF	few	B	mp	O	EM	137
'Salet'	4	3–4	3–4	VF	H	B	mp	R	M	138

Key

Fragrance
SF = slight fragrance
F = fragrant
VF = very fragrant

Hips
H = good fall show
few = enough to notice

Garden Form
smB = small bush
B = bush
lgB = large bush
C = climber
C/B = trained as either
 a climber or bush

Color
ab = apricot blend
mb = mauve blend
ob = orange blend
pb = pink blend
rb = red blend
yb = yellow blend
m = mauve
dp = deep pink
lp = light pink
mp = medium pink
dr = dark red
mr = medium red
o-r = orange-red
r = russet
dy = deep yellow
my = medium yellow
w = white

Frequency of Bloom
RR = reliable repeat
R = remontant
SR = slightly remontant
O = once-blooming

Time of Bloom
E = early spring
EM = early to
 mid-spring
M = mid-spring
MS = mid-spring to
 summer
S = summer

	Coldest USDA Zone Tolerated	Height Range (ft.)	Width Range (ft.)	Fragrance	Hips	Garden Form	Color	Frequency of Bloom	Time of Bloom	Page
China Roses										
'Old Blush'	6	5–8	3–6	F	H	lgB	mp	RR	E	142
'Rouletii'	6	2–3	2–3	SF		smB	mp	RR	EM	144
'Le Vésuve'	7	2–4	2–4	SF	few	smB	pb	RR	EM	145
'Cramoisi Supérieur'	7	3–6	3–4	VF		B	mr	RR	EM	146
'Archduke Charles'	7	3–5	2–4	F	H	B	rb	RR	EM	147
'Hermosa'	6	2–4	2–3	VF	few	smB	lp	RR	EM	148
'Green Rose'	7	3–4	2–3	SF		B	gr	RR	E	149
'Ducher'	7	2–4	2–3	F	H	smB	w	RR	EM	150
'Jean Bach Sisley'	6	4–6	3–4	F		B	pb	RR	EM	151
'Mutabilis'	7	4–7	3–5	SF	H	B	yb	RR	EM	152
'Comtesse du Cayla'	7	3–5	2–3	VF		B	ob	RR	M	153
"Pam's Pink"	7	3–5	3–4	F	few	B	pb	RR	M	154
"Martha Gonzales"	7	1–3	1–3	SF		smB	mr	RR	EM	155

	Coldest USDA Zone Tolerated	Height Range (ft.)	Width Range (ft.)	Fragrance	Hips	Garden Form	Color	Frequency of Bloom	Time of Bloom	Page
Noisette Roses										
'Champneys' Pink Cluster'	7	6–8	3–5	VF	H	C/B	lp	RR	EM	159
'Blush Noisette'	7	4–6	3–4	VF	H	smB	w	RR	EM	160
'Lamarque'	7	>15		VF	few	C	w	RR	MS	161
'Jaune Desprez'	7	>15		VF		C	yb	RR	MS	162
'Jeanne d'Arc'	7	6–8	3–5	F	H	C/B	w	RR	M	164
'Maréchal Niel'	8	>15		VF		C	my	R	M	165
'Rêve d'Or'	7	>15		VF	H	C	my	R	MS	166
'Madame Alfred Carrière'	6	>15		VF		C	w	R	MS	167
'Nastarana'	6	3–4	2–3	VF	H	smB	w	RR	M	168
'Alister Stella Gray'	7	>8		F		C/B	w	RR	M	169

	Coldest USDA Zone Tolerated	Height Range (ft.)	Width Range (ft.)	Fragrance	Hips	Garden Form	Color	Frequency of Bloom	Time of Bloom	Page
Bourbon Roses										
'Souvenir de la Malmaison'	6	3–4	3–4	VF		smB	lp	RR	M	173
'Zéphirine Drouhin'	6	>8		VF	H	C	mp	R	M	174
'Madame Isaac Pereire'	5	5–7	3–5	VF	H	C/B	dp	SR	M	176
'Kronprincessin Viktoria'	6	3–4	3–4	F		smB	w	RR	M	177
'Madame Ernest Calvat'	5	6–8	3–5	VF	H	C/B	mp	SR	M	178
'Honorine de Brabant'	6	5–7	3–5	VF	H	C/B	pb	R	M	179
"Maggie"	6	6–8	3–5	VF	H	C/B	mr	RR	M	180

	Coldest USDA Zone Tolerated	Height Range (ft.)	Width Range (ft.)	Fragrance	Hips	Garden Form	Color	Frequency of Bloom	Time of Bloom	Page
Hybrid Multiflora Roses										
R. multiflora carnea	5	>15		F	H	C	lp	O	MS	183
'Seven Sisters'	6	>15		F		C	pb	O	S	184
'Russelliana'	6	5–8	4–7	F	H	C/B	m	O	MS	185
'Trier'	5	8–12	6–8	F	H	C	w	R	M	187
'Veilchenblau'	5	>12		SF		C	mb	O	S	188

	Coldest USDA Zone Tolerated	Height Range (ft.)	Width Range (ft.)	Fragrance	Hips	Garden Form	Color	Frequency of Bloom	Time of Bloom	Page
Tea Roses										
'Bon Silène'	7	4–6	3–4	F	few	B	dp	RR	EM	192
'Safrano'	6	4–6	3–4	F	H	B	ab	RR	EM	193
'Sombreuil'	7	>10		VF		C	w	RR	M	194
'Duchesse de Brabant'	6	4–6	3–4	VF		B	lp	RR	EM	195
'Marie van Houtte'	7	5–7	4–5	F		lgB	pb	RR	EM	196
'Perle des Jardins'	7	3–5	2–3	F	few	B	my	RR	EM	197
'Souvenir de Thérèse Lovet'	7	4–6	3–4	F		B	dr	RR	EM	198
'Madame Antoine Rebe'	7	4–6	3–4	F		B	rb	RR	EM	199
'Monsieur Tillier'	7	4–6	3–4	F		B	pb	RR	EM	200
'Maman Cochet'	7	3–5	3–4	VF		B	pb	RR	EM	201
'Madame Berkeley'	7	3–5	3–4	F		B	ab	RR	EM	203
'Mrs. B.R. Cant'	7	6–8	5–7	VF		lgB	mp	RR	EM	204
'Lady Hillingdon'	7	4–6	3–4	VF		C/B	yb	RR	EM	205
'Rosette Delizy'	7	3–5	3–4	F		B	yb	RR	EM	206

	Coldest USDA Zone Tolerated	Height Range (ft.)	Width Range (ft.)	Fragrance	Hips	Garden Form	Color	Frequency of Bloom	Time of Bloom	Page
Hybrid Perpetual Roses										
'Marquise Boccella'	4	3–4	2–3	VF	H	B	lp	RR	M	209
'Baronne Prévost'	4	4–5	2–4	VF	few	B	mp	R	M	210
'Paul Neyron'	4	4–6	2–3	F	H	B	mp	R	MS	211
'American Beauty'	4	4–5	2–3	VF	few	B	dp	R	M	212
'Baron Girod de l'Ain'	4	3–5	2–3	VF	H	B	rb	SR	M	213
'Ards Rover'	4	>12		VF	H	C	dr	SR	M	214
'Frau Karl Druschki'	4	6–8	5–7	SF	H	C/B	w	R	MS	216
"Granny Grimmett's"	4	3–5	3–4	VF	few	B	dr	R	M	217

A Brief History of the Rose

Poet Walter de la Mare may be right that "no man knows through what wild centuries roves back the rose," but paleontologists can offer at least a rough idea. Small fossil specimens of roses have been found at sites in several countries, including Austria, Germany, Bulgaria, Japan, China and France, and in the United States in Alaska, Colorado and California. Roses occur naturally throughout the Northern Hemisphere between the latitudes of approximately 20° and 70°, so this is a representative distribution of remains.

These early specimens are dated throughout the Tertiary period of the geologic calendar, meaning that they grew in the time period between 3 million and 60 million years ago, or during the time between the extinction of the dinosaurs and the appearance of early humans. Gerd Krüssman notes in *The Complete Book of Roses* that early roses had probably the same preference for well-drained soil as do modern roses and were not likely to grow in the marshy or alluvial conditions that made fossilization common. This limitation means that only under unusual circumstances, such as a volcanic eruption that covered an area with mud and ash, were rose plants likely to provide fossils. In truth, there are only about two dozen samples from that great stretch of "wild" centuries. Some of the clearest of those samples show very little difference from modern species of roses. This similarity suggests that the plant has not had to change drastically because the rose, like man and the cockroach, had its adaptability built into the original plan.

From Antiquity to the 18th Century: Roses Bred by Nature

The first human connection with the rose is difficult to pinpoint exactly, though it's not hard to believe that early humans recognized the edible and medicinal values of the plant even when gardening was still millennia in the future. Many varieties of wild, or species, roses have traditionally supplied an addition to the menu and are still in use today, whether for the fruit or the sweet and tender tips of the young canes. In cold areas such as Alaska, Japan and Scandinavia, vitamin-packed rose hips are a critical addition to the fruit-poor winter diet. Ancient and modern recipes are available for everything from rose-hip tea, jelly, syrup and tarts to the excellent Swedish rose-hip soup. Gardening has been a practical enterprise longer than a decorative one, and roses have stayed important through the swings of human history in part because they can fill both roles.

It seems likely that the rose was first cultivated as a garden flower in Persia (which we now know as Iran) as long ago as 1200 B.C. At this period, according to Dr. C.C. Hurst, writing in Graham Stuart Thomas's *The Old Shrub Roses*, it had already become a religious emblem. With their adaptability, their prickly beauty, their delicacy and their amazing toughness, roses are so much a floral mirror of our own species that is was only natural we humans found them irresistible in a spiritual way. The symbolism of the rose has spread through religions (from pagan Aphrodite's daughter, Rhodos, to the Catholic rosary), politics (myriad kings and countries have chosen some form of rose as emblem, including the United States, which has recently designated the rose as the national flower) and literature (poets from Anacreon to T.S. Eliot have found the rose a powerful image).

By the time the Greeks and Romans were flourishing, the garden rose was flourishing too. The Greeks delighted in roses, including them in their poetry and religion, but also growing them in silver pots for rooftop gardens and even using rose oil as a preservative for their wooden statues. The Romans, however, had a love affair with the rose that is the stuff of which legends are made.

As the Roman Empire grew more powerful and more decadent, so many roses were in demand for decoration at banquets and orgies that Roman market gardeners learned to force roses to bloom year-round. Columella, a Roman agricultural author, suggested digging a shallow trench around each bush and, when the buds began to show, filling it occasionally with hot water to make the rose think it is summer rather than winter. The great Roman naturalist, Pliny the Elder, offered the same advice, so we once tried it ourselves to see what would happen. Our test rose bloomed but so did several others that we hadn't treated, so we still don't know from experience how the method works.

The garden roses of the Romans, with the single exception of the twice-blooming 'Autumn Damask', flowered naturally only once a year, in the summer, so the forcing process offended some of the more austere philosophers of the day. Seneca asked, "Do they not live contrary to nature who desire a rose in winter?"

Contrary or not, the Romans truly did love roses and were responsible for encouraging and spreading their culture. Dr. Ruth Borchard reports in *Oh My Own Rose* that "to this day, along the old Roman roads in Europe and Britain are to be found wild roses which are not native to the surrounding countryside: descendants of roses planted around the villas of occupying Roman dignitaries." If this is true, it is a nice confirmation of the same type of bond that led settlers in our own country to mark their place in the wilderness with beloved and familiar roses.

The varieties of garden roses that the Romans grew and that continued to be grown in Europe were almost certainly hybrids of *Rosa gallica,* whose Latin name means "rose of the Gauls" (the inhabitants of what is now France) but whose physical roots can be traced back at least to Persia in 1200 B.C. Graham Stuart Thomas, in his book *The Old Shrub Roses,* describes this ancestral family as "all fragrant presentable roses of bushy habit" and agrees that it is no wonder that they "should have been favorites with the Southern European peoples for thousands of years." *R. gallica* is cold hardy, compact and quite willing to preserve itself by suckering new clumps all around the parent plant. This rose is also quite easy to crossbreed with other roses and probably is the common ancestor of the major classes of old European roses: the Gallicas, Damasks, Albas, Centifolias and Moss roses. Nearly all of the European roses have similar traits in terms of cold hardiness but are not quite as sturdy in hot climates. We have described some of our favorites, varieties that perform well for us, in the Encyclopedia; but we have rarely found old European roses surviving in neglected areas in Zones 8 through 10. Those that we have come across are almost always Gallica varieties, which is to the further credit of their tough wild ancestor.

R. gallica was not the only species rose to be intertwined in the parentage of old European roses. In *The Old Shrub Roses,* Graham Stuart Thomas speculates that *R. moschata* ('Musk Rose'), *R. canina* ('Dog Rose') and *R. phoenicia* also played important roles. There was no science involved in the original crossings of these wild roses. Human intervention was necessary only in making the choice of the best of the occasional natural hybrids for garden purposes. A number of species roses have compatible chromosome counts and are capable of interbreeding. It's simply a question of putting them in proximity with each other in an agreeable setting, and a garden would have been ideal for achieving that result.

Another way in which roses voluntarily increased the available number of their varieties before the days of deliberate hybridization was through their well-known tendency to sport, or produce spontaneous mutations, such as double flowers, climbing or dwarf varieties, or a simple change in color. The variability inherent in the genus *Rosa* is one of its most seductive characteristics. John Parkinson, the Englishman whose *Paradisi in Sole, Paradisus Terrestris* of 1629 is one of the great botanical reference books of all time, noted: "The great varietie of Roses is much to be admired, being more than is to be seene in any other shrubby plant that I know, both for colour, forme and smell."

The 19th Century: Scientific Rose Breeding Begins

Given the history of human fascination with roses, it seems quite amazing that until the 1800s there were relatively few varieties in Europe, in contrast to the thousands that we know today. John Gerard's *Herball* of 1597 lists 14 types of roses, and Parkinson's book lists only 10 more. For nearly two more centuries the rose, though grown and cherished, remained fairly static in number of varieties. In 1844 Loiseleurs Deslongchamps, in his book *Recherches sur l'Histoire de la Rose,* was able to express in a contemporary perspective the change that came about in the early 19th century. He writes: "I can well remember back to 1790 and that in those gardens are found only a few roses and rose varieties. They were multiplied only by cuttings or suckers. The vast rose plantations I witness now in my old age, gardens devoted exclusively to roses…did not exist at all. In my youth, roses were grown in quantity only for pharmacy or perfume." A devoted rose gardener, Deslongchamps had collected all the varieties he could find as a young man in the late 1700s, and he totaled them at about 15.

At the turn of the 19th century the number of varieties available began to increase at an astronomical rate, in what Dr. Ruth Borchard in *Oh My Own Rose* calls "an uprush, a burst, a never-ceasing fountain…from Deslongchamps' 15 in 1790

in his garden, to an estimated 100 in 1800, to 250 in 1815 and then, suddenly, to 2,500 about 1830, and again to 5,000 about 1845…." Her rough figures, impressive on paper, are supported by the catalogs and rose books of the period. It is inconceivable that so many varieties spontaneously appeared at once, and, of course, they did not. The three pivotal events that led to our current abundance of roses were Linnaeus's publication in 1753 of his information on the sexual habits of plants, the arrival in Europe of the Chinese roses and the popularization of rose collections from the example of the Empress Josephine.

The role of Linnaeus
The goal of Linnaeus, a young Swede who had trained for medicine as well as botany, was to set in order the confusing mass of information that had accumulated about the natural world: the same sort of task that faced Hercules when he set out to clean the Augean stables. Linnaeus had the ambition and dedication to create a system that would list all the world's known animals, vegetables and minerals so that they could be cataloged in an intelligible fashion and so that new discoveries could be fitted sensibly into the list. For the vegetable kingdom he used a classification that was based entirely on the sexual organs of plants, naming them by the number of male organs, or stamens, and the number of female organs, or styles. Although his system lacked flexibility and has since been much altered, it was a great advance in the study of botany and made an incredible difference in the history of the rose.

That part of the gardening public that wasn't too shocked to function (some naturalists refused to accept sex in plants) became aware that the pollen from the stamens of one rose could be deliberately used to fertilize the styles of another, and that the resultant seeds formed in the hip of the second rose would grow into hybrids of the two plants. Experimentation began to be common, although the laws governing the inheritance of genetic characteristics were still not understood, since Gregor Mendel didn't publish his studies on that subject until 1865. It was also not understood that a controlled environment was necessary to prevent pollen from other, unselected roses from drifting into the breeding area or being carried in by insects. Since each rose seed can have a different pollen donor the way each pup in a litter can have a different dog for a father, the issue from one hip full of seeds can be quite varied.

The contribution of the "stud Chinas"

The real impetus to serious hybridization came when roses from China first began to arrive in the West. These roses, brought back mainly by commercial travelers, were amazingly different from the traditional roses of Europe. While Europeans had to content themselves with roses that bloomed only in spring—unless they wanted to resort to "unnatural" practices like the Romans—the Chinese, with no thought of being unnatural, had roses in their gardens that were everblooming wherever the climate stayed mild in the winter. They painted these roses and wrote some poetry about them and apparently took them for granted, since the once-blooming plum blossom was much more culturally important.

By the late 18th century, the carefully self-isolated Chinese became increasingly involved in trade with the outside world, particularly with the British East India Company, and they began to have to cope with an influx of foreign adventurers. The initial Chinese reaction to these alien guests seems to have been to invite them for tea and a tour of the garden, for all the earliest introductions to the West of Chinese roses were not wild, or species, forms but garden cultivars collected from private homes and nurseries in the south of China. These were varieties that had been selected as desirable over the course of centuries, much as *R. gallica* varieties had been selected in Europe. It makes a nice picture: the intrepid plant hunter staggering wearily home from another dangerous trek into a polite Chinese dwelling, cherishing as the hard-won spoils of his adventure several neatly potted roses carried along behind him by a helpful servant. It wasn't until the British military began wedging their way into the interior of China in the mid-1800s that the wild native roses started to make their appearance in the West.

Like their occidental cousins, the Chinese garden roses could have been described in Graham Stuart Thomas's words: "Fragrant, presentable roses of bushy habit." But the similarity stopped there. The Chinese garden roses had neat pointed leaves and delicate silky petals, whereas the Gallicas tended toward rough leaves and heavier, more fibrous petals. The scent of the Chinese roses was sweet, but unfamiliar. They were not hardy in cold weather because they continued to put on new, tender growth until stopped by a hard frost. And, most fascinating of all, with each spurt of new growth came the formation of new flower buds. They were capable of continuous bloom.

The Chinese roses had an overwhelming effect on the subsequent development of the rose in general. The first four varieties to be shipped back to Europe ('Old Blush' in 1752, 'Slater's Crimson China' in 1790, 'Hume's Blush Tea-Scented China' in 1809 and 'Parks' Yellow Tea-Scented China' in 1824) are known collectively as the "stud Chinas" for their potent influence in the breeding of later roses. Their colors and flower forms brought about great changes when crossed with the old European roses, but the most dramatic characteristic that they passed on was that of remontancy, or repeated bloom. The gene for remontancy is recessive, so the first-generation crosses with once-blooming roses continued to be once-bloomers. Second-generation crosses back to the repeating roses, however, produced new and interesting varieties that could bloom again and again throughout the growing season.

The role of Empress Josephine

At the same time that rose hybridization and the introduction of new varieties from foreign countries began to escalate, Josephine de Beauharnais, Empress of France, stepped into the picture with impeccable timing to indulge her interest in horticulture and her special passion for roses. She created a huge garden at her beloved home, Malmaison, and included in it every rose she could acquire. It is reported that some of her ladies-in-waiting were bored almost to tears by the long daily ritual walk through the garden that included stopping to name every plant and inspect it, but the power of her royal interest was very effective in increasing the popularity not just of roses but also rose gardens among the upper classes. Roses came to her as quickly as they were discovered, even at the height of the Napoleonic Wars, for the garden-loving British gave orders to let plants for the Empress pass unmolested through their blockades.

Josephine's delight in collecting roses was a direct stimulus to French hybridizers to create as many new varieties as possible, and their excellent work in this field continued to set the pace for European nurserymen throughout most of the 19th century, though Josephine herself had died by 1814. Her interest, along with that of other powerful political and scientific figures of the day, was also a motivating force behind the continued exploration of new lands, America included, in order to discover hidden treasures of the plant world that could be sent back to European gardens. These exotics were all the rage, and nurseries that could introduce them did very well financially.

The Spread of Antique Roses through the South

The demand for new plants had a direct effect upon our own local legacy of heritage roses, because where intrepid explorers, plant hunters among them, led the way, groups of settlers seeking fresh land and new opportunities followed. These settlers took with them whatever they envisaged needing for survival in their new home, including roses.

In our part of Texas, many of the early immigrants were second- or third-generation colonists, who moved into new territory from the East. The original English and Scottish settlers had brought their familiar roses with them, including 'Eglantine', the 'Musk Rose' and the Gallica-related garden types. They took these, and many American species roses, with them when they began moving west of the mountains and south to Indian lands after the frontier was opened by the War of 1812. Until the 1830s, the Gallica roses, which were so easy to

propagate from suckers, were favorites with these immigrants, but once the proliferation of new roses reached America, it was the Chinas and Teas (and, later, their progeny) that took over, particularly in the South.

Most rose plants were probably carried on the long, arduous journey west as small rooted cuttings so as to take up the least amount of room. In order to conserve precious water they were likely packed in damp moss or, for short journeys, even stuck into potatoes. Not all roses traveled so informally, however. Settlers often purchased roses and fruit trees from commercial nurseries on their way through the port city of New Orleans, where the latest introductions from both France and England were readily available. Miss Pamela Ashworth Puryear, a historian living in Navasota, Texas, explains that as transportation improved, roses ordered through catalogs and bound for Texas could be sent by ship to Galveston, transferred to steamboats for travel up the Brazos or Trinity rivers and picked up at the landings "by anyone with a wagon heading that way."

Eventually, local nurseries were established in the West. We were fascinated to discover that Thomas Affleck, whose ideas on growing roses in the South correspond so closely to our own, had moved his nursery from Mississippi to Texas, possibly in anticipation of the expansion of the railroad, and had established himself in the late 1850s on a site not five miles from our own current location. We can't help but feel that the presence of a local source of what were then modern roses substantially increased the likelihood of there being so many old roses surviving in this area for us to find, collect, propagate and send out on the next step in their long migration.

Rosa eglanteria

Species Roses
and Their Hybrids

Species roses are generally defined as those that are found wild in nature. Roses are native to the entire Northern Hemisphere, from about the 20th parallel just south of the Tropic of Cancer to inside the Arctic Circle at the 70th parallel, and are bounded only by the most severe extremes of temperature. Their necessary adaptations have made species roses an amazingly diverse group of plants. The differences in prickle, flower, leaf and general habit of growth have fascinated botanists for centuries, as has the question of which are the true species roses and which are the hybrid varieties formed by cross-pollination. In this discussion, we use the term "species" rather loosely to include the hybrids as well. As Linnaeus wrote in 1753, "the species of *Rosa* are very difficult to determine, and those who have seen few species can distinguish them more easily than those who have examined many."

The difficulty in determining species roses explains, to some extent, the way that their names keep changing, not only from one Latin tag to another, but also from Latin back to a "common" name (meaning that they have been taken out of the strict species category). Theoretically, a species rose will reproduce true to itself when grown from seed, but that isn't enough of a universal determining characteristic to define completely what is a species rose and what is not. Since we are not botanists, we prefer to leave the fine details alone and concentrate on generalities that affect garden performance in our selection of wild roses and their very near relatives.

Plant Characteristics

The incredible diversity of flower and plant form that is displayed by species roses will lead some gardeners to rethink their concept of "rose," but this diversity is exactly what makes the whole genus so interesting to work with in the landscape. Species roses can be climbers or shrubs. Their flowers may be the five-petaled wild type expected by many gardeners or they may be very full and double. Fragrance varies from slight to remarkable and is unique for each type of rose.

The most important consideration for most gardeners in a warm climate with a long growing season is that most of these roses bloom only once a year. This isn't always true: *Rosa moschata*, the 'Musk Rose', blooms so late and so long that it is effectively remontant; *R. roxburghii*, the 'Chestnut Rose', repeats sporadically; and the species hybrids 'Mermaid' and 'Stanwell Perpetual' flower throughout the growing season once they are established. If you are used to having roses all year long, however, the varieties that bloom just in the spring require a bit of mental adjustment to appreciate their full value properly.

Once-blooming roses make up for their shorter season by putting all their energy into one overwhelming display. In terms of breeding opportunities, all their ova are in one basket, and the more flowers produced, the more opportunities for making new seedlings to carry on the genes. This attribute of lavish concentration means that once a year you can expect these roses to stop traffic and draw all eyes to the garden, so the trick is to plant them where they can be best appreciated when in bloom but will not leave a gap in the landscape while they are, as theater people say, "resting." Some species roses form attractive hips that decorate the plant after the flowers have fallen, turning color in the fall and lengthening the season of interest.

Culture

Since most species roses are adapted for survival in the wild, they can be planted in a wide variety of settings — within their particular climatic tolerance — and be expected to perform with little fuss. Some of the more vigorous climbers, like the 'Cherokee Rose' or 'Mermaid', seem to thrive on a hard-knock life, and repay tender, loving care by getting out of hand and turning aggressive.

There is no group of roses that provides better subjects for naturalizing, since pruning and spraying requirements are practically nonexistent. The majority of species roses with which we are familiar are remarkably resistant to both insect and disease problems and have handsome, healthy foliage that makes the plant attractive whether it is in bloom or not. (A number of breeders of modern Hybrid Teas are currently working with different species roses, trying to reintroduce some of the health and vigor that is natural to the rose into that beautiful but fragile class.)

We have had a great deal of success with all the species roses included here, with the single exception of 'Harison's Yellow', which is a little difficult to grow this far south (Zone 8) but simply had to be included because of its associations with Texas history. The other roses are all either willing to tolerate our heat or actively prefer it, because it matches the climatic conditions of their original home. This is especially true of the species collected from southern China, and we should caution northern gardeners that some of these, like the Banksias, are not cold hardy below Zone 7. It is theoretically possible to grow any rose in a container and move it into a greenhouse for the winter, or even to grow it in the greenhouse year-round, but it seems a shame to limit the natural enthusiasm of a rose like 'Lady Banks' Rose'.

Landscape Uses

Species roses are scattered throughout our gardens and out to the pasture fence beyond. Some climbing types are formally trained to help cover pergolas, and others fling themselves over entryways or decorate stone walls. In less formal areas, they are used to disguise utility buildings and to break up the stiff lines of the wire fence. The bushier types have found places in garden beds, in large containers and as specimen plants — the 'Swamp Rose', for example, has created a small, natural landscape of its own, growing next to a stream in the middle of our busy display gardens.

Species roses are just roses, after all, and are even easier to grow than most common varieties. If they were not meant to be in our gardens, no doubt we would not find them so fascinating or want them so badly.

Selected Species Roses and Their Hybrids

Rosa moschata
'Musk Rose', 1540

The 'Musk Rose' saga is one of the great lost-and-found stories amongst old roses. This rose fell out of commerce at the end of the 19th century because of a confusion of identity with the 'Himalayan Musk Rose' *(R. moschata nepalensis),* which began to be marketed under the name *R. moschata.* The Himalayan rose is somewhat similar to the true 'Musk Rose', except that it blooms earlier and is considerably more aggressive (climbing to over 30 ft.) and much more cold hardy.

By the mid 1930s, the more tender true 'Musk Rose' was thought to have dropped from commerce. It owes its rediscovery in England to Graham Stuart Thomas and its rediscovery in America to Helen Blake Watkins and a handful of other dedicated rose lovers.

It was vitally important that this rose not be lost because it is, with 'Old Blush' *(R. chinensis)* and *R. gallica,* one of the all-time great rose parents. It seems quite likely that *R. moschata* has the genes for remontancy, for though it blooms late in the season, it continues to produce flush after flush of blossoms for quite a long period. At any rate, the majority of the 'Musk Rose' progeny are repeat bloomers.

It is thought that it was *R. moschata* crossed with *R. gallica* that produced the 'Autumn Damask'

that figures (we think) in Roman history as the "twice-blooming rose of Paestum." And the 'Autumn Damask' made a natural cross with 'Old Blush' to produce the Bourbon roses, making *R. moschata* a likely grandparent of that beautiful class. A direct cross between *R. moschata* and 'Old Blush' created the first American class of roses, the Noisettes, all of which are remontant and nicely scented.

Our *R. moschata* plant is six years old now but has reached only 5 ft. in height—most likely because we were forced to move it to a new bed two years ago and it got cut back severely, both roots and top. It grows quietly, filling its niche in the garden as a thick green shrub until midsummer (sometime in June or July) when it begins to bloom.

The small white flowers are usually double on our plant, borne in corymbs of about seven blossoms. Occasionally there will be a cane that bears single flowers. Predominantly "single" bushes grown by our friends are likely to sport the double form. The fragrance of the 'Musk Rose' releases very freely into the air, forming an invisible cloud around the entire bush in the morning and evening. The lightest breeze will carry the scent a long way.

The density and size of *R. moschata* make it appropriate for use as a specimen plant set back at some distance from the house — a fence corner might be ideal, where its "snowbush" qualities could be appreciated while the bloom season lasted. We have found it to be a good backbone plant for our largest bed of mixed roses and perennials, but if it begins to stretch toward its potential recorded height of 12 ft., we may want to move it.

The 'Musk Rose' would work well in a large naturalized hedge of mixed species roses. The delayed bloom season, midsummer through fall, would spread out the flowering potential of such a hedge and do wonderful things for its fragrance.

We understand that *R. moschata* does not begin to bloom until August in colder climates, perhaps because it is a little tender and hopes to protect itself and its potential seedlings by flowering in the warmest season.

Zone 6 / 4 ft. to 6 ft. high / 3 ft. to 4 ft. wide / very fragrant / white / remontant

Stephen Scanniello

Rosa eglanteria
'Eglantine', possibly cultivated before 1551

Martha Washington loved flowers and cultivated a number of roses, though she left no record of their names. Her husband George was the journal keeper, and he had no interest in any plants that he didn't perceive as useful, so we know a lot about his vegetables and fruit trees but nearly nothing of the flowers that filled the vases on his table. He did, however, order at least one rose for himself—the 'Eglantine' or 'Sweet Brier Rose'.

We can only assume that the traditional useful characteristics of this European species, a member of the 'Dog Rose' (*R. canina*) family, made it seem appropriately functional rather than frivolous. The hips, which are high in Vitamin C, can be used to make soothing syrups, and the foliage is not only refreshingly scented but edible. Samuel B. Parsons noted in 1888 (*Parsons on the Rose*) that "the ends of the young shoots of the sweet briar, deprived of their bark and foliage, and cut into short pieces, are sometimes candied and sold by confectioners."

R. eglanteria is a large and rambling shrub with dark green, slightly rough foliage that gives off a wonderful clean apple scent. The fragrance is especially noticeable in the spring while the rose is actively growing, but it is also released anytime you brush against the plant and after every rain shower or watering. The flowers are sweet rather than showy, not more than 1 in. or 2 in. across, with five pink petals and a rosy fragrance of their own. They are borne separately, or occasionally in small corymbs of a few flowers, studded like polka dots over the plant during the three- or four-week spring flowering.

It is tempting to include 'Eglantine' in an herb or fragrance garden, but there are several points to consider first. One is that the canes are very prickly, another is that the natural height of the plant is 7 ft. or 8 ft. It wouldn't hurt to prune it back part way every year just after it flowers, however. The plant can be kept at roughly a 4-ft. or 5-ft. height, and the new growth will be full of the characteristic fruity scent. On its own roots, this rose spreads slowly into a clump by means of suckers, but these can be removed once or twice a year, potted up and given to a friend if you are trying to keep *R. eglanteria* somewhat restricted.

We like to see this rose used in a garden where there is room to let it fill out, perhaps at the corner of a fence where it will be lightly brushed now and then by passers-by. It is a good, carefree rose, requiring no spraying at all to stay healthy, so it naturalizes well. It has, in fact, naturalized in the northeastern United States, where it was planted by early settlers. 'Eglantine' makes a good informal hedge and would be lovely in combination with the 'Musk Rose' along a country lane. The contrasting flower colors and opposite bloom seasons (one blooms in spring, one in late summer) would ensure a long period of interest, and the combination of fragrances would be formidable.

In the photo above 'Eglantine' is at left, with a hybrid *R. eglanteria* at right.

Zone 4 / 7 ft. to 12 ft. high / 5 ft. to 8 ft. wide / very fragrant / light pink / once-blooming

Rosa laevigata
'Cherokee Rose', 1759

R. laevigata is known not just in America but around the rose-growing world as the 'Cherokee Rose', though it is a Chinese native. No one knows precisely when it came to North America, though Dr. Ruth Borchard, a Swiss rosarian, records in *Oh My Own Rose* that a botanist named Plukenet mentioned *R. laevigata* in 1696 and made a dried specimen of it that is now in the Sloane collection at London's Natural History Museum. At any rate, the rose got here early and managed to naturalize throughout the Southeast.

It was first thoroughly described from a specimen growing in Georgia, and it has been adopted as that state's official flower. The "Cherokee" appellation came, so the story goes, from one of the nastier episodes of American history. In 1838, when the Cherokee Nation was forced from its homeland in the East on the basis of a highly questionable treaty, the people apparently took slips of the familiar rose with them as living mementos. These slips got planted here and there along the "trail of tears," quite possibly to mark some of the many graves, and the rose spread this way as far west as the new reservation in Oklahoma.

The 'Cherokee Rose' migrated even farther west when it was discovered that it made an excellent cattle-proof hedge. *R. laevigata* was one of two Chinese species roses advertised by nurseries in the late 19th century for use as hedging; the other, with which the 'Cherokee Rose' is often confused, was *R. bracteata*, the 'Macartney Rose'. (The latter is very invasive and not at all suited for a well-mannered garden.) In his 1860 *Almanac*, western nurseryman Thomas Affleck gives specific advice on how to plant such a hedge for livestock and erosion control and when and how to prune it — as if it were a thing everybody needed and could be expected to be growing. A number of plants of both these roses can still be found along old fence lines, although their purpose has long since been replaced by barbed wire. Our own theory is that barbed wire was invented by someone who was familiar with these roses.

R. laevigata is really a very beautiful climbing or mounding rose, and it is not at all unmanageable if you are careful with the large, curved prickles. It blooms for four to six weeks quite early in the spring, usually beginning sometime in March for us. The nicely scented flowers are wide and very flat, consisting of five white petals around a large central crown of bright gold stamens. The petals drop cleanly from spent flowers so that there are never any brown tatters hanging on the plant. The foliage is very healthy and shiny, with each leaf made up of three pointed leaflets, light green in color.

The 'Cherokee Rose' will not tolerate cold weather, but it is one of the best roses for naturalizing in the South. It is carefree once established and offers an outstanding spring floral display that is visible from quite a distance. It will spill over a fence or ramble up a tree with equal enthusiasm, and the neat, shiny foliage is attractive even when the rose is not in bloom.

Zone 7 / 5 ft. high by 10 ft. wide (mounded) / over 15 ft. as a climber / fragrant / white / once-blooming

Rosa banksiae banksiae
'Lady Banks' Rose', 1807

In the Indonesian language, the way to signify a plural is to repeat the noun: Two dogs, for example, would be "dog dog." We assume that *R. banksiae banksiae* is botanical nomenclature's equivalent of that interesting rule, for this rose is the double white form of the species and the single form is simply designated *R. banksiae.* The double-flowered form was the first of the Banksias to be described by botanists, however, and it was introduced to England from China in 1807 as a specimen collected by William Kerr for Kew Gardens. The rose was named to compliment the wife of Sir Joseph Banks, director of Kew at that time, and it is still most commonly referred to as 'Lady Banks' Rose'.

'Lady Banks' Rose' is not at all cold hardy, resenting temperatures below 15°F, but where it will grow, it grows with a passion. Both the white and the yellow (*R. banksiae lutea*, 1824) forms can be seen filling up large trees in the South, causing confusion for passers-by who think that the trees are miraculously in lavish bloom during the roses' spring extravaganza.

The white 'Lady Banks' Rose' holds several records for size, the largest of all roses being the Tombstone Rose in Tombstone, Arizona. This specimen, now spreading thickly across a supporting arbor that covers 8,000 sq. ft., was planted by a young Scottish bride, Mary Gee, not long after her arrival in 1855 at what was then a raw mining camp. Her family back home must have had a very sheltered garden, for they sent a slip of 'Lady Banks'

Rose' from Scotland along with other starts of plants she had requested to ease her homesickness. The rose must have been thrilled to be back in a warm climate, because it has expanded steadily ever since and in April fills the air of Tombstone with the fragrance of many thousands of blossoms.

The double-flowered Banksia roses have very dainty leaves and no thorns and are frequently mistaken for climbing vines rather than roses. The massive spring display doesn't help to establish identity, because the myriad tiny flowers, just 1 in. across, look more like a drift of snow than like roses until you get very close. The yellow form has no scent to speak of, and for that reason alone we prefer the white 'Lady Banks' Rose', which has a delicious fragrance strongly reminiscent of violets that carries well on the air for some distance. Both color varieties are excellent for naturalizing in Zones 8 to 10, needing no care at all once they are established.

The Banksias grow much too large to be included in a small garden, but anywhere there is a good-sized tree or an outbuilding or a high fence to submerge, they are too easy a pleasure to do without. If they must be pruned for reasons of space, they should be thinned by

removing entire canes to the base of the plant instead of cutting them back part way. Thinning will preserve the graceful lines of the rose instead of creating a schizophrenic bush/climber. (For more information on pruning climbing roses, see pp. 90-91.)

'Lady Banks' Rose' is very long-lived and can be expected to be a legacy to the grandchildren of any gardener who plants one.

Zone 8 / 15 ft. to 20 ft. high or more / very fragrant / white / once-blooming

Rosa roxburghii
'Chestnut Rose', cultivated before 1814

In the early 1800s, strange new plants from foreign lands were all the rage among European gardeners. Tantalizing specimens, including a handful of roses, were sent back from the few accessible gardens of China. The market for exotics was so large that the East India Company set up its own Botanic Garden in Calcutta, India, as a relay station to handle many of the plants being brought out of China. One of these plants was the double 'Chestnut Rose'. (The single form was not discovered until 1908 when the Chinese interior had been opened up for exploration.)

Originally found in a garden in Canton, this rose reached Calcutta by 1820 and attracted the attention of the superintendent of the Botanic Garden, surgeon William Roxburgh. It is his name that is now attached to the rose, though this was a second choice. The original designation was *R. microphylla*, a comment on the many (up to 15) small leaflets that form each leaf. This description was so apt that even though it was officially dropped (the name had already been used for an unrelated European species) many early rose books feature *R. roxburghii* as *R. microphylla*: "the Chinese small-leaved rose."

The common names of 'Chestnut', 'Burr' and 'Chinquapin' are a result of the curious, thick, prickly calyx and large, prickly hips, both of which are reminiscent of the fruits of the chestnut tree and its southern near-relative the chinquapin. (We have heard this rose called 'Moss Rose' by gardeners who have never seen a real Moss rose with its softer, glandular fuzz.) Another distinctive characteristic is the peeling light-brown bark, rather like the bark of a crape myrtle, that covers the angular branches.

We have heard the flowers described as being "like the French silk roses Mother used to sew onto her hats," and the petal-crammed, bright lilac-pink blossoms do have an almost artificially artistic appearance. These features,

combined with the handsome, long, pinnate leaves, caused Philadelphia nurseryman Robert Buist to write in *The Rose Manual* in 1844 that "the plants…are very beautiful" and that a hedge of them was "the *beau idéal* of the flower garden." He also gave excellent advice on the cultural requirements, saying that the 'Chestnut Rose' prefers a well-drained soil and does not like to have its roots disturbed. As we have found this curious rose in every part of the South that we've visited, we are quite willing to believe that an uncared-for, undisturbed 'Chestnut Rose' will last a very long time.

This rose is fairly hardy, growing in the open as far north as Zone 6. Even though it slowly makes large plants (to 7 ft.) in the ground, it can be pruned back to grow in a large pot or tub and be brought indoors during cold spells. Since the 'Chestnut Rose' is one of the rare species varieties to repeat its bloom sporadically during the growing season, it is worthy of a position as a specimen rose whether in the ground or featured in a container.

The only significant failing of this rose is that it has no discernible fragrance, but the "French silk" flowers in their prickly cup, set off by the long, neatly divided leaves and strange pale bark will keep most gardeners too intrigued to notice the flaw.

Zone 6 / 5 ft. to 7 ft. high / 4 ft. to 5 ft. wide / slightly fragrant / medium pink / slightly remontant

Rosa palustris scandens
'Swamp Rose', cultivated before 1824

It is common knowledge that roses require good drainage and hate wet feet, but there is one exception, *Rosa palustris*, whose Latin name can be translated literally as "swamp rose." It is a native American species that can be found in moist swampy areas throughout most of the eastern United States from Louisiana across to Florida and northward from Minnesota to Nova Scotia, Canada. It tolerates extreme heat and extreme cold with equal grace and does not appear to care at all about drainage.

R. palustris was discovered and described by some of the best-known early botanists in the Colonies, including Marshall (who introduced it in 1726), Michaux (who called it *R. pensylvanica*) and Bigelow (who called it *R. caroliniana*). In the early 19th century, Empress Josephine of France included this rose in her outstanding collection of the world's roses at Malmaison. It was painted there by the great flower portraitist Redouté and described by his botanist partner, Thory, as *R. hudsoniana*. This variety of place names gives an idea of the rose's

wide distribution. Thory also described the same rose elsewhere as *R. salicifolia*, which means "willow-leaved rose."

The species variety that we prefer to grow is *R. palustris scandens*, which differs from the basic *R. palustris* mainly in that it has double instead of single flowers and is almost completely thornless — two obvious advantages in a garden setting. The flowers of our 'Swamp Rose' are pink, about 2 in. across, and have a sweet scent when they first open. The 'Swamp Rose' waits to bloom until most other species

roses have already finished for the year, filling in a gap between the first overwhelming garden display of spring and the second flush of repeat-blooming varieties. For us in Texas, this means anywhere from late April to early June, but in cooler Zones it can come as late as August. The bloom period is relatively long, usually lasting at least six weeks.

With their narrow, willowlike leaves, dark, smooth bark and gracefully arching form, the canes of the 'Swamp Rose' are particularly beautiful. In fact, the plant is so handsome that the flowers are more a decoration than a necessity. This is a rose that even looks good in the winter garden—it has that quality of "good bones," a timeless beauty whether clothed or bare.

We have one bush of the 'Swamp Rose' planted at the edge of a small stream, with its roots half in the water and its branches arching in a canopy above. Unpruned and uncared-for it has reached a height of between 3 ft. and 4 ft. and is completely healthy. In late spring it looks like a miniature pink-flowered willow and draws visitors like a magnet.

Another specimen is planted in a regular well-drained garden bed where it has reached 5 ft. in height and forms the backbone of the plantings as a leafy shrub even when not in bloom. Here we prune away only a few canes to emphasize the arching form and otherwise leave it alone. It is also the main interest of this bed in the winter— truly a plant for all seasons.

Zone 4 / 4 ft. to 6 ft. high / 4 ft. to 6 ft. wide / slightly fragrant / medium pink / once-blooming

'Harison's Yellow'
circa 1830

This hybrid of *Rosa foetida,* probably a cross between the 'Persian Yellow' (*R. foetida persiana*) and the 'Scotch Rose' (*R. spinosissima),* is the only bright yellow Old Garden Rose that is easy to grow. At least it's easy to grow from Zone 7 temperatures down to those of Zone 4. A large number of early settlers seem to have carried this rose with them on their migration to the West during the mid-1800s, when it was first popular. 'Harison's Yellow' is so hardy and independent that it can still be found in areas where it was planted 150 years ago. It has naturalized completely in some areas of California and New Mexico, spreading by suckers and unaffected by disease.

'Harison's Yellow' is often referred to in rose literature as the "Yellow Rose of Texas," probably because of its early and extensive spread in the West. Unfortunately, it would have to be the Yellow Rose of North Texas, because it doesn't grow at all well in our central area (Zone 8) or in the southern part of the state. The rose seems to prefer a dry, cool climate and resents our combination of high humidity and a long hot growing season. If its roots are well drained and the cold

dormancy period is long enough, 'Harison's Yellow' will thrive anywhere with minimal care. Otherwise, as with our specimens, it will gradually die back until it is completely gone.

Another argument against designating 'Harison's Yellow' as the Yellow Rose of Texas is the fact that it was first found as a spontaneous hybrid in the garden of attorney and amateur rose breeder George F. Harison in what is now downtown Manhattan. Anyway, the true Yellow Rose of Texas was a mulatto indentured servant (not a slave) named Emily Morgan. She accompanied her boss, Captain James Morgan, from New York to the front of the Texas War of Independence from Mexico, where she earned admiration for her Mata Hari-like befuddlement of Mexican general Santa Anna. She kept the general busy enough to allow the Texan army to win the crucial battle of San Jacinto and thus the war. Though a fellow New Yorker, Emily Morgan, performed well in Zone 9 (where the battle was), 'Harison's Yellow' does not.

'Harison's Yellow' is a charming, though extremely prickly plant. The small, semidouble flowers are

bright yellow with yellow stamens. They are fragrant, with a scent that is somewhere between fruit and linseed oil, and they are borne very freely on the bush throughout the spring. The leaves are small and dark green, reminiscent of *R. spinosissima* foliage, on an open, rather gaunt bush that generally reaches 4 ft. or 5 ft. in height and width, though it can get somewhat larger under ideal conditions.

'Harison's Yellow' is difficult to root from cuttings, but it does sucker, so new plants can be acquired that way or by layering. It can be confined to a half barrel or similar container to prevent misbehavior in a small garden, but this rose is at its best when planted in an area where it can be left alone, such as an informal hedge or a corner of a fence where it will slowly form a small, healthy thicket, hosting birds on its prickly oval hips in the fall and covering itself with a treasury of bright flowers every spring. 'Harison's Yellow' is pictured in such a setting in the photo at left, paired with the Rugosa rose 'Hansa'.

Zone 4 / 4 ft. to 6 ft. high / 3 ft. to 5 ft. wide / fragrant / deep yellow / once-blooming

Joyce Demits

'Stanwell Perpetual'
1838

A happy accident, 'Stanwell Perpetual' sprang up all on its own with no human hand to guide the breeding. Although it has no recorded pedigree, it is thought by most rosarians to be a hybrid of *Rosa spinosissima*, called the 'Scotch Rose' or 'Burnet Rose', most likely crossed with 'Autumn Damask'. This makes it a sort of kissing cousin to 'Harison's Yellow', and as with 'Harison's Yellow' the name is derived half from point of origin and half from the most striking characteristic of the rose.

'Stanwell Perpetual' was discovered as a seedling at Stanwell, in Middlesex, England, and it is truly a constant bloomer throughout the growing season—which is more than can be said of many roses with "perpetual" in their names, including the entire Hybrid Perpetual class. The genes for repeat-flowering are recessive, so it was quite a stroke of luck that the right combination came up to give 'Stanwell Perpetual' this characteristic. Unfortunately, another chance combination of genes made this rose sterile, so its sterling qualities begin and end with itself—it can't be bred.

In *Old Roses*, Ethelyn Keays says of 'Stanwell Perpetual' that "the foliage and the growth are Scotch," meaning that they are characteristic of *R. spinosissima*. The Scotch roses as a class are very hardy and adaptable, thriving and spreading even in sandy soil and needing little care. 'Stanwell Perpetual' is just as tough, but is more suited to the garden because it doesn't sucker. It makes a relaxed, mounding bush that is usually 3 ft. or 4 ft. high in our gardens, though we have seen specimens like the one in the top photo that reached 5 ft. and more.

The greyish foliage is dainty in appearance with paired, small leaflets giving it a ferny look. During the most stressful days of summer the leaves will sometimes fall away, leaving the reddish-brown, very prickly stems exposed to view, but the rose keeps blooming quite steadily and the blossoms don't seem to be much affected by the heat.

The flowers are a pale Damask pink that fades to blushed cream in the summer. They are double, rather flat when fully open, and they often have a knot of smaller petals hiding the yellow stamens in the center. The flowers are listed in *Modern Roses* 9 as "slightly fragrant," but for us, they are heavily and exquisitely perfumed with a tangy Damask scent.

'Stanwell Perpetual' needs no pampering but is supposed to prefer a cool soil and some afternoon shade in our hot summers, making it a good candidate for a north-side planting. We have grown it completely exposed, however, with no trouble except some foliage loss in high summer if we don't give it extra water. Because of its sprawly, mounding habit of growth, 'Stanwell Perpetual' is very decorative in large containers, especially in tubs of weathered wood that heighten the soft effect of the pale pink flowers and greyish foliage. It also looks natural planted near the edge of a water feature, blending into the whole picture instead of creating a discordant note of harsh color or form. As an added bonus, the leaves show some autumn coloring, turning maroon when the weather is cool enough.

Zone 3 / 3 ft. to 5 ft. high / 3 ft. to 5 ft. wide / very fragrant / white / reliable repeat

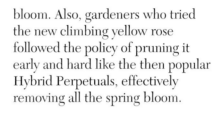

'Fortune's Double Yellow'
1845

"I found this rose in the garden of a wealthy Mandarin in Ningpo where it had completely covered a wall and was a mass of bloom. The Chinese call it Wang-jang-ve or 'yellow rose.' I sent it to the R.H.S. in 1845." So wrote Robert Fortune (quoted in the 1983 *American Rose Annual),* an enthusiastic Scots plant hunter who accepted a commission from the Royal Horticultural Society to explore the areas of China accessible to Europeans with the idea of collecting new plants to introduce into England. He made several trips to China, lasting three or four years each, and brought back a number of important plants, including at least five remarkable roses and a much-sought-after yellow camellia.

Thought to be a possible hybrid of *Rosa odorata* and *R. chinensis* (also called *R. indica* in some books), 'Fortune's Double Yellow' was originally given the Latin name of *R. x odorata pseudindica.* Unfortunately the English did not immediately see the value of this rose. It is not cold hardy, and a hard late frost can burn away some of the

bloom. Also, gardeners who tried the new climbing yellow rose followed the policy of pruning it early and hard like the then popular Hybrid Perpetuals, effectively removing all the spring bloom.

It was in the southern United States, where it was treated more gently and warm enough at last, that 'Fortune's Double Yellow' finally lived up to Robert Fortune's enthusiasm. Here, this rose will form a large and vigorous plant that needs no pruning at all except to remove any dead wood. The canes are well armed with sharp prickles, but any scratches they inflict are forgiven during the inspiring spring display. The foliage is neatly arranged and is a memorable pale apple-green color that makes this rose easy to spot even when it's not in bloom.

The flowers are double and very sweetly scented, a rich apricot-yellow in color with a blush of rose or crimson on the outer petals. Interestingly enough, 'Fortune's Double Yellow' is excellent for cutting, because the flowers are borne in small groups at the end of long (though prickly) stems. They last for several days in water, which is unusual for most species varieties.

'Fortune's Double Yellow' blooms very early for us with a huge flush in March or early April, and everyone who sees it in our gardens wants one immediately. In fact, it has been such a popular rose in the warm climates that it is loaded with appreciative nicknames such as 'Beauty of Glazenwood' and 'Gold of Ophir' and, commemorating the fact that it has naturalized in California, 'San Rafael Rose'.

'Fortune's Double Yellow' can be allowed to grow on its own in the open as a tangled mound of a specimen plant, or can be grown near a fence or other support for its clawed arms to drape over. We have trained one specimen up the side of a rough stone chimney, using only nails driven into the mortar as supports on which to fasten the canes. The result (shown in the photo on p. 4) is deceptively beautiful, since it looks as though the blush and gold rose has climbed up the tawny stone all by itself in a naturally graceful fashion.

Zone 8 / 12 ft. or more / very fragrant / yellow blend / once-blooming

'Fortuniana'
1850

This apparently natural hybrid of *Rosa banksiae* and *R. laevigata* ('Cherokee Rose') also bears the name of Robert Fortune, who collected it during his second plant-hunting expedition to China (1848-1851). Fortune had a great deal of enthusiasm for the plants he sent home for introduction, and one of his letters (quoted in the 1983 *American Rose Annual*) contains the following description of his discovery of 'Fortuniana':

"The white climbing rose referred to is cultivated in gardens about Ningpo and Shanghai, and is held in high esteem by the Chinese; indeed it is one of the best white kinds which I have met with in China. It is frequently seen of a large size, covering trellis work formed into alcoves or built over garden walks. For this purpose, it is well suited, as it is a luxuriant grower and it blooms profusely and

is no doubt well worth cultivation in English gardens. It may not please in every respect Rose-fanciers, but it is very beautiful nevertheless, and it has some advantages peculiar to itself."

'Fortuniana' did not, in fact, please all rose fanciers because it was too tender for the English climate outdoors — though it was grown very successfully in greenhouses. As did 'Fortune's Double Yellow', 'Fortuniana' really came into its own in a warm climate. By the turn of the century, this rose, listed in most literature of the period as *R. x fortuniana*, was being used as an understock for less vigorous roses in Australia and New Zealand and later in the United States. 'Fortuniana' is extremely disease resistant and thrives even in poor, dry or sandy soil, so it is the understock of choice for much of the deep South, especially Florida.

Because we do not grow any roses that won't survive on their own roots, we have no need of 'Fortuniana' as an understock. We grow it as a climbing rose and hold it in at least as high esteem as did the Chinese.

The plant itself is beautiful, with long, vigorous, graceful canes decorated with the shiny three-leaflet leaves so reminiscent of the 'Cherokee Rose', and it has relatively few prickles. The white flowers are like those of the 'Lady Banks' Rose' but larger (about 2 in. across), and they are very double, with a distinctive knot of white petals in the center. They also have the fragrance of the white 'Lady Banks' Rose', a delicious violet scent that carries well on the air. 'Fortuniana' blooms only in the spring, but it puts all its energy into a lavish and memorable display that lasts four or five weeks.

This rose can be planted anywhere warm and will naturalize easily, requiring no care at all once established. It is slightly less rampant than the Banksias or 'Cherokee Rose', so it can be used to add a little wild grace to a trellis or gazebo closer to the house. It can even be pruned back, after blooming, to form a mounding shrub 6 ft. to 8 ft. in height — though it seems a shame to waste the full display potential. 'Fortuniana's' colors of vivid green and bright white are very clear and sharp in contrast, making it stand out in any garden setting.

Zone 7 / 20 ft. or more / very fragrant / white / once-blooming

'Mermaid'
1918

S.J. Derby

"Rampant" is a word that keeps coming up in connection with 'Mermaid', but in spite of its excess vigor the rose has been a favorite with many gardeners ever since the English nursery of William Paul introduced it in 1918. This is the only hybrid of *Rosa bracteata*, the pestilentially invasive 'Macartney Rose', that is widely available in commerce, and there are several reasons for its continued popularity. Foremost is the fact that 'Mermaid's' other parent was a double yellow Tea rose, and the combination produced a plant that blooms intermittently throughout the entire growing season. In addition, 'Mermaid' does not make a nuisance of itself by suckering and spreading seedlings (like *R. bracteata*), though it does grow extremely large and carries full body armor in the shape of wicked, curved prickles.

"How can I move this rose?" is a question that comes up every time an incautious gardener plants 'Mermaid' too close to the house. We recommend taking its eventual size into account before planting, because battling this rose into submission in order to dig it up can be a rather painful and occasionally bloody ordeal. We know of an experienced rose rustler who recommends 'Mermaid' instead of burglar-proof bars.

In spite of its overwhelming energy, or perhaps because such enthusiasm is contagious, 'Mermaid' is a very attractive rose. The shiny, apple-green foliage is remarkably healthy, and the dark bronze, well-armed canes are sleek and glossy. The flowers, which have only five petals but are a good 4 in. or 5 in. across, are in scale with the rest of the plant. They are distinctly yellow in the bud and upon first opening, then fade to cream in the sun and finally drop their petals cleanly, leaving a thick crown of gold stamens centered in a star of sepals. The fragrance is fruity and sweet rather than dry like that of the Teas. In 1917, just before its official introduction, 'Mermaid' won a Gold Medal from the National Rose Society of England for its excellent qualities.

This rose is limited by cold tolerance, but we have seen it growing everywhere from the dry inferno of central Texas to a pasture fence at the top of Virginia's Blue Ridge Mountains. It is susceptible to an out-of-season hard freeze, but otherwise it seems hardy to the limits of Zone 7.

'Mermaid' can be planted anywhere there is a support for it to climb—a fence or tree or even a stone wall—and it is a natural for smothering ugly outbuildings. It will make a handsome, tangly mound if planted in the open as a specimen, but it is also quite easy to train up a building

(use gloves) if there is room enough for it to grow without getting in the way. The effect can be stunning—like a wall full of harvest moons. 'Mermaid' needs no pruning except for occasional removal of dead wood, and the wise gardener will choose a site for it that leads to the optimum enjoyment of its beauty and a minimum of physical contact.

Zone 7 / 20 ft. or more / fragrant / medium yellow / remontant

Peter Haring

Rosa setigera serena
'Prairie Rose', 1924

Native to North America, where it grows from the Atlantic coast to the Rocky Mountains, the 'Prairie Rose' is this country's only species in the Synstylae group (see the class description for Hybrid Multiflora roses on pp. 181-182) and the only indigenous rose that can be trained as a climber. In the wild, *R. setigera* can be found growing in clumps, or colonies, with its 12 ft. to 15 ft. arching canes spreading out in all directions. Although it does not sucker, it has the ability to propagate by seed as well as by self-layering.

The hardiness, grace of form and self-reliant nature of this rose made it a natural for early breeding experiments. In the mid-1800s several varieties, including the still-popular 'Baltimore Belle', were in general commerce and much

admired. Another burst of interest in the 1930s produced the lovely rose 'Doubloons', which won an American Rose Society prize in 1936. We can't help but feel that there is still a lot of untapped potential here.

The species type of *R. setigera* was described and introduced by the botanist Michaux in 1810. The selection we grow, *R. setigera serena*, differs very little from the type and has the advantage of being thornless—a quality always welcome in a garden plant. The canes are long, slender and whiplike, with faintly downy leaves that have a soft, matte look to them. The flowers are deep pink when first open, fading over several days to pale pink or white. They are five-petaled and are borne along the length of the canes in corymbs of three or four blossoms each.

The question of fragrance is interesting. Ellen Willmott, in *The Genus Rosa*, writes that the flowers are "deficient in scent." *Modern Roses 9* describes them as "almost scentless." But Graham Stuart Thomas, the most eminent rosarian of our time, states positively in *Shrub Roses of Today* that the "broad petals…are very fragrant in spite of numerous statements to the contrary." It must be a question of

luck and weather—so far we have detected only a very light perfume in our own plants.

The 'Prairie Rose' is excellent for naturalizing, forming a graceful thicket of curving canes that need no attention after the first period of establishment. If the propensity to root and spread is a problem, the newly formed plants can be removed periodically and planted elsewhere. The bloom season is very late, coming in June for us in Zone 8 and as late as August in colder climates, so the 'Prairie Rose' will greatly expand the display period of wild roses in the garden if it is used in a mixed planting.

We like this rose as a pillar, too, for use in a more intimate setting. Its only flaw is the very occasional attack of rust that can render it almost leafless for as long as a month. Since none of the other roses seems to catch this disease, we tend more toward watching it with interest than treating it, but no doubt it could be stopped with a mild fungicide. Even if it defoliates, the 'Prairie Rose' is always clothed again in soft green in time to bloom from top to bottom of its graceful canes.

Zone 3 / 8 ft. or more / slightly fragrant / medium pink / once-blooming

Old European Roses

Old European roses, a composite class of our own creation, is made up of garden rose varieties that were grown in Europe before the coming of the China roses at the end of the 18th century. Because these roses are more cold hardy than they are heat tolerant, we find few of them remaining in the old gardens of the deep South. From Zone 7 northward into the colder Zones, however, they appear to thrive, and they are so attractive in form, foliage and flower that we feel they deserve a place in the gardens where they can grow well.

We have included in this section some varieties from each of five well-known classes—the Gallicas, Damasks, Albas, Centifolias and Mosses—that do reasonably well in our own Zone 8 gardens. These roses require a little extra fuss, but their fragrance is unmatchable and their nostalgia value is irresistible, as novelist Katherine Anne Porter reveals in this passage taken from the essay "The Flower of Flowers" in her book *The Days Before:*

> Once in California, in a nursery, lost in a jungle of strange roses, I asked an old gardener, no doubt a shade too wistfully, "Haven't you a Cabbage Rose, or a Damask, or a Moss Rose?" He straightened up and looked at me wonderingly and said, "Why, my God, I haven't even heard those names for thirty years! Do you actually know those roses?" I told him yes, I did, I had been brought up with them. Slowly, slowly, slowly like moisture being squeezed out of an oak, his eyes filled with tears. "So was I," he said, and the tears dried back to their source without falling. We walked then among the roses, some of them very fine, very beautiful, of honorable breed and proved courage, but the roses which for me are the very heart of the rose were not there, nor had ever been.

The old European roses fell out of favor primarily with the development of the Hybrid Perpetual class, their once-blooming varieties losing ground before roses of a similar hardiness that were able, by crosses with the Chinas, to bloom more than once. This trait of remontancy was of deep interest not only to gardeners but also to participants in rose shows. By the late 19th century, with a focus on flowers and their availability for show dates, the garden form of the rose bush ceased to be an issue of primary importance. Even Dean Hole, the British cleric and champion of roses, was willing to let the old slide away in favor of the new. "The Albas and Gallicas," he says in an 1896 article quoted in Lesley Gordon's *Old Roses*, "have almost vanished from our gardens, nor do I plead for their restoration, because, beautiful as they were, we have gained from the development of selection and culture more charming roses in their place."

We cannot accept this. There are other roses that are perhaps as charming in their individual ways, but there are none that have more share in human history and more right by long tradition to be restored to garden use.

Plant Characteristics

In treating the old European roses as one class we are responding to their similarities in season of bloom and cultivation requirements, but a brief note of their differences needs to be made to prevent confusion.

Gallica roses   Gallicas are perhaps the oldest class, descendants of the wild *Rosa gallica* that is native to central and southern Europe and western Asia. In general, these roses are between 3 ft. and 5 ft. in height, loosely upright in habit, and have a covering of thin, hairy prickles and a habit of spreading into thick clumps by suckering (sending up new canes from the roots). Their flowers tend to open fairly flat, are often extremely double and have excellent fragrance. Their colors run the gamut of pinks and crimsons with mauve (or bluish) tints, and they are famous for a multitude of streaked, striped and spotted sports. Other common names for Gallicas are French roses (*Gallia* is Latin for Gaul, that part of the Roman Empire that included France) and Provins roses (from the French city of Provins). These are almost the only class of old European roses that we have found specimens of in old gardens and cemeteries in Texas and Louisiana.

Damask roses   Damask roses are of two types, the once-blooming varieties that are thought to be progeny of *R. gallica* and *R. phoenicia;* and the remontant 'Autumn Damask' and its sports, thought to descend from a *R. gallica/R. moschata* cross. The name Damask comes from Damascus, in Syria, and these roses are common in the Middle East. It has been suggested that they were spread into Europe by returning Crusaders, though this has always been open to question. The once-blooming or "summer" Damasks tend to be tall and leggy, in the 4-ft. to 6-ft. range, and they are known for their habit of leaning on nearby plants for support. The 'Autumn Damask' varieties are more compact and self-contained. Both types generally have wide pink flowers (ranging in tone from pale to warm) with crinkled, silky petals and an exquisite fragrance (strongest in the once-blooming Damasks) that is the basis of many commercial rose perfumes.

Alba Roses   Albas are famous as white roses, though they are quite often blush or warm pink. Their heritage is thought to be Damask crossed with the 'Dog Rose' (*R. canina*) that is native throughout Europe. Albas tend to be tall, 5 ft. or 6 ft. in our garden, and form soft, graceful bushes with scattered prickles and interesting blue-green foliage. Their flower forms are particularly lovely, often cupped with neatly overlapping petals, and their fragrance is strong and sweet.

Centifolia roses   The Cabbage roses of antiquity, these roses can be found under that name in much rose literature. *Centifolia* is Latin for "hundred leaves," and many varieties of this class are notable for being very double. The "cabbage" designation comes from their neatly layered, globular form with the bottom petals reflexing out like the lower leaves of a cabbage. Not all varieties of Centifolia have this form, and not all roses with cabbagy flowers are Centifolias, so it is a confusing name. Also confusing is the other name for the class, Provence roses, which gets mixed up with the Gallica/Provins designation. Provence is a region of southern France where Centifolia roses are grown, but the class is thought to have originated in Holland in the 16th century as the result of crossing *R. gallica* with *R. phoenicia, R. canina* and *R. moschata.*

Centifolias are tall and rather sprawly, in our experience, mounding into large bushes (some 6 ft. tall by 4 ft. wide) with grey-green foliage and sweetly scented flowers in the pale to dark pink range. Centifolia roses are second only to Damasks in commercial cultivation for perfume.

Moss roses   Moss rose varieties are sports either from the Centifolias or from one or the other of the two types of Damasks. Their basic habits are comparable to whichever plant they sported from, but their distinguishing characteristic is the mossy growth of enlarged glandular hairs covering the calyx and sepals and, sometimes, the flower stem. This moss is interesting visually and is very fragrant, with a musky, earthy scent that lingers in a sticky resin on the fingertips when the bud is touched. Moss varieties that have sported from the 'Autumn Damask' type can be remontant.

As can be seen from these short biographies, the old European roses we have included here are all related through the original *R. gallica*. With the single exception of the 'Autumn Damask' (and its Moss rose descendants), they bloom only once a year. They are all cold hardy, but not all are equally at home in our southern heat and humidity. They suffer from the lack of proper dormancy and are more susceptible to disease at their weakest point, mid to late summer, than are the heat-tolerant roses.

Culture

We have learned that old European roses perform best in our gardens if they are on their own roots (though they are difficult to root from cuttings) and if they are well planted when first put in the ground. The ideal location would be one with very rich, fertile soil, good drainage, six to eight hours of sun (with some protection in the afternoon) and a deep, regularly applied mulch. A thorough watering once or twice a week during the summer will also help to keep the roots cool and the plant in good spirits. Our soil is fairly alkaline, so we add a dose of aluminum sulfate to the old European rose bed in June when the leaves are starting to look yellow and weak, and that seems to bring them back to prime. With these roses, we have found that concentration on the overall health of the plant, especially with fertilization, watering and mulching, keeps them fit enough to avoid having to spray for disease. Gardeners who demand perfect foliage may choose to treat with a mild fungicide if and when problems occur.

Old European roses respond fairly well to hard pruning and can be cut back by one-half after they have bloomed. We usually wait and prune in mid-September so that the new growth will not have to survive the worst heat of summer. Some varieties, such as 'Madame Plantier', have such an attractive natural form that we prune them very lightly, for we are willing to sacrifice some of the potential output

of flowers to our enjoyment of the graceful shape of the plant. It is up to the individual gardener to decide whether or not to prune hard for aesthetic reasons and when to go ahead and cut a straggly looking rose way back in order to preserve its health.

Landscape Uses

We find that old European varieties look most natural in a garden setting when combined in beds with other roses and soft-colored perennials. Some can be grown successfully as container plants and others make handsome specimens on their own in the landscape, but they need to be planted where they can get proper care or they will draw visitors' eyes for the wrong reasons. Also, old European roses in a warm climate seem to have much shorter life spans than when grown in their proper environment. We have tried to compensate for this intolerance to heat by layering a few branches of most varieties so that when the original plant begins to fail there will be a healthy young replacement waiting in the wings.

The life span will vary according not only to the variety and health of the specimen, but also to the microclimate of each garden, so we can give no figures for others to plan by. The Gallicas seem by far the best survivors in the South, and in our garden the Damask roses also seem to do quite well. In the other classes it is very much hit and miss, but half the fun is in the experiment. By all means, try some of these roses in your own garden and experience firsthand the flowers whose range of rich fragrance got humankind addicted to the rose.

Selected Old European Rose Varieties

'Apothecary's Rose'
Gallica: probably cultivated before 1600

Some roses seem to be even more deeply rooted in human history than they are in the ground. The 'Apothecary's Rose' is one of those roses whose continued popularity is in many ways a result of a shared past that stretches back more than 400 years.

The 'Apothecary's Rose' is probably the oldest form of *Rosa gallica* in cultivation, and legend has it that it was brought to Provins, France, in the 13th century by the count of that region, Thibaut le Chansonnier. (He was the author of

66 songs, several of which have verses that refer to roses.) He is thought to have collected the seed hips of this plant in Damascus during the Seventh Crusade, though *R. gallica* is native to much of Europe, including France.

Thibaut's variety was adopted by the apothecaries and grown for their use in conserves and medicines because of its special ability to retain its scent when dried. This led to the commonly used title of *R. gallica officinalis*, signifying by the "officinalis" that this rose was sold as an herb. The specimen shown in the photo below was deliberately planted at the restored Pest House Infirmary at the Confederate Cemetery in Lynchburg, Virginia, to emphasize the connection between roses and medicine.

The 'Apothecary's Rose' startled us the first time we saw it. We understood that it would be the color that passed for red in the roses of the Middle Ages, but we didn't expect that color to be vivid cerise pink. (It was not until the 18th century that "pink" came into use as an adjective. One presumes that the ancients settled for calling the rose "red" because that was a color they could describe.) The bright flowers are semidouble, opening as flat as those depicted in old woodcuts, with a center of yellow stamens. They are produced only in the spring, but at that time they cover the top surface of the plant and look very showy indeed.

'Apothecary's Rose' is a small plant in our garden, only 2 ft. to 3 ft. in height, with stiff little canes that have relatively few prickles. It fits very nicely into our garden of useful herbs, adding vivid color in late spring with a bonus of fat hips to follow. It is not very enthusiastic

about our heat, shedding most of its rough, dark green foliage in the summer and increasing in size at a slow rate, but it will gradually throw up a few suckers and thicken into a sturdy clump once established and acclimated. In cooler climates this rose will reach 4 ft. in height (it tends to sprawl if it gets tall enough) and may spread more rapidly. 'Apothecary's Rose' is a good candidate for growing in a container, either to keep it accessible for pampering in a hot climate or to keep it neatly confined in a cold one.

There is a famous striped sport of this rose, a variety called 'Rosa Mundi' (also found in literature as *R. gallica versicolor*). It is the same vivid cerise pink as the 'Apothecary's Rose', but with irregular white streaks splashed across the petals. Both roses are identical in habit, and they are very showy planted together in the garden. Quite often both types of flowers will occur on the same bush.

Zone 3 / 2 ft. to 5 ft. high / 2 ft. to 4 ft. wide / very fragrant / deep pink / once-blooming

'Cardinal de Richelieu'
Gallica: 1840

The French nurseryman Laffay is usually credited with this most purple of Gallicas, but it seems that the rose was first raised in Holland and was originally known as 'Rose Van Sian' after its breeder there. It is thought that Laffay received the rose from Van Sian and reintroduced it with a new name, though why he chose 'Cardinal de Richelieu' is a mystery. As everyone knows, cardinals dress in red, not purple, and Richelieu was not a particularly savory character in French history. He was, however, memorable, and so is his namesake rose.

Of all the Old Garden Roses, only Gallicas are truly purple, and 'Cardinal de Richelieu' is one of the purplest. Its flowers are sweetly scented and of medium size (between 2 in. and 3 in. across), and they are very double, with a knot of petals in the middle that conceals most of the stamens. They are dark crimson-purple with blue highlights upon opening, and they fade to a handsome greyish-mauve. We find this last coloring very elegant, but some people don't care for it and should probably avoid the Gallicas, since it is a habit of this class to assume some shade of greyish-purple as the flowers fade. Since the petals of 'Cardinal de Richelieu' are paler on the backs, there is a changing pattern of light and dark colors as the flower gradually turns from a round little ball of a bud into a reflexed purple pompom. In full bloom in midspring, the bush is a study in shades and textures.

At about 3 ft., 'Cardinal de Richelieu' is a very convenient height for a small garden, and it tends to drape itself in several directions, suckering and sprawling about in a pleasant, informal way.

The canes are not terribly prickly and the foliage is neater and takes the heat better than many Gallicas, but after the plant has become established at a certain size, we dig out the multiple new suckers once a year to keep from having too much of a good thing. Gallicas that are grafted onto a rootstock will not sucker (though the rootstock might), but the roses do so much better on their own roots in our unsuitable climate that it is worth the little effort it takes to keep them controlled.

Like most of the European varieties, 'Cardinal de Richelieu' needs to be planted where it can be tended with extra water and fertilizer if it is to thrive in Zones 8 and 9. Zone 10 is really too warm, and Zone 7 is cool enough for old European roses to grow well without any fuss. Pruning is very simple, involving removal of dead wood and cutting back between one-third and one-half of the bush either right after flowering or just at the end of summer. It is not a requirement that the bush be cut back, but it will bloom more heavily with this treatment.

Since 'Cardinal de Richelieu' blooms only once a year, we like to plant it in a mixed bed with other roses and perennials. That way it becomes part of a changing pattern of bloom. In season it's such a splendid, glowingly purple rose that we can't resent it for resting the remainder of the year.

Zone 4 / 3 ft. to 5 ft. high / 2 ft. to 4 ft. wide / very fragrant / mauve / once-blooming

'York and Lancaster'
Damask: cultivated before 1629

The badge of the royal house of York in England was a white rose, *Rosa alba,* and the badge of the royal house of Lancaster was a red rose, *R. gallica.* Their opposing claims to the throne led to the Wars of the Roses (1455-1485), which ended with a marriage uniting the two factions and creating the house of Tudor. The Tudor Rose became the badge of reconciliation—a double rose with the white superimposed upon the red.

With all this turmoil symbolized by roses it is not surprising that the discovery of a bicolored Damask rose called the whole conflict to mind, and the rose was dubbed 'York and Lancaster'. This rose is often called *R. damascena versicolor* in the literature, and it is often confused with the early variegated Gallica 'Rosa Mundi'—though the two roses are really very different. 'Rosa Mundi' is bright

cerise pink streaked with white, whereas 'York and Lancaster' is all soft colors. The petals vary between cream white and pale pink, sometimes one, sometimes the other, sometimes half and half. The flowers are double, but not extravagantly so, and from a distance it is hard to see why they are so interesting—the whole effect is simply pastel pink and you have to get close to see the "York." The bush is very attractive, however, fuller and more branching than the other Damasks that we grow, with many small prickles and lightly downy, matte-green leaves that complement the softness of the flowers.

We have one specimen of 'York and Lancaster' planted by a low stone wall in the corner of a vegetable garden that adjoins the herb garden. It looks perfectly at home next to the zucchini. The grey of the wall is a fine background for the rose, which spills over to offer its fragrance on both sides. 'York and Lancaster' can also be grown in

a large container, such as a weathered wooden tub, with very attractive results.

'York and Lancaster' begins blooming very early in the spring, early or mid-April for us, and continues for six weeks or more. The long bloom season, combined with the heady Damask fragrance, makes this rose worthwhile even for those who are not impressed by its subtle color.

'York and Lancaster' is remarkably healthy in our garden and keeps its foliage much better than we had expected—possibly in response to the extra-fertile, well-worked soil of the vegetable garden. The Damask roses in general have done fairly well for us in Zone 8, as long as they are fertilized and watered, and they seem to require little or no pruning. Farther south, even 'York and Lancaster' has some trouble with the heat and will do a little better in the cooler soil of the north side of the house, sheltered from the late afternoon sun. If the plant begins to lose vigor, which it may do even on its own roots, replacements can be started by layering some of the longer canes (see Chapter 3).

Zone 3 / 3 ft. to 5 ft. high / 3 ft. to 5 ft. wide / very fragrant / pink blend / once-blooming

'Celsiana'
Damask: before 1750

Painted by the Dutch artist Van Huysem and later by the French flower portraitist Redouté, 'Celsiana's' career as an artist's model parallels its path of distribution. It was grown extensively in Holland for a number of years before its introduction to France, but it is from the French nurseryman Jacques-Martin Cels that this rose takes its name.

'Celsiana' is one of the Damask roses that forms a vigorous, upright bush 4 ft. or 5 ft. high, perfect for the back layer of a mixed flower border. When it is in bloom in the spring, the long, prickly canes arch over with the weight of the flowers and make an extremely graceful picture. The flowers come in clusters of three or four, and each one is large—up to 4 in. across. They are semidouble, with the crinkled pink silk petals arranged around a huge central crown of golden stamens, and when the light is behind them they glow with translucent color. One of our acquaintances says they remind her of the pink light bulbs her grandmother always used when she gave a party so that everyone would look young and beautiful.

The fragrance is the special Damask citrus-and-spice blend that is one of the finest perfumes invented by nature, and 'Celsiana' has it in full measure. There is something really addictive about the scent of Damask roses, so it is not surprising that they are the

source of most commercial rose oil. Apparently, either they have more scented oils in their petals than do other roses, or the oil can be separated more easily by the distillation process. It takes hundreds of pounds of petals to make just one ounce of rose attar, however; a single bush will supply the same perfume in the garden.

An interesting characteristic of Damask roses is that their foliage often has a scent as well, very faint but distinctly musky. 'Celsiana's' smooth, dull-green leaves have this trait, and they are also nearly disease-free. In climates where Damask roses don't have to struggle with the heat and humidity, they are often extremely vigorous and can be left to grow pretty much on their own. 'Celsiana' has done very well in our garden, however, in spite of high temperatures and a rather alkaline soil, and we are happy to recommend it as a specimen rose that will more than justify its care when it blooms each spring.

Zone 3 / 4 ft. to 6 ft. high / 2 ft. to 4 ft. wide / very fragrant / light pink / once-blooming

'Ispahan'
Damask: cultivated before 1832

This rose has been reported growing wild in the hills of Iran, especially between Shiraz and the old caravan trading center of Isfahan (the modern spelling), so its romantic-sounding name is a product of common association, though it is listed in some literature more royally as 'Pompon des Princes'. Residents of Shiraz apparently still grow this variety in their walled gardens, where plants and pools are a relief from the hot, dry land outside. In fact, that city is still visited for its gardens, and Iran has a long history of fondness for roses.

It is easy to see why 'Ispahan' would remain a favorite. It is one of the toughest and most carefree of the Damasks, even for us, and it blooms for a long season — six or seven weeks at least. The rich pink flowers are quite amazingly fragrant. They are broad and loosely double, with the wrinkly petals typical of a Damask and a knot in the center that hides most of the stamens.

Damasks are often criticized in rose literature for their relaxed growth habit and their tendency to lean on nearby plants for support, but 'Ispahan' is gracefully top-heavy. The long canes bow just enough under the weight of foliage and flowers to give the impression of a loosely held bouquet. Even in

winter, when the small, rough, grey-tinged leaves have fallen and the plant is bare, it still has attractive lines to add to the texture of a winter garden.

We have seen 'Ispahan' used in several gardens both toward the back of a large mixed-flower border and set out on its own as a cherished specimen where it can be approached more easily for smelling. It has a place in any herb garden, perhaps near a wall or fence corner where its height will seem in proportion, because the scented flowers are useful for potpourris, rose beads, distilling or even sprinkling onto salads. 'Ispahan' and the other Damasks are wonderful in flower arrangements even though they don't last for more than a day or two after they've been cut. They have a sensual beauty that lasts in the mind's eye from one spring to the next and makes each bloom season eagerly awaited.

Zone 3 / 5 ft. to 7 ft. high / 2 ft. to 4 ft. wide / very fragrant / medium pink / once-blooming

'Autumn Damask'
Damask: before 1819

'Autumn Damask' is thought to be a cross of *Rosa gallica* with the repeat-blooming *R. moschata*, or even with *R. chinensis*, rather than the *R. gallica/R. phoenicia* combination that produced the once-blooming Damask varieties. Until the introduction of the Chinese roses, 'Autumn Damask' was almost the only rose known to Western civilization that bloomed more than once each year, and it got mentioned frequently in botanical literature because of this peculiarity. The Roman poets praised a "twice-blooming" rose found in the city of Paestum that may very well have been this plant.

'Autumn Damask' can be found in rose books under several names: *R. damascena bifera* and 'Rose des Quatre Saisons' are the most common, but we are more intrigued by the appellation 'Rose of Castille', because it is under this name that the 'Autumn Damask' can be found growing nearly wild in New Mexico and California. The story is that Bishop Lamy, who brought the Catholic religion from Spain to that part of the West in the 1600s, also brought with him this pink rose. Both 'Autumn Damask' and 'Harison's Yellow' have naturalized in some areas around the older, Spanish-settled towns, and in Taos at least, either one may be meant when 'Rose of Castille' is mentioned, though by right the name belongs to the pink rose, not the yellow.

'Autumn Damask' differs from the other Damasks in growth habit as well as in remontancy. It is generally a shorter and more compact plant, with flowers borne in clusters of three or four at the ends of prickly canes. The leaves are typically Damask—rough, dull green and serrated on the edges. Both the foliage and the powerful Damask scent are traceable in the descendants of this rose, the Bourbons and the Hybrid Perpetuals. Those classes also share with 'Autumn Damask' the habit of blooming profusely in the spring, very little in summer, and then having a modest but very fine display in the fall.

The flowers of 'Autumn Damask' are not particularly shapely, but they are sweet, pink, double and very fragrant. Since this rose doesn't make a very large plant, it can be grown in a container and placed where the perfume of the flowers will be accessible whenever it is needed to lift the spirits. The grey-green foliage and pastel-pink flowers blend softly with most backgrounds and with any color of pot except the common orange clay.

We have 'Autumn Damask' planted in one quadrant of our stone-walled herb garden, balancing in size and history with a plant of the 'Apothecary's Rose' and one of the Persian Musk 'Nastarana'. These old and very fragrant roses act as specific focal points in the garden in the spring, and the herbs fill out and carry the ball all summer.

Zone 4 / 3 ft. to 5 ft. high / 2 ft. to 4 ft. wide / very fragrant / medium pink / remontant

'Madame Plantier'
Hybrid Alba: 1835

The breeder of this rose, Monsieur Plantier, named it after his wife — presumably a sign of the best and most desirable varieties. A good rose can keep the name of the nursery alive in the mind of the public, so for reasons of common sense as well as loyalty, the finest roses often bear the names of the breeders, their wives and children. In truth, this one rose is the only posterity that Plantier achieved — without it, his part in the history of the rose would have vanished with no trace, but with it his name (or rather, that of his wife) may live forever.

'Madame Plantier' is thought to be a hybrid of *Rosa alba* and *R. moschata,* and it is without question the best Alba variety for the South. When we first acquired this rose we had never seen an Alba, so we didn't know that our specimen was not the Bourbon rose, 'Coquette des Alpes', that we had ordered. It looked nothing like the other Bourbons, however, so we

asked rosarian visitors about it. They were surprised that we hadn't recognized it immediately, and now that we are familiar with 'Madame Plantier' (as an Alba rather than a fake Bourbon) it would be very hard to mistake.

The form of the bush is distinctive, with long arching canes that are very smooth (almost without prickles), dark and glossy and that curve slightly back and forth from bud to bud — a graceful, wavy look. The foliage is dull green with the handsome blue tinge that is so characteristic of Alba roses, and it covers the plant just thickly enough to look attractive without hiding the good bones.

The buds of 'Madame Plantier' are also memorable, showing delicate, leafy sepals that are reminiscent of the 'Musk Rose' in their projecting calyx lobes. The flowers show a touch of creamy pink on the outside petals that is quickly lost as they reflex back to expose the pure white inner petals, arranged in neat layers around a central knot accentuated by a green eye. The flower is loosely cupped, sliced off flat on top and filled with a sweet fragrance.

'Madame Plantier' blooms very heavily right in the middle of the spring season, mid-April for us, and makes an outstanding specimen plant. It is extremely healthy in our garden, and we have heard good reports of it from all over the South. In fact, the *Fruitland Nurseries Catalog* of 1913-14 from Augusta, Georgia, describes this variety as "desirable for massing and as hardy as an oak."

Back when we thought it was a Bourbon, we planted 'Madame Plantier' in our pegged-rose bed, so we are in a position to know that it performs well when pegged down and that the beautiful canes show to advantage under this training. This rose does not grow as large for us as it does in cooler climates — we've heard of specimens growing 15 ft. or 20 ft. up into trees in England — but this just makes it easier to handle. When grown as a shrub, we find that the only pruning 'Madame Plantier' really needs is removal of dead wood, but we often cut away a few of the bottom canes so that the cascading shape can be seen clearly.

Zone 4 / 4 ft. to 6 ft. high / 6 ft. to 8 ft. wide / very fragrant / white / once-blooming

'Celestial'
Alba: before 1848

Supposedly one of the oldest of Alba roses, 'Celestial' (or 'Céleste') has very little recorded history — perhaps because its admirers all seem to be moonstruck before its beauty. Graham Stuart Thomas, our most reliable source, suggests in *The Old Shrub Roses* that this rose was originally from Holland, arriving in France at the end of the 18th century. Flower portraitist Redouté painted it as a Damask, *Rosa damascena* 'Aurora', and though he mistook the class, he caught the unique beauty of the rose by including the stages of the bud as it opens. Gertrude Jekyll wrote that 'Celestial' is "a rose of wonderful beauty when the bud is half-opened." Graham Stuart Thomas adds: "Apart from *R. virginiana plena* and the earliest Polyanthas like 'Cécil Brünner', I know of no rose of such exquisite charm when unfurling its petals."

We find that 'Celestial' is also beautiful when the double, sweetly scented flowers are fully opened. The gentle cup is balanced by the reflexed outer petals, and the center is filled with a golden circlet of stamens. The color is clear and pure, as if white porcelain flowers had been glazed with translucent paint. The foliage sets a standard for other Albas to strive toward, a particularly elegant grey-green hazed with blue that has been described as "leaden." The bush is a moderate 4 ft. in size with relatively few thin, sharp, reddish prickles. To add one final word of praise, Vita Sackville-West is quoted in H.L.V. Fletcher's *Rose Anthology* as saying that 'Celestial' is "one of the loveliest shrubs one could ever wish to contemplate."

Peter Haring

In landscape form, 'Celestial' is very much like the 'Autumn Damask' pictured on p. 133. In our garden this rose is planted by a stone wall in a bed containing several old European roses and several varieties of thyme, and it is one of the prettiest features.

We have been both surprised and grateful that this particular Alba grows so well for us when so many of its cousins have a struggle here. We have had no problems with it so far except for a few leaves lost in the summer. Pruning has been minimal, just removal of dead wood and any unwanted branches, and watering and fertilizing are on the same regular pattern that we offer the other European types.

In the warmest parts of the South, it might be well to plant this rose on the north side of the house for a slightly cooler soil, or to try growing it in a container that can be moved into the afternoon shade. In cooler Zones 'Celestial' will make a gorgeous shrub to 6 ft. in height.

Zone 3 / 4 ft. to 6 ft. high / 3 ft. to 4 ft. wide / very fragrant / light pink / once-blooming

'Fantin-Latour'
Centifolia: date unknown

This is the only Centifolia we have had success growing, and we suspect that is because it is not a Centifolia after all. It was rescued from obscurity and reintroduced about 1900, and it can be found in catalogs of that period with no background or breeder's name given. Graham Stuart Thomas records (in *The Old Shrub Roses*) having found it once in a garden labeled simply 'Best Garden Rose', and that is virtually the limit of 'Fantin-Latour's' history.

The Centifolia designation is more than a little arbitrary. Thomas speculates that the rose shows signs of some China blood, whereas other rosarians suggest that it may be a Hybrid Alba. We lean toward the Hybrid China idea because that would explain the rose's cheerful tolerance of our hot and humid climate.

The name that was chosen for this rose is most appropriate: Henri Fantin-Latour was a 19th-century Romantic artist who painted many studies of flowers, roses among them. His namesake rose has the sort of rich sensuality that he would have appreciated, and surely painted, had the two been contemporaries. As it is, 'Fantin-Latour' deserves a place in every garden planned for fragrance and romantic effect.

The blush-pink blossoms open flat to display a swirl of cupped petals and a knotted center. The outer petals reflex backward in typical Centifolia fashion, but the fragrance is even richer than most Centifolias, though not, to our noses, quite as potent as the Damasks. The peculiar beauty of this rose is in the contrast between the large, light-pink flowers and the very dark green, broad, rounded leaves that thickly cover a bush as wide as it is tall. There are

Peter Haring

interesting plummy tones to the foliage that make the color combination even more noticeable.

This is a rose that should be planted where you wish to draw attention, a classic specimen type. 'Fantin-Latour' doesn't clash with other roses, but it does stand out amongst them in a striking fashion. It begins to bloom between the middle and the end of April for us, shows no ill effects from the gradually increasing heat of the approaching summer and continues the display for four or five weeks.

The bush in our garden is about 3½ ft. in every dimension, so we have kept it near the front of a bed that includes some 5-ft. and 6-ft. tall rose varieties. We have experienced no problems with its health or vigor under the full Texas sun, but have to admit that we have seen larger, lusher specimens in areas of New York and California where the nights are cooler.

Zone 3 / 4 ft. to 6 ft. high / 3 ft. to 5 ft. wide / very fragrant / light pink / once-blooming

Charlotte Haring

'Crested Moss'
Moss: 1827

Although introduced in 1827 by the French nurseryman Jean-Paul Vibert, 'Crested Moss' was not bred by him but by nature. The original seedling of this odd variety was discovered about 1820 growing in a crack in the wall of a ruined convent near the town of Fribourg, Switzerland, where it was most likely planted by a passing bird.

'Crested Moss' is notable primarily for the excessively developed growths on the edges of the sepals that give this variety a unique, frilly-looking bud. This characteristic has determined all the names given to the rose, from the sober Latin designation of *Rosa centifolia cristata* to the slightly disrespectful 'Chapeau de Napoléon'. The buds are not as distinctly three-cornered as Napoleon's hat, but they do project their peculiarities with a similar cockiness.

According to the research of Dr. C.C. Hurst, whose work on the background of roses was published in Graham Stuart Thomas's *The Old Shrub Roses*, 'Crested Moss' is not properly a Moss rose at all but a parallel development. The true Moss roses sported from Centifolia and Damask roses and have calyxes covered with scented glandular hairs, or moss, whereas 'Crested Moss' lacks this trait. It is also a Centifolia sport, but with moss that is leafy rather than glandular and has only a little of the delightful musky scent that makes true Moss rose buds so appealing. Nonetheless, 'Crested Moss' is a delightful oddity and takes up very little space in the garden—at least in the South.

We keep 'Crested Moss' planted near the front of a bed that features varieties of old European roses. It stays at about 3 ft. in height, regulating itself by a little dieback after a hot summer. We've learned to prune this rose in early fall rather than immediately after the late spring blooming, because this way it has a larger canopy of canes and foliage for its own protection in the heat. 'Crested Moss' does not bloom heavily for us, but the flowers are satisfyingly fat, pink and very fragrant.

Keeping 'Crested Moss' where it can be easily noticed makes the most of its particular beauties and makes it accessible for a little extra care in terms of water, fertilizer and mulch to keep its roots cooler. The dull-green foliage is relatively disease resistant in the full sun, but it is not heatproof, and during July and August a neglected plant tends to look like a bristly plucked chicken.

This rose would be an ideal container specimen in the South, where it could be brought out as a conversation piece while in bud and flower and tucked into an out of the way spot while resting. In the cool

Stephen Scanniello

North, we understand, this same rose is quite vigorous and reaches up to 7 ft. in height.

Zone 4 / 3 ft. to 5 ft. high / 2 ft. to 4 ft. wide / very fragrant / medium pink / once-blooming

Bill Bennett

'Salet'
Moss: 1854

In the Victorian language of flowers, a Moss rosebud given to a sweetheart was taken to mean a confession of love. The musky scent of the glandular hairs, or moss, is a surprisingly earthy fragrance to have appealed so much to the chaste (or chastened) women of that era, but perhaps it is one more clue to the secret sensuality that flowed beneath the frozen surface of those times. Taken for its own worth, with no hidden meanings, the scent of the moss is a pleasant and interesting addition to the already wonderful fragrance of the flowers.

Of all the Moss roses, 'Salet' seems to be the hardiest in the South and to repeat the most. These qualities are probably both linked to the fact that 'Salet' is the sport of a Damask perpetual rose (like the 'Autumn Damask') rather than a Centifolia. These repeat-blooming Damasks are thought to be products of *Rosa gallica* crossed with *R. moschata*, and it is the 'Musk Rose' blood that would make them both remontant and heat tolerant—or at least

relatively so. We have seen 'Salet' in a number of gardens where few other old European varieties are included, and the consensus is that it looks wonderful in spring and fall, "half-dead" in the summer, and is a real survivor in most situations.

Moss roses in general have a history of susceptibility to fungal diseases, especially mildew, but we have seen little of this disease on our plants of 'Salet'. They are grown in full sun, with plenty of air movement, and we try not to let them get stressed for lack of water or fertilizer.

One of the reasons we prefer 'Salet' to some of the prettier Moss varieties is that it forgives inadvertent neglect, as we feel a garden-worthy rose should. So far it has recovered from every setback, and our best specimen has formed a bush about 4 ft. high by 3 ft. wide. It was originally planted in the middle of a flower bed, but we soon moved it to a more accessible position since there is no point in having a Moss rose if you can't rub your fingers on the mossy buds and enjoy the musky scent of the glandular resin.

The moss on 'Salet' is green and lightly covers the stems, calyx and sepals of buds that appear in groups of three. The flowers are fairly a good size, 3 in. or 4 in. across, medium pink and very double. Their form is a little muddled and irregular, but pleasing for all that, with a knot of petals in the middle and a nice Damask fragrance. The foliage is plentiful, most of the time, on lightly prickled canes, and the rough, dull-green leaves provide a quiet background that keeps the attention focused on the buds and flowers.

In our garden, 'Salet' blooms quite well in the spring, has a few uncertain flowers in the summer and produces its prettiest efforts in the cooler weather of the fall.

Zone 4 / 3 ft. to 4 ft. high / 3 ft. to 4 ft. wide / very fragrant / medium pink / remontant

Mary Rae Mattix

China Roses

And China opened her shut gate
To let her roses through...
—Vita Sackville-West, "The Garden"

Every time you step out into an October garden and inhale the scent of roses, thank the Chinese. Not for the fragrance itself, because China roses aren't best known for their scent, but for the simple presence of roses after the summer is over. Until the coming of Chinese roses, Europe had just two roses that could bloom in the fall. One was the not very cold-hardy *Rosa moschata*, and the other was the 'Autumn Damask', which didn't always repeat very enthusiastically. All other known European roses bloomed once during the short summer growing season, and that was it.

There are two reasons why the Chinese roses repeated their bloom and European roses did not. The first and most important was completely natural. Roses in a cold climate prepare for winter by going dormant for protection—flowers and leaves are discarded, and all the starchy energy is stored in the root so that no matter how the top of the plant fares in the cold it can be sure of survival down below. Roses in a warm climate, on the other hand, have different survival tactics. Dormancy is not such a requirement—the roses can go on growing and blooming safely for most of the year. Resistance to disease and insects is vital, however, because disease organisms and pests thrive in a long warm season.

Chinese roses, including the Chinas, Teas and their closest descendants, have a marvelous ability to shed damaged leaves and replace them quickly without any apparent loss of vigor. In Zones 8 and warmer, we find that the majority of old European roses suffer a lot from disease because they were not selected to withstand its continuous onslaught. Losing their leaves can send them into a tailspin from which they take months to recover. Sometimes they don't begin growing new foliage until fall, just before they're supposed to go dormant. Except for selected varieties, old European roses need as much cosseting of their health in the South as the tender Chinese varieties need protection against cold in the North.

The second reason European explorers in the 18th and 19th centuries were able to find remontant roses in the Chinese gardens has to do with human selection. When a once-blooming climber has a dwarf sport, occasionally that bushy sport will be a remontant type. With at least a 2,000-year head start on Western gardening, Chinese rose lovers had plenty of time to notice, evaluate and collect these useful mutants that were the ancestors of all our present-day remontant roses. Although the chrysanthemum and the plum blossom may have been more important in their culture, the rose was never neglected. Confucius (551-479 B.C.) records that a large number of roses were planted in his day in the Imperial Gardens at Beijing, and rosebushes with both single and double flowers are shown in Chinese art at least from the 10th century onward. Perhaps the Chinese took their long-blooming roses for granted; in spite of some of the appealing varieties that were brought out of that country to the West, it's hard not to regret what roses they could have created if they'd ever gotten serious about them.

Plant Characteristics

Chinese roses of this bushy remontant type were divided into two classes: the Chinas, which we discuss in this section, and the Teas, which we discuss on pp. 189-206. The two classes are closely related in many ways, but they differ visibly in color (Chinas tend toward pink or crimson, Teas run the gamut of pastels) and flower form (Teas are often long-budded and full of petals, Chinas are looser in shape and more open). There is also a distinct difference in fragrance: Teas smell like orris root, whereas the Chinas that are strongly scented have a fruity, astringent, raspberry-like perfume, and most have a black-pepper scent to their foliage that lingers on the fingers after handling. Of the two authors of this book, one finds the scent of China roses the most appealing in the rose kingdom, whereas the other can barely detect it and much prefers the cool rich scent of Tea roses. But we both agree that these two classes are without peer for their performance in southern gardens.

From an article in *The American Cotton Planter* dated July 3, 1855, we gleaned the following: "Among all the shrubs which are cultivated in the Southern garden, the ever-blooming roses unquestionably hold the highest rank....In fact, nothing is more interesting to a Northern horticulturist than our ever-blooming rose." (The author, Robert Nelson, was with the Troup Hill Nurseries in Georgia, so although he can be presumed prejudiced, he can also be presumed informed.) That interest led to a remarkable number of crosses, especially from the easy-to-breed 'Old Blush' (brought to Europe in 1752) and the other China "stud rose," 'Slater's Crimson China' (introduced to the West about 1790). The blood of the China rose now flows through almost all other classes from Noisettes and Bourbons through Hybrid Perpetuals, Hybrid Teas, Hybrid Musks, Polyanthas and Floribundas.

Fortunately, many of the fascinating old Chinas still exist in rural gardens, in cemeteries and in quiet neighborhoods where they were shared as gifts among green-thumbed neighbors with a taste for older plants. They are easy to collect, very easy to propagate from cuttings and hard to kill once they have settled in. Chinas are in bloom for at least three weeks out of every six during the growing season, and it is rare to catch them completely bare of flowers. Most varieties in this class are hardy to Zone 7. They can be grown in colder areas with appropriate winter protection or as container specimens. The flowers are mostly crimsons and pinks with some coppery-orange shades. Most bushes are at least as wide as they are tall and range from 2 ft. for 'Rouletii' to 7 ft. or more for 'Mutabilis'.

Culture

China roses are an excellent choice for water-restricted gardens, because they can and do survive long periods of drought once they are well established. They will respond enthusiastically to the lightest of care (pruning, watering and fertilizing), and they should be the first selection for any gardener who has been frightened by the demands of Hybrid Teas. Some varieties will get a touch of mildew if warm days are followed by cool nights and the roses don't get the first morning sun—they need at least six to eight hours of full sun. Except for mildew, which doesn't seem to affect their overall health, we have rarely seen a China rose suffer from any disease. There is no reason we can think of to spray them.

The bush of most China roses is a chunky affair characterized by smooth, angular branches, lots of twigs, neatly pointed leaflets and thin, curved prickles. Chinas do not absolutely require pruning, but they take well to it in moderation. Cutting them back by about one-third two times a year thickens them up and encourages even greater flower production. They don't have to be pruned carefully, however—hedge shears are faster than hand clippers, and the result is the same. New growth follows a clipping so quickly that no scars or mistakes will show for long.

Landscape Uses

Plants from this class are especially useful as specimens and for hedges, borders and container planting. The crimson Chinas and some of the more compact pink varieties make excellent bedding plants since they can be shorn uniformly and kept in vigorous bloom. For the same reasons they are also perfect for hedges and foundation plantings. The flowers of the China rose have the interesting trait of turning darker in the sun instead of fading to a paler shade. This quality is almost unique among roses and makes for some very interesting color effects in the landscape. Some varieties grow large and glorious enough to feature as specimen plants decorating an otherwise bare area of the garden. Others are petite or unusual enough to feature in containers as patio or roof-garden decor. Their silky petals and dainty leaves give them a delicate and cultured look, but they are tough as nails and will do whatever is asked of them. Thomas Affleck summed up the performance of China roses perfectly in his *Southern Nurseries Catalog for 1851 and 1852*, saying simply: "They are so constantly in flower during the summer and autumn, and give so little trouble."

Selected China Varieties

'Old Blush'
1752

It's difficult to know where to begin with this fascinating rose. 'Old Blush' is important in rose history as the first of the Chinese everblooming varieties to make its way to Europe and as the great "stud" rose that lent its genes to the majority of remontant roses from that time forward. ('Old Blush' is certainly an appropriate name for such a promiscuous flower.) But it is also the familiar rose of a thousand gardens,

known by popular names such as 'Common Monthly', 'Common Blush China' and 'Old Pink Daily' (in reference to its schedule for producing new flowers).

The date of 1752 records the introduction of 'Old Blush' into Sweden. It was not until some years after that date that the rose began to catch the attention of English gardeners, but when it did, they were fascinated. In her book *Old Time Gardens,* Alice Morse Earle quotes Henry Phillips, author of *Sylva Florifera* (1823), who records that this rose was initially considered so tender that "it was kept constantly in the stove, and the smallest cuttings were sold for many guineas each." But 'Old

Blush' is so very easy to propagate that the populace was soon disillusioned on this point. It was shared about, says Phillips, and "every country casement had the pride of sheltering this Chinese prodigy, until the cottager, for want of pence to purchase flower pots, planted it in the open ground, where it blooms happily throughout the summer and may often be seen, 'its petals pushing through a veil of snow in the month of December.'"

'Old Blush' really is a superb plant in the landscape. The loose, semidouble lavender-pink blooms with lilac veins keep repeating their rich display throughout the growing season: nine, ten or even twelve months a year, depending on winter temperatures. The flowers are lightly scented but are not useful for cutting as they press upon each other's heels too quickly, one flush falling away to make room for the next. Fat, orange hips begin to appear by midsummer if the spent flowers are not pruned away, and they add their touch of color (and testimony of fertility) well into the winter.

The neatly pointed leaves thickly cover a chunky shrub that can be pruned to grow in a large container or allowed to reach (as one early Texian lady phrased it) "the size of a hogshead"—about 5 ft. or 6 ft. in every dimension. A single bush of this rose adds color to any setting, while a whole hedge can be truly spectacular. It would be nice to see dull, green foundation plantings of box or pittosporum replaced with the colors of willing roses like 'Old Blush'.

There is also a climbing sport of this rose, and once established, it blooms nearly as much as the bush, so 'Old Blush' can be used to fill very nearly all landscaping needs.

Best of all, 'Old Blush' thrives in almost any conditions with almost any sort of care and shows a remarkable resistance to disease. An easy, easy rose.

Zone 6 / 5 ft. to 8 ft. high / 3 ft. to 6 ft. wide / fragrant / medium pink / reliable repeat

'Rouletii'
before 1818

One of the major mysteries of rose history is how this little pink rose got from China to the Swiss village in which Major Roulet chanced upon it. Sent home by a sailor son, perhaps? Or shared around by a retired tea trader with a green thumb? At any rate, the Major (a physician in the Swiss army) found it in 1918 and gave notice of it to Geneva nurseryman Henri Correvon.

The original plant was quite tiny, only 2 in. tall, and had reputedly been grown in the same window box for more than a hundred years, blooming throughout each season. The story is that when Correvon went to collect the rose, he arrived just after a fire had destroyed the village. Fortunately, the rose was also found growing at the nearby village of Onnens, and Roulet and Correvon were able to get a start of it there.

Correvon introduced the little rose in 1922, under the name of his friend, the finder. For a long time it was considered to be a species, and

it can be found in many books as *Rosa rouletii.* It is actually a variety of *R. chinensis minima,* however, and as such is not entitled to a Latin name of its own. 'Rouletii' has figured as a major rose parent in the breeding of Miniature roses and is still in use for that purpose today.

We find that 'Rouletii' responds to our warm climate by expanding in size. Our plants average between 2 ft. and 3 ft. in height, perhaps because they are never cut back by the cold. The plant is very compact and bushy, with half-size leaves and flowers that rarely get as big as a quarter. The petals are lavender pink with slightly darker veins, and the neat bud formation opens into a blousy flower remarkably like a

down-scaled version of 'Old Blush'. 'Rouletii' stays neat with a minimal amount of pruning (once or twice a year) and never shows any signs of disease. It is a little slower to come out of dormancy in the spring than is 'Old Blush', but only by a week or two, and then it blooms frequently until late in the fall.

This is a rose that was designed by nature to be grown in a container, and it can be tailored to fit almost any sort of receptacle (except those that are the orangy color of some clay pots, for orange does not go with lavender pink). In a half barrel or a pot of glazed ceramic or even a blue enamel basin with holes punched in the bottom for drainage, 'Rouletii' will be steadily decorative as a focal point for any patio or small garden. It also makes an excellent edging plant for outlining a flower border or circling a mailbox or sundial, because it stays well covered with foliage to the base of the canes as long as it gets pruned back a little now and then. The flowers can even be used in potpourris. They have very little scent, but their diminutive size makes them a nice visual addition to a fragrant mixture.

Zone 6 / 2 ft. to 3 ft. high / 2 ft. to 3 ft. wide / slightly fragrant / medium pink / reliable repeat

'Le Vésuve'
1825

The breeder of 'Le Vésuve', Jules Laffay, was clearly interested in experimentation. The parents of this rose are not listed, but it shows characteristics of Teas as well as Chinas. Laffay went on to become a leader in the breeding of Hybrid Perpetuals, which incorporate a handful of genes from many different classes, so it isn't surprising that this little China variety looks somewhat mixed. There are no clues, however, as to why he named the rose after a volcano, unless because it regularly erupts with flowers.

'Le Vésuve' is a remarkably handsome bush in our garden, and though very few of the early rose authors bother to mention it, it is one we wouldn't be without. The plant grows in a softly mounded shape that is so thoroughly covered with apple-green leaves that the branches are barely seen. Flowers on this rose are quite large for a China, and they are fully double with wonderfully muddled centers, as if someone had casually stirred them with a finger while the petals were going on. The color varies from dark to pale pink, depending upon sun, climate and time of year.

This is one of those Chinas that is only occasionally fragrant, when the temperature conditions are perfect for a slow release of rose oil from the petals, but then it has a sweet, soft, fruity scent. In fact, the whole character of 'Le Vésuve' is to seem lush and soft, hiding the fact that it is tough and sturdy underneath. We have heard from a friend on the Gulf Coast that 'Le Vésuve' was a "martyr to spot" in his garden, but it has not shown this behavior in ours, so perhaps blackspot is a factor only in conditions of extreme humidity.

We have used 'Le Vésuve' (which grows about 3 ft. tall for us) in a mixed bed of several of the smaller China varieties. Each rose in the bed was chosen for its restrained behavior and constant bloom, and the roses are planted roughly 3 ft. apart so that there is room to underplant with narcissus and a changing display of annuals. We usually prefer the longer-lasting perennials, but the pinks and crimsons of the Chinas are irresistible with a spring blanket of Texas bluebonnets, so for this one small bed we don't mind the extra work of seasonal replanting between the rose bushes.

'Le Vésuve' is quite similar in size and form to the specimen of 'Hermosa' pictured on p. 148, and like 'Hermosa', is a natural for container planting. We've seen it set out in half barrels around a swimming-pool area, where it did a lot to soften the harsh look that chlorinated water surrounded by concrete can have. If you do grow 'Le Vésuve' in a container, be aware that all container-grown plants have a greater need for water than they would if planted in the ground. 'Le Vésuve' can survive some drought, but it looks much nicer with all its leaves lush and intact.

Zone 7 / 2 ft. to 4 ft. high / 2 ft. to 4 ft. wide / slightly fragrant / pink blend / reliable repeat

'Cramoisi Supérieur'
1832

"Oh what a tangled web was knotted / When the first red China rose was spotted!" Forgive us our poetry, but after struggling for years to separate the varieties, it is a great relief to admit finally that there's not a single red China rose grown today whose identity is unquestioned. Not only did rose authors and catalog compilers of the 19th century shortchange us on clear descriptions, but the red Chinas as a group are masters of self-alteration. They grow readily from seeds that spread by natural means, and the seedlings can vary in size, shades of color and number of petals. As a result, there are many genetic variations on this one theme in existence throughout the South.

The rose that we grow as 'Cramoisi Supérieur' is a variety that can be collected under that name in old gardens all over Texas, and it does match the existing written descriptions of 'Cramoisi Supérieur' quite closely. Identification is not final, however, because it also looks almost identical to the rose that is grown throughout the Southeast as 'Louis Philippe', and both of them match the same inexact descriptions.

'Louis Philippe' was introduced only two years after 'Cramoisi Supérieur', in 1834, and we know it was grown in Texas because Lorenzo de Zavala, an early statesman for the Republic of Texas, collected it during his term as Minister to France and brought it home to plant at Lynchburg. It is possible, therefore, that the two plants are one and the same variety. We can't even say that for sure, though, because one of our friends in New Mexico is growing a plant of 'Cramoisi Supérieur' that he got

from us and a 'Louis Philippe' that he got from another nursery and he says they look "quite distinctly different," and he doesn't understand the controversy.

Our 'Cramoisi Supérieur' is one of our favorite roses. It is a vivid glowing crimson in color, with an occasional white streak in one or more of the petals. The color and size change a little with the temperature. Flowers in midsummer are smaller, dark red all over and have fewer petals. In the cooler temperatures of spring and fall, the flowers are larger (about 2½ in. across), more double and shaded with blush in the center. They are always very cupped, with globular buds that never open all the way flat, and they are extremely fragrant. 'Cramoisi Supérieur' is probably the single most fragrant rose in the China class, with a delicious raspberry scent. The flowers are usually borne singly on fairly long, smooth stems, making them easy to cut and rewarding to arrange.

When young, the bush responds well to firm cutting back (by one-third to one-half) to thicken up its angular, twiggy growth. After that, it requires only minimal shaping to stay healthy and full of blooms and will grow, as we have seen it in graveyards, with complete neglect. 'Cramoisi Supérieur' is very easy to grow as long as it gets plenty of sun (six to eight hours). Shady settings produce plants with too little foliage and too few flowers.

This is an excellent rose for growing in a container, as a specimen to accent some garden feature, or trained and neatly pruned as a heavily blooming hedge.

Zone 7 / 3 ft. to 6 ft. high / 3 ft. to 4 ft. wide / very fragrant / medium red / reliable repeat

'Archduke Charles'
before 1837

'Archduke Charles', like 'Le Vésuve', is an interesting-looking China introduced by the French rose breeder Laffay. Thomas Rivers, a 19th-century rose authority, called this rose "changeable as the camelion," and so it is if he means our little Southern chameleon, a lizard that changes only from green to brown. 'Archduke Charles' doesn't display a wide variety of colors, but it changes quite reliably from pink to crimson. The buds are dark, but when they open it can be seen that the red outer petals guard a full center of the palest pink. As the sun shines on the fragrant flowers, they follow the peculiarly China habit of getting darker and darker until they are crimson all over.

China roses are the only class whose blossoms naturally "fade" darker instead of lighter, and any modern variety with this trait is certain to have China blood in its background. Cultivators of this rose have always had trouble accepting this backward behavior, in spite of the evidence of their own eyes. In his book *Beauties of the Rose* (1850), Henry Curtis, a painter of roses who ought to have had a good eye, lists descriptions by four prominent authorities who say 'Archduke Charles' gets darker with age and then gives his own opinion that it opens crimson and then turns "pale pink or nearly white." The rose is well worth growing just to prove that many rules—in this case, the rule of fading to a lighter color—are improved by their exceptions.

We have used 'Archduke Charles' extensively as a hedge rose and for foundation plantings. (There is a

photo of it at our display garden on p. 36.) This is not to say that it won't make a good specimen, but the healthy, neat and erect bush and constant bloom work so well in a hedge that it is hard to resist. Besides, it has the interesting advantage of being bicolored in the cool spring and fall and crimson all through the hot days of summer.

'Archduke Charles' is much less chunky in form than most of the other China roses. In fact it leans toward the vase-like shape of the Teas. If it is pruned or sheared back by about one-quarter three or four times a year, it will stay very leafy and full in appearance (much like the 'Cramoisi Supérieur' shown in the top photo on the facing page). If left alone to fill out naturally, this rose can be a little bare on the bottom. We think of this not so much as a flaw but as an opportunity for underplanting with colorful perennials.

Zone 7 / 3 ft. to 5 ft. high / 2 ft. to 4 ft. wide / fragrant / red blend / reliable repeat

'Hermosa'
1840

'Hermosa', also to be found in old rose literature as 'Armosa', is a neat little rose that has been shunted back and forth between the Bourbons and the Chinas and is probably equally at home in either class. Thomas Affleck, whose Southern Nurseries had branches in both Texas and Mississippi, includes it in his *Catalog for 1851 and 1852* as a Bourbon and describes it as "cupped, very double and perfect, a delicate rose."

Eighty-five years later, Bobbink and Atkins (at that time almost the only American nursery selling old-fashioned roses) list 'Hermosa' as a China or Bengal rose with "medium-sized, symmetrically double flowers of soft pink." The most current authority, *Modern Roses 9,* lists it definitely as a China,

and that is the way it must be labeled if it is ever shown at an American Rose Society show.

Hermosa is the Spanish word for beautiful, which fits this rose to a T. The plant is small, rarely reaching over 3 ft. tall in our garden, and the flowers are scaled to match. They are beautifully formed, very cupped and double, with a neat interior arrangement of petals and a strong fragrance that mixes Bourbon and China characteristics. The flower color is soft pink with a bluish tone (the same lavender pink so characteristic of 'Old Blush' and its progeny), and the foliage is a handsomely contrasting bluish-green.

This rose is tailor-made for container gardening. It flushes with bloom at regular intervals throughout the growing season and adapts well to most conditions. Friends of ours on the West Coast and the Gulf Coast have complained of blackspot problems (neither party ever sprays with chemicals), but they continue to grow the rose because they like it so much. We believe that high humidity is the culprit here rather than lack of light (due to fog), because 'Hermosa' usually does fine for us in as little as five hours of sun.

Another friend of ours gave 'Hermosa' to his mother-in-law as a present, and she has grown the rose for four years on a shady porch in the original small container, praising it highly for its good behavior and constant, fragrant bloom. Our own plants are grown in 12 to 16 hours of direct sun and stay completely healthy, though they tend to defoliate out of self-defense in the hottest part of summer. But

they keep blooming and grow back plenty of blue-green leaves after a few weeks' rest.

The Bourbon in 'Hermosa's' breeding has given it extra cold hardiness beyond any of the China roses except 'Old Blush'. It can be planted in the ground as a bedding rose or as the central focus of a small herb garden well into Zone 6 and needs only normal winter protection. It can be grown as a potted rose in any Zone, of course, and is a good choice for anyone just getting started with gardening. 'Hermosa' is one of those tough and rewarding plants that can quickly lead to old rose addiction.

Zone 6 / 2 ft. to 4 ft. high / 2 ft. to 3 ft. wide / very fragrant / light pink / reliable repeat

'Green Rose'
before 1845

Easy to grow, hardy for a China, always in bloom, never a victim of any disease and unfortunately quite, quite green, this rose has a long history of inspiring distress as well as admiration. "Rosa Monstrosa" is one early name for it, and even the garden writers who like it tend to damn it with faint praise.

"A natural curiosity" is Robert Nelson's description of the 'Green Rose' in an article from the *American Cotton Planter* in 1855. He goes on to say that the flower is merely a tuft of green leaves or a double calyx, but he is kind enough to add that "it does, however, bloom in this way from early spring until Christmas, and is almost indispensable for bouquets." Why does this remind us of being set up for a blind date with someone who has an awfully nice personality?

The 'Green Rose' is not offensive in the garden, especially since it is hard to see. It grows as a typical twiggy China with neat pointed leaves exactly the same color as the flowers. A little light clipping now and then will keep it shapely and full of new growth and blossoms, but it will manage fine if left alone, growing happily unkempt as if it truly believes that surface appearances don't matter.

It's not until you get close to this rose that you can begin to see its deeper possibilities. The tufted flowers (which really are composed of petals, leafy as they look) have an enthusiastic and jaunty appearance and a spicy scent of black pepper. In cool weather they turn bronze green, responding to the season as if they were modest poinsettias. These are the qualities that make flower arrangers treasure this fascinating rose, whereas flower growers see it as an "empty spot" in the border. The 'Green Rose' lasts very well in water and makes a good accent for other flowers, especially yellow flowers of any sort. It has even been known to win awards at rose shows, though usually only from judges with an educated eye. To quote Kermit the Frog: "It isn't easy being green."

In the garden, the 'Green Rose' grows much like a smaller version of the 'Cramoisi Supérieur' pictured on p. 146. If you don't feel like sacrificing a spot in the garden to this interesting but somewhat invisible variety, it can easily be grown in a container (see the photo on p. 51) and displayed to unsettle any friends who think they know all about roses. And the 'Green Rose' is no trouble to start from cuttings, so you can share it with anyone who might appreciate such a changeling.

Zone 7 / 3 ft. to 4 ft. high / 2 ft. to 3 ft. wide / slightly fragrant / green / reliable repeat

'Ducher'
1869

The fact that French nurseryman Joseph Ducher chose to name this rose for himself leads us to believe that he must have been a practical man rather than a great romantic. 'Ducher' has a clean, handsome appearance and a thrifty habit of growth. It makes a good impression rather than an overwhelming one, and it is only after growing it in your own garden that its sterling reliability can be appreciated.

As far as we know, 'Ducher' is the only white China rose left in commerce. Its landscape form is much like that of 'Cramoisi Supérieur' (see p. 146), but its flowers are very double, like those of 'Archduke Charles', and they open from shapely buds to a loosely cupped form that holds a full measure of the sharp, fruity China scent. The color of the petals is that of raw cream, a rich yellowish-white that shows up very well against thick, dark-green foliage. 'Ducher' doesn't seem to have the most irritating habit that might be expected of a white rose — it doesn't cling to its faded petals but lets them drop fairly cleanly when the flowers are past their peak. (There's nothing worse in the garden than a white rose with browning petals hanging on the branches like soiled and sodden tissue.)

We have noticed that people pass over white roses and white flowers in general when they are planning their gardens, insisting that they want lots of color. This is a great mistake and seriously limits the potential enjoyment to be had from a flower bed. In full sunlight, white roses do tend to look like overexposed spots in a garden picture, but most of us are not out in our gardens when the sun is at its peak. The time to enjoy a southern garden is in the morning, when white roses sparkle with a sharp clarity that accents all the other colors and makes them seem brighter, or in the cool of the evening. There's nothing quite like sitting out on the porch when the faint evening breeze has started up, watching all the red roses fade into the dusk while the white ones begin to glow with reflected light. Street lights, house lights or moonlight will all suffice to bring out the ghostly beauty of white roses.

With its compact shape and constant bloom, 'Ducher' is one of the most useful white roses for the landscape. It can be massed as a bedding plant to fill in an area such as the center of a curved driveway. It makes an excellent low hedge, tidy and full of scented flowers, to line a pathway or hide a foundation. 'Ducher' mixes well with most other roses in a border, especially the bright crimson globes of 'Cramoisi Supérieur'. It even does well as a container plant, especially with a strongly contrasting background. A tub on each side of the door of a red-brick house would be strikingly handsome.

**Zone 7 / 2 ft. to 4 ft. high /
2 ft. to 3 ft. wide / fragrant / white /
reliable repeat**

'Jean Bach Sisley'
1889

We were very pleased that *Modern Roses 9* moved this rose out of the Bourbon class, where it doesn't belong, but we were surprised to see that it is now classified as a China, since from the form and habit we had always thought of it as a Tea. In fact, there is still some controversy about whether the plant now in commerce is actually the China rose 'Jean Bach Sisley', because it is very similar to an old Tea called 'Rhodalogue Jules Gravereaux' that has been acquired by one of our expert rosarian friends. Whether these two varieties are one and the same and which name is correct are not questions that affect the performance of this rose in the garden. Fortunately, the nurseries of which we're aware all carry the same plant as 'Jean Bach Sisley', so whatever it really is, we can all enjoy it by that name — and as a China, until it gets changed again.

Jean Sisley was an eminent French rosarian, responsible, among other things, for introducing the Multiflora rose into Europe. His namesake rose was introduced by the French nurseryman Dubreuil, and the plant that we grow matches fairly well most of the descriptions we've seen. It is outstandingly handsome, with a sturdy, spreading bush that grows as wide as it is tall.

The lightly Tea-scented flowers are long-budded, double but not full, so the bicolored petals are well displayed when they open. The outer color is salmon rose, veined with carmine, whereas the inside color is a pale silvery rose. This elegant arrangement is enhanced by a setting of dark-green foliage with occasional spurts of the wine-purple new growth typical of Teas. The whole effect is both striking and sophisticated.

'Jean Bach Sisley' will certainly blend well in a bed with other roses, but it makes a wonderful specimen plant out on its own. We picture it in a small bed with silver-foliaged lamb's-ears (*Stachys byzantina*) and dusty-blue mealy sage (*Salvia farinacea*), hiding an air-conditioning unit from view or improving a dull corner of the house. The only drawback is that the flowers are not at their best for us during the heat of summer — not an unusual characteristic, but an irritant on a rose that looks so good when it's in top form. We've never experienced any disease problems with 'Jean Bach Sisley', and it has withstood sudden freezes without any damage, so we grow it and use it with great pleasure and will continue to do so no matter how the experts arrange its past.

One caution: Prune this rose like a Tea, that is, as little as possible. Removal of dead twigs and a minimal amount of shaping are all that's necessary. The rose will resent it if you prune away more than a third of the bush.

Zone 6 / 4 ft. to 6 ft. high / 3 ft. to 4 ft. wide / fragrant / pink blend / reliable repeat

'Mutabilis'
before 1894

One of the nice things about this rose is that it is so distinctive that its identity is (currently) unquestioned. It was even thought to be a species rose for a long time, so it can be found in most old rose books as *Rosa chinensis mutabilis.* Peter Beales suggests in *Classic Roses,* and we agree, that it is more likely a garden hybrid from China and is much older than the date given. Other names for this rose are 'Tipo Ideale' and the 'Butterfly Rose', and all three names fit quite well.

'Mutabilis' is the "ideal type" of China rose, twiggy and vigorous with healthy, neatly shaped leaves of dark bronzy green. It can grow quite large if left alone, more than 6 ft. in every direction, but it has little understanding of dormancy and occasionally gets cut back in full bloom by a hard freeze. (This may be just as well. Ethelyn Keays reports in her book *Old Roses* that a plant growing in a sheltered spot made it as high as a second-story window.) We have never lost this

rose, or any other China, to cold. If they are damaged, China roses almost always grow back quickly from the root.

In areas where the seasons are more defined, 'Mutabilis' seems to be a little better prepared for the freezes than here in Texas. We've seen a handsome old specimen growing in a garden on top of one of Virginia's Blue Ridge Mountains, at the farthest limit of Zone 7.

The 'Butterfly Rose' appellation has to do with the flowers, which have only five petals and look as if they have been clipped out of raw silk. Bright orange buds open sulfur yellow then darken as they "fade" in a color show that is excessive even for a China, moving through apricot to a rich pink and finally to crimson. The bush in full bloom looks as if a cloud of multicolored butterflies had settled on it. The flowers have no perfume, but butterflies don't need it. The changeable color explains the definitive name of 'Mutabilis'.

We grow this rose as part of an informal mixed border in a cottage-style garden. It is planted by a weathered picket fence so that it can poke its flowers through on either side, and it is surrounded by other roses and old-fashioned perennials in a haphazard fashion. In spite of its odd combination of colors, or perhaps because of it, 'Mutabilis' seems to blend well with all of its companion plants. It is a natural choice for a specimen plant, especially in an area where there is room for it to grow. 'Mutabilis' seems to have no disease problems. Its minimal faults are those of the other China roses — shedding part of its foliage at the height of the summer to protect itself from the heat and producing less colorful flowers at that time because the sun darkens them too quickly. Also, the foliage can take on a yellowish tint in our alkaline ground, and though that doesn't affect the flowers, it is worth spending time to prepare the soil well so this outstanding rose will be at its best.

Zone 7 / 4 ft. to 7 ft. high / 3 ft. to 5 ft. wide / slightly fragrant / yellow blend / reliable repeat

'Comtesse du Cayla'
1902

The charming woman for whom this rose was named was mistress to Louis XVIII — a challenging position when you consider that her King was the first to be placed back on the throne after the French Revolution, only to lose it again temporarily when Napoleon returned from the island of Elba. None of this uncertainty shows up in her rose, however, unless it is in the fact that 'Comtesse du Cayla' grows a little slowly until it is properly established.

The flowers of 'Comtesse du Cayla' are semidouble or near single, averaging about ten petals each. The burnt-orange buds are particularly lovely in form as they unfold into barely cupped roses of coppery pink. The shades of color are most vivid in spring and fall, when the flowers have the bright but subtle glow of watered silk. Their fragrance is very strong, especially in the early morning of a warm day, and the charm of this rose is enhanced by its having almost no prickles to defend itself. (Very few so-called "thornless" roses are entirely without prickles, but it is always pleasant when the danger of a scratch is at least reduced.) 'Comtesse du Cayla' bears no prickles on the new growth (perfect for cut flowers) and relatively few on older canes.

The foliage of this rose is dark and coppery, and the branches naturally have an open, airy pattern. If 'Comtesse du Cayla' is pruned regularly (about one-third to one-quarter of the bush sheared back twice a year) it will grow as thick and bushy as required. The form and color of the flowers are so delicate, however, that the plant also looks very artistic and oriental if allowed to follow its natural habit of growth. Sheared back and made more bushy, it makes an excellent container rose or bedding plant, blending with pinks, blues, yellows and creams or even softening the intense orange of modern Hybrid Tea roses like 'Tropicana'. Left unpruned, it will resemble in form the 'Mutabilis' shown in the photo at left on the facing page.

If allowed to grow large and airy as a specimen plant, the fragrant 'Comtesse du Cayla' will look best in a highly groomed site with a dark background of shrubbery, fencing or a house wall. This way the eye will be led to follow the artistic lines of the rose without being distracted by weedy grass or visual clutter.

Zone 7 / 3 ft. to 5 ft. high / 2 ft. to 3 ft. wide / very fragrant / orange blend / reliable repeat

"Pam's Pink"

Not every old rose that gets collected can be identified, but we have always felt it unfair to keep a good rose out of the garden because it lacks a recognized name. We have taken the step, with the advice of the Heritage Rose Foundation, of re-registering, under their study names, certain particularly useful old roses that we have been growing for a number of years and would like to see back in commerce. This way they can be propagated and sold by nurseries and shown in American Rose Society shows without confusion, and, most important, they can be saved from extinction by being brought back into garden use.

"Pam's Pink" is one of these excellent roses. It is named for rosarian and historian Miss Pamela Ashworth Puryear, who found it in two locations in Texas about ten years ago. One plant, from which our cuttings were taken, was in the garden of an old house in Navasota. The house has since been torn down and replaced by a trailer park, and the garden area was bulldozed to level it. That plant no longer exists.

The other plant was spotted by Pam in North Zulch, also at an old house. The neighbors told her that the owners of the house, then in their nineties, had moved to a rest home, but they remembered having been told that the rose was planted when the couple first set up house.

"Pam's Pink" has large, lightly scented blooms that are similar in shape to those of 'Archduke Charles' except that the petals reflex as the flower opens, forming an inside-out globe. The inner petals are dark pink, the outer petals a lighter pink with dark veining (like 'Old Blush'). It is a sturdy bush that grows easily with no special requirements except light pruning now and then to keep it tidy.

The broad leaves and reflexed petals suggest that "Pam's Pink" is a China/Bourbon cross, so it may be susceptible to some blackspot or fungus in humid coastal conditions. For us, it sheds a layer of leaves in midsummer but shows no signs of decline and grows the leaves back quickly. Extra water during summer can prevent this common rose behavior, but a certain amount of dormancy is natural during temperatures that stay above 90°F. It doesn't hurt the plant and it does save water to let some shedding occur and just keep on with a regular watering schedule.

"Pam's Pink" closely resembles 'Hermosa' in form (see p. 148), though it is somewhat larger. "Pam's Pink" is a wonderful container rose, producing its fat pink flowers throughout the growing season. It also performs dependably in a mixed border and can be shaped into an everblooming hedge to soften the line of a porch or house foundation.

Zone 7 / 3 ft. to 5 ft. high / 3 ft. to 4 ft. wide / fragrant / pink blend / reliable repeat

"Martha Gonzales"

Like "Pam's Pink", our vivid "Martha Gonzales" is another unidentified product of rose-rustling activities on the part of Pam Puryear. She insists, however, that the credit for collecting this rose belongs to Dallas rosarian Joe Woodard. The two of them were visiting the yard of Martha Gonzales in Navasota, Texas, to enjoy that lady's display of large bushes of 'Old Blush' and 'Mrs. Dudley Cross', when they spotted this little rose in the same garden. Pam was, she says, trying to ignore anything that looked like yet another red China seedling, but Joe

went into "his golden retriever pose" and rescued a valuable rose from potential oblivion. Sra. Gonzales has since passed away, and the only other known specimens of this variety were in the few gardens tended by Spanish-speaking ladies in Navasota with whom she had shared her plants.

"Martha Gonzales" is a small rose with a flair for color. The bright scarlet, nearly single flowers open flat, like wild roses, to display their stamens and an occasional white streak in the petals. The bush is low-growing, rarely exceeding 3 ft.

in height in our garden, and the foliage is scaled down to match. The leaflets are neatly pointed and dark green in color with a dark-red tinge to the new growth that contrasts attractively with the scarlet flowers.

We grow "Martha Gonzales" both as a container specimen and as a particularly handsome low hedge on one side of a gravel path. When it has been lightly sheared and the new growth is sprouting over the whole surface of each plant, the hedge is lost in a beautiful haze of dark red—not unlike crimson barberry.

"Martha Gonzales" is becoming a favorite with local landscape contractors because it is so compact, vivid and easy to care for. We have never seen it display any signs of disease. There is virtually no fragrance, but the scarlet flowers are produced on a regular cycle throughout the growing season, and the profusion makes up for the lack of perfume.

"Martha Gonzales" is a good rose for adding color to small gardens and a great rose for massing in showy beds — around a sundial or birdbath, or perhaps in the center of a circular driveway.

Zone 7 / 1 ft. to 3 ft. high / 1 ft. to 3 ft. wide / slightly fragrant / medium red / reliable repeat

Noisette Roses

How do I love thy Rose fit emblem rare
Of all that's modest, smiling, soft and fair!
Such charms more please me than those brilliant dyes
Her flaunting sisters spread for vulgar eyes.

The verse above is from "Epistle to Mr. Noisette" translated from the French in 1834 by an anonymous friend of the breeder of Noisette roses. The florid praise goes on for several pages, reflecting the many achievements of this "Agriculturist and Botanist."

The history of the Noisette roses reads like the plot for a southern novel, something along the lines of *Gone With the Wind*. In 1793 or 1794 Philippe Noisette left Haiti in a hurry to avoid a slave rebellion and moved to Charleston, South Carolina, with his Haitian wife, Celestine. The move didn't do *her* status much good: Since the laws of that state prohibited interracial marriage, she became legally a slave. But Noisette was able to find himself a prestigious position as Superintendent of the South Carolina Medical Society Botanical Gardens, no doubt aided by the fact that his father and his brother were well-known horticulturists back in France.

Among Philippe Noisette's Charleston acquaintances was wealthy rice planter John Champneys, who had a taste for gardening and the wherewithal to indulge it. About 1802, through Philippe and his brother Louis in Paris, Champneys acquired a specimen of the new exotic rose 'Parsons' Pink China' ('Old Blush'). He somehow crossed this rose with the 'Musk Rose' (*Rosa moschata*) and apparently gave some of the resultant plants (or their seeds) to Noisette out of friendship. In 1811 Champneys sent a barrel of cuttings to another horticulturist friend, William Prince, so that Prince's New York nursery could handle the commercial introduction. With the creation of this one rose—the first American hybrid ever recorded—Champneys faded quietly out of the picture and left the future to the professionals.

Philippe Noisette has been accused of stealing the glory that properly belonged to John Champneys by giving the Noisette name to a class of roses that sprang from 'Champneys' Pink Cluster'. This is unfair, however, because Champneys' rose has always retained his name, while the Noisette rose lineage was probably most strongly influenced by a seedling, a visibly different plant, that Philippe Noisette grew from a 'Champneys' Pink Cluster' hip. In 1817 Philippe sent seeds and a seedling of his rose, 'Blush Noisette', to his brother Louis, who introduced it to French nurserymen. It is this rose, painted in 1821 by the artist Redouté as *R. noisettiana*, that was crossed with 'Parks' Yellow Tea-Scented China' in 1830 to begin the long line of yellow-tinted climbing "Tea-Noisettes" that are so important to the class.

Philippe Noisette died in 1835, not long after petitioning the state of South Carolina for the freedom of Celestine and their seven children. His property, a large tract that is now contained within the city of Charleston, is still known as The Rose Garden. It is now a residential district, but, as one local newspaper account recalls, "within the memory of living Charlestonians his descendants sold roses from the gardens started by him." Many of those descendants still live in Charleston, among them his great-granddaughter, Louise Noisette Merrell, who shared with us from her personal files the "Epistle" quoted on the previous page. In 1976 the Noisette Rose Garden, designed to feature Noisettes, Chinas and Teas, was planted in the city in the rose breeder's honor. The right of John Champneys to some of this recognition has not been overlooked, however. Of all the Noisette varieties, it was 'Champneys' Pink Cluster' that received, in 1986, designation as "The Charleston Rose."

Plant Characteristics

Noisette roses are still commonly found throughout the South, where they comprise some of the most rewarding landscape varieties available. There are two basic types: the mounding, loosely formed, cluster-flowered bushes and the larger-flowered, enthusiastic climbers—all in pastel shades of yellow, pink and cream. There are variations, of course, and plenty of unknown foundling varieties that may be seedlings or sports of the recognized types.

One writer of the last century made a point of recommending to southern gardeners that they all grow seedlings of 'Champneys' Pink Cluster' since it did so very well in warm gardens, and there is no way to know how many enthusiasts took him up on the suggestion. The Palmetto Garden Club of Columbia, South Carolina, which has the longest tradition of Old Garden Rose shows in the United States (dating back to the 1950s), has a special division just for "early Noisettes." These are varieties of the cluster-flowered type, mostly unidentified, which look a lot like Champneys' original *R. moschata*/'Old Blush' cross. Whether they've lost their names or are seedlings that never had names, they represent a very good and useful type of rose, and it is nice to know that one group of gardeners thoroughly appreciates them.

We have not yet encountered an unscented Noisette variety, and their perfume is especially fine. The cluster-flowered types tend to mix the earthy Musk scent with the sweet, astringent fruitiness of Chinas. The larger-flowered varieties show their Tea blood to differing extents in their fragrance as well as in their form. Each variety is slightly different, but all of them are delicious, and it would be a terrible waste to walk past a Noisette of any kind without stopping to smell it.

Culture

Cultural requirements for the class as a whole are not very demanding. Good soil, good sun and good drainage are beneficial, but the Noisettes will do well even in less than ideal conditions. A little shade during the worst of the afternoon sun will help preserve the delicate colors of the flowers. Pruning is necessary mainly to remove dead wood—otherwise, it is up to the individual taste of the gardener. We don't feel that Noisettes need to be sprayed, unless you want them to have perfect foliage for show purposes. Proper watering and fertilizing go a long way toward correcting their occasional tendency to blackspot, and if they should lose some foliage, they generally grow it back without any loss of vitality or bloom.

Landscape Uses

Noisette roses fill many niches in the garden. Unlike the "brilliant dyes" mentioned in the panegyric to Noisette, their soft colors blend well with almost any other plant, and they have the advantage of being able to do so from every height that a rose can reach. Since some of the finest climbers in the rose world are members of this class, we find that you can put a Noisette virtually anywhere you want a rose, from down in a container to up past the second-story window. Noisettes are, in fact, generally so well foliaged and so free with their scented flowers that they epitomize the lush and generous character of the South. If a rose is needed to encrust a pillar with bloom or to sway tantalizingly down from an arbor, a Noisette can be found to handle the job.

Selected Noisette Varieties

'Champneys' Pink Cluster'
circa 1811

'Champneys' Pink Cluster' is not a rose to provoke "oohs" and "aahs," but its creation was and is a very good idea. John Champneys should get a lot of credit for the idea since he was responsible for crossing one of the oldest known remontant roses, *Rosa moschata*, with the most newly discovered (in his day) remontant rose 'Old Blush' (which he acquired as 'Parsons' Pink China', according to various sources). Whether or not he had a hand in the actual cross, only he and nature know for sure, but as an educated and enthusiastic amateur horticulturist, Champneys was able to nurture it along and recognize the value of the result.

His 'Pink Cluster' retained the repeat-blooming habits of both parents, flowering through the

spring on its China blood and into the fall and winter like a 'Musk Rose'. He himself called the plant *R. moschata hybrida*, very clear and pragmatic, but William Prince had the courtesy to introduce it from his New York nursery with the author's byline attached to the more marketable name of 'Pink Cluster'.

The rose that we grow as 'Champneys' Pink Cluster' is the subject of an exciting rediscovery story. It was as lost to commerce as its parent, the 'Musk Rose', and was not recovered until the 1970s. At that time, a rose growing in the Virginia garden of Jack Tatum was sent to the Huntington Botanical Gardens for study and was identified by several experts as the real thing. This plant has the narrow, graceful leaves and delicately formed clusters of small, pale pink flowers that are described in rose literature as typical of the first member of the Noisette class, and it blooms on schedule. It grows thickly to a height of about 4 ft. if pruned as a bush, or 7 ft. to 10 ft. if allowed to increase slowly over time.

We find that 'Champneys' Pink Cluster' makes a fine pillar rose when allowed to grow tall enough to submerge a post in its canes and foliage. The flowers range up and down the post in staggered clusters, so their sweet scent is almost always at the right level to be inhaled and admired.

Unless it is used as a pillar, 'Champney's Pink Cluster' is more a working rose than a show rose. It fills in middle or back areas of the flower border very well and, especially if lightly pruned now and then, is rarely without at least one pale pink flower cluster in the process of unfolding bud by bud.

The scent moves fairly freely in the open air in the morning or evening of a warm day, so even at some distance the pleasure of the fragrance will not be lost.

The only real drawback we've noticed is that 'Champneys' Pink Cluster' has a tendency to acquire fungal diseases in conditions of low light and poor air circulation. As long as the plant gets plenty of sun and space, fungal diseases should not be a problem.

This first American rose, created upon the sound principle that more of a good thing (i.e., remontancy) is better, was officially proclaimed "The Charleston Rose" in 1986, an honor both for the rose and for the memory of John Champneys, who made that "better rose" a reality.

Zone 7 / 6 ft. to 8 ft. high / 3 ft. to 5 ft. wide / very fragrant / light pink / reliable repeat

'Blush Noisette'
1817

'Blush Noisette', a seedling of 'Champneys' Pink Cluster', is a fine example of how unpredictable rose genetics can be. Instead of being identical in form and flower to its parent, 'Blush Noisette' is more compact in size, has more petals in its small cupped blossoms and has an even more intense fragrance. Also, the flowers are less susceptible to fungal diseases, and the plant is a little more cold hardy than is 'Champneys' Pink Cluster'. It may do well into Zone 6 if planted out of the north wind.

Rose botanist Dr. C.C. Hurst speculates in Graham Stuart Thomas's *The Old Shrub Roses* (1979) that 'Blush Noisette' is the product of Mendelian segregation, having inherited the alternate characteristics of some of the many pairs of genes it shares with Champneys' rose. This theory is hotly disputed by at least one

rosarian who believes that the changes come from the introduction of another rose parent, possibly 'Hume's Blush Tea-Scented China', into the family. As we are gardeners and not scientists, we are quite willing to agree that many things are possible and concentrate on the way the plant behaves in the garden.

John Champneys gets full credit for having the first of the class, but the Noisette brothers got the better rose from its seeds. 'Blush Noisette' is a classic. It produces clusters of dark pink buds mixed with barely pink cupped blossoms attractively displayed against rich green foliage. The flexible, slender canes (in the 4-ft. to 6-ft. range, for us) make it very tempting to add this rose to the historic and fragrant collection in our herb garden by espaliering it along the low grey stone wall. Since we have already pruned the specimen growing in a half barrel into the short, thick, heavily blooming bush shown in the photo above right, this gives us an excuse to plant another and train it up

from scratch. The main difficulty with 'Blush Noisette' is to remember not to plant too many bushes of it when there are so many other varieties that also need garden space.

It's not hard to think of ways to include 'Blush Noisette' in the landscape. Leafy, compact and frequently in bloom, this rose would make an attractive hedge, or you might consider planting a single bush by the kitchen door, where the fragrance could drift in through the screen on warm days. For those who like to get the most from their roses, the buds of 'Blush Noisette' are a perfect size and warm pink color to dry for adding to potpourri, and the thin, well-scented, cream-colored petals are good for making into rose beads or sprinkling onto a salad.

**Zone 7 / 4 ft. to 6 ft. high /
3 ft. to 4 ft. wide / very fragrant /
white / reliable repeat**

'Lamarque'
1830

There was a change in the Noisette class in the 1830s. Until that time, Noisette varieties had been recognized as much for their large clusters of small, fragrant flowers as for their extended season of bloom, but the introduction of 'Parks' Yellow Tea-Scented China' in 1824 and its subsequent use in breeding brought about a new line of "Tea-Noisettes." 'Lamarque' and its seed-sister 'Jaune Desprez' are the direct result of a cross between 'Blush Noisette' and the new yellow remontant rose. These two varieties don't look particularly alike, but they do have traits in common that none of the other Noisettes of the time shared. They both have larger flowers, up to about 3 in. across, that are carried in clusters of no more than three — often simply with one rose per stem. They also both display the color yellow, which was extremely rare in roses at that time.

'Lamarque' was bred in France and named for a French general of some distinction, but there is something of southern feminine purity — a fresh crinoline petticoat — about it. The flowers open from yellow buds to fully double blossoms of clean white with a hint of lemon in their hearts, and they smell delicious.

This rose is very free-blooming and keeps on going long after other roses have slipped into winter dormancy. It's a rare year that doesn't see an arrangement on the Christmas table of red-berried yaupon holly and scented white 'Lamarque' roses. Though 'Lamarque' is historically tender to the cold, it has shown no weakness for us (in Zone 8), except one year when an unusually hard and early

freeze caught it in full bloom. Even then it didn't die but came back vigorously from the root.

Vigor is something that 'Lamarque' has in abundance, along with the ability to survive hot summers and, in our experience, human error. We first planted it on a willow arch over the gateway shown in the photo at right. In two years' time it had flung itself gracefully over the top of the arch. Unfortunately, two years' time was enough for the flimsy arch to disintegrate, and it came down in a storm. A new arch was built of long-lasting (we thought) 2x2 cedar, and it lasted one year more. We stayed with 2x2 material, but now it is wrought iron.

'Lamarque' is easy to grow, easy to train and easy to like. It is a good climber for a beginner to choose because it grows rewardingly fast and creates a really satisfying effect on any wall, trellis, fence or arbor. Even if it is planted in an area where freeze damage occasionally cuts it down, the canes grow long enough in a season for 'Lamarque' to be used as a pillar rose. At its best, 'Lamarque' will change a mundane garden into a place of special magic where you can lift your eyes and restore them on the

profusion of scented white roses in the leafy green. For us in the warm Zones, it is all a climbing rose should be. In the words of Ethelyn Keays (*Old Roses*): "The southern moon sheds a lovely light over 'Lamarque'."

Zone 7 / 15 ft. or more / very fragrant / white / reliable repeat

'Jaune Desprez' is not in bloom quite as often as its sister, but the spring and autumn flushes are fairly heavy, and there is almost always at least one rose to be seen on any well-established plant. The foliage seems to stay on well all summer and to resist common diseases with no trouble. We have never seen any frost damage on our specimen or heard about any where temperatures remained above 10°F—typical Zone 7 weather. ('Lamarque' is more tender. The sturdy blood of *Rosa moschata*, hardy to Zone 6, seems to bless members of this class somewhat irregularly.)

There is almost no pastel color that will not blend well with the soft pink and yellow of 'Jaune Desprez', so it makes a fine backdrop for bushes of everblooming Teas and Chinas mixed with various perennial flowers (blue salvias, pale petunias, garden pinks and bearded iris). 'Jaune Desprez' will spill along a white picket fence to great effect, and it is equally happy, according to one correspondent, growing up into trees to the height of second-story windows, though the blooms, she says, "have greater appeal when you can look right into them and put your nose in them." We heartily agree.

Zone 7 / 12 ft. or more / very fragrant / yellow blend / reliable repeat

'Jaune Desprez'
1830

When siblings look remarkably unalike, the "milkman" often jokingly gets the blame. 'Jaune Desprez' seems to be a product of that same genetic milkman factor, being as warm a rose as its sister 'Lamarque' is pale and cool. *Jaune* is, of course, French for yellow (Desprez was the breeder's name), and the blossoms are yellow as peaches, flushed on the outer petals with a sun-warmed pink. Even the scent seems fruitier, with less of a citrus tang than the fragrance of 'Lamarque', but that may simply be an odor illusion influenced by the color.

When we first planted 'Jaune Desprez', it was very small, nearly hidden in a bed of 12 in. tall bouncing bet (*Saponaria officinalis*). It seemed at least a year before the little rose fought free of the shade and crowding and began to head up the trellis, but since that slow beginning, there has been no end to its vigor. It grows so thickly on the freestanding trellis that after four years of weaving the canes back and forth, the structure has begun to look like a wall of roses dividing two areas of garden.

'Jeanne d'Arc'
1848

Saint and soldier, Joan of Arc has always had a firm hold upon the imagination of her chosen people, the French. Her living character may have been complex, but her legend remains pure. Of the three roses introduced in her name over the span of nearly a century, all three came from French breeders and all three had flowers of spotless white. Our 'Jeanne d'Arc', a Noisette, was the second of these introductions, brought out by Victor Verdier's nursery in 1848. (The other two were an Alba from Vibert in 1818 and a Polyantha from Levavasseur in 1909.)

'Jeanne d'Arc' is the 'Musk Rose' all over again, but with slightly larger flowers on a smaller plant. The individual blossoms are double but rather primitive in appearance with loose, tousled petals. They make a much greater visual impression in their snowy clusters than they do individually, but their musky scent is noticeable whether you sniff one flower or a group of them. The foliage is dark green and heavy, making a handsome backdrop for the clean white flowers. Like the class prototype, 'Champneys' Pink Cluster', 'Jeanne d'Arc' will sometimes shed a few of its leaves when attacked by blackspot or mildew unless it gets plenty of fresh air and sun, but the leaves are quickly replaced even on a plant that never gets sprayed.

We have grown this rose as a 6-ft. tall pillar with great success, though there is one drawback to training it in this form. The clustered flower stems, when their bloom is past, tend to protrude and interrupt the

grace of line that a pillar rose should have. It is difficult to resist pruning off the spent stems, but they must be left alone if you want the hips. 'Jeanne d'Arc' has the nice habit of producing small, bright red hips that decorate the plant at the same time as the flowers, and both displays continue well into late fall or early winter. These dainty, open clusters of fruit can do double duty, for they are also attractive and long-lasting in cut-flower arrangements.

The problem of form vanishes if 'Jeanne d'Arc' is allowed to grow as a bush. It needs no training to form a mound 4 ft. to 5 ft. tall and nearly as wide, making a handsome accent in the middle or back of a mixed bed of roses and perennials. Our favorite way to see it grown is by a garden pond. There it becomes one of the most attractive of roses, especially when the moon accents the white clusters to match the dapples of light on the water.

Zone 7 / 6 ft. to 8 ft. high / 3 ft. to 5 ft. wide / fragrant / white / reliable repeat

'Maréchal Niel'
1864

'Maréchal Niel' is consistently the most requested rose at our nursery, particularly by the elderly. One charming lady came in to say she had prayed we would have a 'Maréchal Niel' for her, for she had grown up with that rose, was now 87 years old and hoped to see and smell it again. Unfortunately, we had to disappoint her (and many others), because this rose is very difficult for us to grow from cuttings. They take root but fail to thrive, and we have not been able to determine why. Yet we know 'Maréchal Niel' will grow here, for we've seen many thriving established plants—not only in our neighborhood but throughout the South.

Once well established, 'Maréchal Niel' seems healthy and vigorous, but it may always have been difficult to get this plant to grow. The introducer of this rose is reported to have asked customers buying one plant to take several, in order to cover expected losses. 'Maréchal Niel' is also sensitive to cold weather. Indeed, this may be the most tender of the Noisettes, and we recommend it only for Zone 8 or warmer. The flowers' color and form were so desirable at the time of introduction, however, that 'Maréchal Niel' became one of the darlings of Victorian gardeners, who grew it under glass in England and introduced it to India, where it still thrives.

Said to be a seedling of 'Chromatella' (which grows well for us and is a very good substitute for its offspring), 'Maréchal Niel' was introduced by the French nurseryman Pradel in 1864. Rather

incongruously, it bears the name of Napoleon III's Secretary of War. Apparently, Monsieur Niel saw and admired the rose before it was named. Pradel offered to name it for Niel's wife, only to discover that the Secretary was a confirmed bachelor as well as a fine judge of roses.

'Maréchal Niel's' Tea-rose-like flowers are borne in great profusion on rather weak stems, giving them a charming nodding appearance. The flowers have been described as having a "soft yellowness" or resembling "summer butter." This is an extremely fragrant rose, and the smell alone may be why it is so well remembered from childhood and so often requested. The scent is that of Tea roses, but many people can smell raspberries in the blossoms as well. The plant blooms heavily in spring and fall as well as sporadically in between. The foliage is a light, very distinctive yellowy-green.

In the garden, 'Maréchal Niel' will perform much like 'Lamarque' (see the bottom photo on p. 161). It is a large climber and needs room to travel. We have seen it in California gardens growing up and over arbors to well over 25 ft. In our own garden, we find that a height of 15 ft. is a reasonable expectation for a mature plant. It is the perfect companion for lemon-white 'Lamarque' on a garden arch, but a fair amount of training has to be done to get two such large roses to fit gracefully without overwhelming a small structure. The important thing is to get 'Maréchal Niel' well up into the air, so that the big golden goblets of its flowers can hang down and spill their scent on admiring passers-by.

Zone 8 / 15 ft. or more / very fragrant / medium yellow / remontant

'Rêve d'Or'
1869

Introduced by the famous Ducher nursery in 1869, 'Rêve d'Or' is a rose that deserves a feature spot in the garden. The French name translates as "dream of gold," but "dream of butterscotch" might be more accurate to describe its tawny petals. The flowers are large and well formed, with deceptive buds that look as if they contain an amazing number of petals but then open into handsome, barely double blossoms that allow the central stamens to show through.

As with most roses in our miserably hot climate, 'Rêve d'Or' is larger and fuller in the cool fall weather than at any other time. Roses do change their appearance somewhat from spring through summer and into fall. They can also fluctuate in color, size and number of petals with the effects of local climate and soil. This changing display adds interest to the garden and confusion to the aficionados trying to identify the roses. This sort of confusion has lead some writers to label 'Rêve d'Or' a climbing sport of 'Safrano', the Tea rose. The flowers are a close color match and do sometimes look fairly similar, but 'Rêve d'Or' is almost always larger and has more petals—besides, its "green parts" are different than those of the more pure Tea variety.

We have trained 'Rêve d'Or' on the stone wall of a kitchen that was built in about 1870. The flowers are only one shade lighter than the stone, and the rose looks as if it's been there forever, trailing over the kitchen door so that you can look up onto the blossoms as you enter. This kind of adaptive grace makes 'Rêve d'Or' and the other Noisettes perfect complements for old southern houses. Since this rose will climb effortlessly to 15 ft. or 20 ft. and is not very thorny, it is an easy rose to work with in many other garden niches as well. Grey makes an excellent background color for the flowers, so a weathered fence or garden shed would be an ideal support.

The only complaint we have heard about this rose is that it blooms too infrequently until well established, a process that takes about three years. For this "dream of gold," we think it's worth the wait.

Zone 7 / 15 ft. or more / very fragrant / medium yellow / remontant

'Madame Alfred Carrière'
1879

Alfred Carrière was an eminent 19th-century scientist whose principal claim to fame among rosarians is that he recorded the appearance of the remontant white Moss rose that sported from the pink 'Autumn Damask'. It was in compliment to his achievements that this white Noisette rose was named for his wife. The breeder, Joseph Schwartz of Lyon, France, introduced 'Madame Alfred Carrière' in 1879, and the following year brought out a Tea rose, 'Madame Joseph Schwartz', that was very similar in the color and form of the flowers.

The parentage of 'Madame Alfred Carrière' is not known, but most rosarians accept that this rose shows traits that link it to the Bourbon and Tea classes almost more closely than to the Noisettes. We have wondered if 'Madame Joseph Schwartz' might not have been at Schwartz's nursery for some time (it was a sport of the 1857 Tea, 'Duchesse de Brabant') and might not have figured into the breeding of 'Madame Alfred Carrière'.

We have found that this rose tolerates a number of climatic conditions, surviving hot summers as easily as sudden freezes. Yet in spite of its cold-hardiness, it is one of the last to go dormant and pays tribute to its late-flowering *Rosa moschata* blood by giving us flowers in January, when almost nothing else is in bloom. In spite of its hardiness, however, we would suggest that it be planted where it can get at least six to eight hours of sun, since one of our specimens in a shady location was too often attacked by mildew and blackspot when others of the same variety were not.

The flowers of 'Madame Alfred Carrière' are cupped and quite double, moderately large (3 in. or 4 in. in diameter) and cream white in color with a warm blush of pink at their heart. They often show pale pink all over in cool autumn weather. Their fragrance is very sweet but intense, and more like the rosy scent of Bourbons than the musk scent of *R. moschata*, though there are hints of other influences as well.

Foliage is a little sparse on this rose, at least in our garden, but the smooth, stiff canes are not unattractive and have very few prickles. The stiff canes make 'Madame Alfred Carrière' easier to train flat in a fan shape on a wall or trellis than to weave back and forth laterally, but with patience and strong ties to secure unwilling branches almost any effect can be achieved with it. We have seen 'Madame Alfred Carrière' pruned back to 8 ft. and grown as a tall bush, but it does seem a shame to cut away half of the flowers to do this. With a growth potential of 15 ft. to 20 ft., this is a second-story rose par excellence, and the scent of the sweet flowers drifting on the breeze into an upstairs room will more than make up for the effort of the training.

Zone 6 / 15 ft. or more / very fragrant / white / remontant

'Nastarana'
1879

'Nastarana' is reported to have been around for many years before being introduced in the West, and its other name, 'Persian Musk Rose', certainly suggests a long and romantic history. Unfortunately, we will never know—its past is lost, and only the name remains.

'Nastarana' is probably an early hybrid of *Rosa moschata* and some form of *R. chinensis* (not necessarily 'Old Blush', but at the least a close relative). It was long classified as a Hybrid Musk, but rosarians recently realized that this classification was incorrect. The Hybrid Musk class (which doesn't merit the Old Garden Rose designation, having begun around the turn of the 20th century) consists mainly of roses bred from a cross between the Multifloras and the Noisettes. It is the Noisettes themselves that are actually direct crosses with *R. moschata*, so 'Nastarana' is now classified much more accurately as a Noisette. This is the sort of classification tangle that goes on all the time with old roses, much to our fascination.

'Nastarana' is a small bush for us, 3 ft. to 4 ft. in height and just the right size for a compact garden, an herb bed or a container near a favorite chair on the patio. It is not difficult to grow and blooms quite steadily with semidouble, flat, pure white flowers that open from clusters of pink buds. The fragrance is completely of musk, very earthy and intoxicating, highly suggestive of the gardens and covered markets of the Middle East. 'Nastarana' is well worth planting in a spot where it will be noticed often and its fragrance will not be wasted.

This is such a favorite rose that we don't mind cleaning it up now and then—it seems to get a lot of small dead twigs in it, though this habit doesn't interfere with growth or blooming. The leaves of 'Nastarana' are particularly attractive—narrow, pointed and a little exotic looking. They drop in the late fall in our gardens, since this rose is fairly cold hardy and actually has the sense to go dormant at a reasonable time of year instead of blooming through Christmas. Small, dark red hips add a piquancy to the naked bush, like Christmas lights strung irregularly around it.

Zone 6 / 3 ft. to 4 ft. high / 2 ft. to 3 ft. wide / very fragrant / white / reliable repeat

'Alister Stella Gray'
1894

Not much is known about the history of this rose, except that it was bred in England by a man named Gray and introduced by William Paul's nursery. Presumably it is named for a member or members (surely Alister is a man's name and Stella a woman's?) of Gray's family. The name is both too long and too little descriptive to catch on easily, and for years this rose was known familiarly by the common name of 'Golden Rambler', which is much more to the point.

'Alister Stella Gray' has buds the dark orange-yellow color of egg yolks scattered in clusters through the equally dark green foliage. When the buds open, the little flowers fade quickly to a warm glow the color of some white wines (a sauterne, perhaps). This rose is another throwback to the *Rosa*

moschata side of the family, with rather primitive little double blossoms in great quantity. One of our rosarian friends calls it "probably the most continuous-blooming rose that I have," and we'd agree that it is right at the top of the list in flower production.

'Alister Stella Gray' is also one of the healthiest of roses, with plenty of foliage throughout the growing season and no unusual disease or insect problems, although, like many Noisettes, it may suffer from blackspot or mildew if not given plenty of sun and air movement.

'Alister Stella Gray' is not one of the largest Noisettes but falls in the middle range at about 7 ft. to 12 ft. It is a perfect subject for a pillar and would look striking with one plant trained up each side of a gateway arch, preferably with a house in a contrasting dark color as a backdrop. Grown as a free specimen in the garden, it will form a soft, loose mound of leaf and flower to 5 ft. to 6 ft. high and almost as wide. 'Alister Stella Gray' carries a typical good Noisette scent, which seems to be a blend of many things but is always strong on the musk, so it's nice to plant this rose within convenient smelling distance.

Since 'Alister Stella Gray', 'Jeanne d'Arc' and 'Champneys' Pink Cluster' are of much the same style and habit, they would make a memorable picture if planted together as a pale gold, white and pink group. Such an arrangement would be especially effective in the corner of a garden large enough to allow the roses to reach their full size and be seen in perspective from a distance. 'Alister Stella Gray' is of a color that mixes well with dark red roses, too, so it would make a handsome focal point as a pillared or trellised rose behind a group of crimson Chinas.

Zone 7 / 8 ft. or more / fragrant / white / reliable repeat

Bourbon Roses

The study of rose breeding provides some fascinating sidelights on human history. On the Ile de Bourbon (now renamed Réunion) off the coast of Madagascar in the Indian Ocean, the French colonists of the early 19th century commonly planted hedges and windbreaks of two kinds of roses. The preferred varieties were *Rosa chinensis* (either 'Old Blush' or 'Slater's Crimson', depending upon your literary source) and 'Autumn Damask', both of which had the trait of blooming more than once a year. This charming and practical habit of forming hedges from sturdy remontant roses must have made the Ile de Bourbon a delightfully colorful place, and we would probably know nothing about it were it not recorded as part of the history of the Bourbon roses. This snippet of information may not be as important historically as the date of a famous battle, but it is uplifting and offers both precedent and inspiration to a gardener wondering whether an attractive rose hedge would be a suitable way to enclose her yard.

The first of the Bourbon roses was discovered in 1817 by Monsieur Bréon, director of the Royal Botanical Gardens on the island. According to the account of a contemporary, the rosarian Loiseleur-Deslongchamps, this rose "appeared naturally at the base of a hedge of the property of M. Édouard Perichon and since it seemed to present several unique characteristics, M. Bréon dug it up and transplanted it to the botanical garden....Three months after M. Bréon replanted his rose it flowered and since he had found it at the base of a mixed hedge of Bengals [China roses] and Damasks and also judging from the characters that it possessed, he

formed the opinion that it was the result of a Bengal having been fecundated by a Damask." (From an account in *The American Rose Annual*, 1953.)

In 1819 Bréon sent seeds of the new rose to a Monsieur Jacques who was gardener to the King at the Château de Neuilly. The new type of rose was quite different from the ordinary China roses, so French horticulturists gave it the name of 'Rosier de l'Ile de Bourbon', and the breeders went to work with it. The rose reached England by 1822 and was in the United States by 1828. In 1844 Philadelphia nurseryman Robert Buist recorded in his book *The Rose Manual:* "It is about six years since we predicted that this group of roses would be the most popular of the 'Queen of Flowers'." His foresight did not fail him, for good Bourbon roses continued to be produced at least into the early 20th century ('Gipsy Boy', or 'Zigeunerknabe', was introduced in 1909) and were so admired that their bloodlines were bred into the Hybrid Perpetuals and thus into our modern Hybrid Teas.

Plant Characteristics

The original Bourbon rose had flowers of a rich, deep rose color with many rounded petals in an interlocking, or imbricated, pattern. These petals reflexed backward as the flowers opened fully, creating a globe. The broad, slightly tough-looking leaves were a healthy blue-green, and the bushy plant was of compact and vigorous habit. Old records show that the first gardeners to grow this variety coddled it as if it were delicate. They soon gave up, however, because with too much tender loving care it was likely to take over the garden.

The Bourbon varieties that we have included in this book retain many of the fine qualities of their early parent. They are husky, vigorous shrubs with full, richly colored flowers that have an old-fashioned cupped and often quartered form and more than their fair share of potent fragrance. Bourbon roses combine the best of two worlds, with their handsome, heavy flowers reminiscent of the old European garden varieties like Gallicas and Damasks but with silkier, thinner petals and the remontant bloom habit of the China rose. Their scent is also a combination, but it is distinctively their own, and some rosarians state that Bourbons have the most intense true rose fragrance of any class.

Culture

The majority of Bourbon roses are remontant, and we do not describe the few exceptions here. They tend to bloom profusely in the spring (usually at least two good displays in our Zone 8 garden before the heat of summer slows them down), and then they put on a smaller show of their very finest flowers in the fall. This final blooming is produced mainly on the long new canes that grew in the spring, so it is well worth saving these leggy shoots even if they look awkward and seem to beg for pruning. The entire plant can be cut back in the early spring, by one-third to one-half if it is being grown for a shrub, or just the dead and twiggy growth removed if it is being used as a pillar or pegged specimen. In the words of British rosarian Graham Stuart Thomas (*The Old Shrub Roses*), "these Bourbons are all vigorous bushes, and it is little use trying to keep them down." We have found this to be quite true. Bourbons seem to have the ambition to reach their full height every growing season, pruned or not, and we have discovered that they bloom reasonably well even if their clipping is overlooked.

Bourbon roses do wonderfully well in the South because of their China blood, and a number of varieties can still be found in old southern gardens. They do tend to get some blackspot if planted in poor soil, but if conditions are to their liking, disease will rarely be a problem. Ideally, they want rich, well-drained soil, open air, at least six to eight hours of sun and periodic deep watering. They will tolerate the full strength of our summer sun without either leaves or blossoms burning and without the color of the flowers fading. Due to the Damask influence, Bourbon roses are also reasonably cold hardy and can be grown outdoors through Zone 6 and possibly even colder (depending upon the microclimate).

Landscape Uses

The Bourbon roses available today are characterized mainly by varieties with a leggy growth habit, such as 'Madame Isaac Pereire' and 'Honorine de Brabant'. These varieties can fill a number of niches in the garden: They can either be trained as small climbers for pillars, lampposts or trellises, or they can be pruned back and used as shrubs. We have found Bourbons to be the best varieties for pegging, though the long new shoots will make the plant look a little peculiar and out of control until they are no longer too tender to risk bending them down for fastening.

The smaller, chunky varieties such as 'Souvenir de la Malmaison' and 'Kronprincessin Viktoria' are eminently suitable for container gardening or use in a more confined area of the garden. Given the variety of Bourbon growth habits, there seems little need to do without their rich and scented flowers somewhere in the garden. The only trouble is, in the words of Thomas Affleck (*Southern Nurseries Catalog for 1851 and 1852*) that: "The Bourbon, a charming family of roses, 'now almost perfect,' forms a group of beauty most difficult to select from."

Selected Bourbon Varieties

'Souvenir de la Malmaison' 1843

Empress Josephine did not grow this rose herself at Malmaison, for she was dead by 1814, but it was named in honor of her passion for roses and the wonderful garden she made of them. Roy Shepherd records in *The History of the Rose* that a Russian grand duke obtained a specimen of this rose following his visit to the late Josephine's garden, and that he is responsible for having changed its name from 'Queen of Beauty and Fragrance' to 'Souvenir de la Malmaison' when he introduced it to the Imperial Garden in St. Petersburg. This Bourbon rose deserves the tribute implied in either name, for it is remarkably fine.

Both 'Souvenir de la Malmaison' and its climbing sport (introduced in 1893) have identical flowers — large, full and quartered blossoms whose tissue-paper petals are the palest of pinks. This is the quintessential cabbage-type rose, with the advantage of remontancy (the true 'Cabbage Rose', *Rosa centifolia*, blooms only once). The flowers of 'Souvenir de la Malmaison' are perfectly photogenic and frequently win awards at rose shows. They have also been known to inspire authors of rose descriptions to adjectival madness. Our favorite piece is taken from an article written in 1855 for the *American Cotton Planter* about the roses at Troup Hill Nurseries in Georgia. 'Souvenir de la Malmaison', the author writes, has "a face as delicately beautiful and softly tinted as the full-orbed moon rising through those light mists that

float about the horison [sic] of a calm summer sea." Ah, yes. And it is very fragrant, too.

Such perfection is ephemeral, however — rain and high humidity can quickly make a sodden brown mess of the delicate petals. Nature has a way of striking a balance. 'Souvenir de la Malmaison' blooms often enough that a few flowers lost to such balling can be forgiven. The flowers can also be rescued, if one is obsessive, by peeling off the damaged outer petals so they can't trap the rest of the flower in a stiff brown crust.

The bush form of 'Souvenir de la Malmaison' is slow growing and chunky in form, with large, leathery leaves. It will hold its own as a specimen in a small garden or in a tastefully chosen container. It rarely reaches more than 3 ft. or 4 ft. in height, so if planted in a large border it should be near the front so that it doesn't get lost in the undergrowth.

The climbing sport has the same name, flowers and leaves, but reaches 8 ft. to 12 ft. easily and will grow larger with time. The climber has its best display in the fall, but will bloom nearly as often as the

bush (once established for several years) and seems to be less prone to blackspot than any of our other Bourbons. Both bush and climber should be included in any garden that aspires to fragrance, beauty and elegant taste.

Zone 6 / 3 ft. to 4 ft. high / 3 ft. to 4 ft. wide / very fragrant / light pink / reliable repeat

'Zéphirine Drouhin'
1868

Most sources blandly record that 'Zéphirine Drouhin' was raised by the breeder Bizot in 1868. In *The Old Shrub Roses* Graham Stuart Thomas provides further information, citing a report that this rose was found growing wild in Turkey, which adds an element of surprise and mystery to an already attractive plant.

We have no information at all about the identity of the Zéphirine Drouhin for whom the rose was named, but she must have been both enchanted and flattered by the association, because her rose is not only beautiful and fragrant but completely without prickles. There are a number of roses that are nearly "thornless," but they almost always throw out a prickle or two somewhere—at the base of the canes, on the new growth or perhaps under the midribs of the leaves. (Rose "thorns" grow on the surface of the plant, from the cambium layer rather than from the wood beneath, so they are more properly called "prickles.") Even the famous *Rosa banksiae banksiae* has been caught producing an occasional barbed cane, but 'Zéphirine Drouhin' has no blot, as far as we know, on her unarmed reputation.

'Zéphirine Drouhin' grows naturally as a sort of climber, producing many canes 8 ft. to 12 ft. in length from a thick base. The canes are sleek and a rich chocolate-brown in color, with an abundance of dark green foliage that hides them almost entirely from view. The highly visible new growth is wine-purple, making a striking contrast with the vivid cerise-pink flowers. The color combination would be in questionable taste in clothing, but it works remarkably well for the rose. 'Zéphirine Drouhin's' buds are long and shapely, opening to beautifully formed semidouble flowers that have an intense and satisfying fragrance—sweet, spicy and "rosy" all at once.

We had heard that this rose bloomed only once a year, but we were quite happy to find out otherwise. In our garden, 'Zéphirine Drouhin' took three years to get properly rooted out and established, and during those first years we saw only the single yearly flush of bloom we had expected. Once settled, however, 'Zéphirine' began blooming several times each spring and fall, and even in summer there is always a flower or two to admire. We understand that farther north, even in areas of Zone 7, this rose adheres to its once-a-year program, so we feel quite lucky.

'Zéphirine Drouhin' is an extremely workable rose, able to pull its weight as an eye-catcher in any sunny location. We have used it as a pillar rose with great success. (It's the pillar in the foreground in the photo on the facing page.) The lack of prickles makes it very pleasant to train, even though it grows so thickly that it has to be taken down and thinned out almost every year. We also have a beautiful specimen fanned out on a pale grey picket fence. It gets minimal care because it is hard to reach. 'Zéphirine Drouhin' needs no pruning except to thin the number of canes and remove any dead wood, but it can be cut back and encouraged to grow as a large and showy bush.

Zone 6 / 8 ft. or more / very fragrant / medium pink / remontant

Stephen Scanniello

'Madame Isaac Pereire'
1881

'Madame Isaac Pereire' appeared when Bourbon roses were at the height of popularity, at the same time as the Hybrid Perpetuals and just before Hybrid Teas began to hit their stride. Undoubtedly 'Madame Isaac Pereire' was an asset that helped the class stay in favor for a longer time. It was introduced by a breeder named Garçon and named in honor of the wife of a French banker—a fairly bourgeois-sounding beginning for a strikingly beautiful rose.

The flowers of 'Madame Isaac Pereire' are inspiring when they are at their best in the cool weather of spring and fall. They begin as petal-packed, quartered cups of deep rose madder shaded with purple lights, and reflex as they open so that the final stage is a big globe of petals turned inside-out. At their worst, muddled and smaller in a warm spring or during the summer, these flowers are still among the most intensely fragrant in the rose world. It is possible to forget completely all the "slings and arrows of outrageous fortune" as long as your face is buried in a scented bloom.

The bush that accompanies these wonderful flowers is far less refined and requires a little thought to cope with. The canes are leggy—too long and lax for proper upright growth, but not really long enough to qualify 'Madame Isaac Pereire' as a climbing rose. The foliage is large and typically Bourbon—a little rough and somewhat prone to blackspot.

Some gardeners prune this rose down to a manageable size and keep it compact, cutting off the ungraceful whips of new growth when they unbalance the bush. This is probably how it was handled to achieve the bush in the photo above, shown with its paler sport, 'Madame Ernest Calvat'. 'Madame Isaac Pereire' can be trained as a moderate pillar rose to good effect, or it can be used to decorate a section of fence or a low trellis, as long as there is enough sun and air movement to prevent serious blackspot problems.

We find that 'Madame Isaac Pereire' is most interesting as a pegged rose, and it could have been bred for that specific purpose. (It's shown as a pegged rose on p. 53.) The 5-ft. to 7-ft. flexible canes are the perfect length to arch over and pin to the ground, and the horizontal training stimulates extra foliage and flowers as the nutrients and sunlight circulate more evenly to every bud instead of being focused in just the ends of the canes. Pegging requires a little extra fuss and bother, but it transforms 'Madame Isaac Pereire' from a gawky rose with lovely flowers into the *pièce de résistance* of the garden.

**Zone 5 / 5 ft. to 7 ft. high /
3 ft. to 5 ft. wide / very fragrant /
deep pink / slightly remontant**

'Kronprincessin Viktoria'
1887

Crown Princess Victoria was the eldest daughter of Queen Victoria, and to name a rose after her required permission from the Queen and her advisers—a group renowned for caution in their endorsements. As if this mark of approval were not enough, 'Kronprincessin Viktoria' is a sport of the classic 'Souvenir de la Malmaison', so it is royal in blood as well as in name. (As a historical footnote, the name of the rose is probably German in form to honor the German background of much of the Queen's family. Crown Princess Victoria herself went on to become the next to last Empress of Germany.)

'Kronprincessin Viktoria' is a particular favorite of ours because it was first added to our collection as a local foundling and was later identified without any possibility of mistake—a rare occurrence. Our cuttings came from a garden in the nearby, German-settled (quite appropriate) town of Brenham, and the rose was known simply as "Brenham White" for several years. The flowers closely matched the descriptions of 'Kronprincessin Victoria', but the final proof was an unexpected bonus. One of our bushes of 'Souvenir de la Malmaison' fortuitously sported a branch that bloomed with white roses. We knew these to be genuine 'Kronprincessin Viktoria', because it is the only known white sport of that rose. They matched our "Brenham White" to perfection, and we finally knew for certain the true name of our foundling.

Matching found roses to recognized sports is an excellent way to cross-reference and confirm two old roses at once, and one of the few ways to be certain of identity, since the natural behavior of the plant is much more reliable than the variable descriptions found in old rose books.

'Kronprincessin Viktoria' is a small bush. In our garden it grows slowly and rarely passes 3 ft. in height. It is a stocky, open bush with large, rounded, slightly rough leaves that will occasionally develop blackspot in humid weather. The flowers, which are quite rewardingly fragrant, are similar to 'Souvenir de la Malmaison', just slightly smaller and lemon-white rather than pale pink. They seem huge on such a small bush, however. In garden form, 'Kronprincessin Viktoria' is much like 'Souvenir de la Malmaison' (see the top photo on p. 173).

'Kronprincessin Viktoria' can be used to stunning effect as a low border by any gardener who has the patience to grow the small bushes to a uniform size. A very light pruning will encourage growth and fullness without delaying the plant's progress unduly.

We ourselves prefer to grow 'Kronprincessin Viktoria' in a pot. The large, pale flowers are even more dramatic when the plant is set apart by being framed in a container and raised above its natural level. The rose looks good against the softly weathered wood of an old barrel, but it also makes a fine specimen when housed in a colorful pot—bright blue, for example, or a cheerful green. Best of all, when this rose is grown in a container you don't have to bend over quite so far to smell it.

Zone 6 / 3 ft. to 4 ft. high / 3 ft. to 4 ft. wide / fragrant / white / reliable repeat

growth is a wonderful plummy color, which contrasts beautifully with the pale, bluish-pink flowers with darker pink centers, and the leaves have a silvery sheen. The blooms are just as large and nearly as fragrant as those of 'Madame Isaac Pereire', and the two varieties are very handsome together both in the garden and in the vase.

We had originally thought that 'Madame Ernest Calvat' bloomed less often than 'Madame Isaac Pereire', but now that both varieties are mature plants, there is not much to choose between them in enthusiasm. Both are at their best in the fall, when the cool weather encourages the largest and most perfectly formed flowers of the growing season and discourages the tendency toward blackspot. The canes of 'Madame Ernest Calvat' are a little longer, by a foot or two, than those of 'Madame Isaac Pereire', but it is equally suited to training as a pegged rose.

These two varieties combined with the softly striped 'Honorine de Brabant' would made a beautiful grouping pegged together in a bed with some contrasting clumps of perennials in blues, purples and greys. 'Madame Ernest Calvat' can also be trained as a pillar rose or cut back to form an informal bush (as pictured with 'Madame Isaac Pereire' on p. 176).

Zone 5 / 6 ft. to 8 ft. high / 3 ft. to 5 ft. wide / very fragrant / medium pink / slightly remontant

'Madame Ernest Calvat'
1888

Sometimes called the 'Pink Bourbon' (as if there were no other of that color), 'Madame Ernest Calvat' is in fact the sport of 'Madame Isaac Pereire'. It was introduced by the Schwartz nursery in France and is a credit to the directing hand of the widow Schwartz, who was in charge at the time. Madame Schwartz introduced several excellent roses, making her mark in the essentially male-dominated field of 19th-century rose breeding.

There is no information on the identity of Madame Calvat herself, but the rose that Madame Schwartz named for her is lovely. The unique coloring of 'Madame Ernest Calvat', in particular, has inspired some writers to poetic heights. The new

'Honorine de Brabant'
date of introduction unknown

With no date, no parents and no breeder known, it is difficult to place this rose in any historical perspective. All we can do is speculate that Honorine was the same Duchesse de Brabant for whom the beautiful pink Tea rose was named. If so, she was either a much-admired woman or she had some kind of hold over the rose breeders of her day, for both varieties are exquisite.

'Honorine de Brabant' is a cheerfully frivolous rose, bearing flowers of a very soft pink, striped and splashed with violet and mauve. They are medium-sized, double and loosely cupped, with a full measure of the heavy rose fragrance typical of the Bourbon class. The bush is more compact and branching than some of the Bourbons, not too thorny, and well covered with large, leathery leaves.

This rose is the most rewarding striped variety we grow. It is not the most brightly marked, but it blooms steadily throughout the entire growing season (unlike the striped Gallicas) and is remarkably healthy and easy of culture, which can't be said of the Hybrid Perpetual varieties or even of some of the more strikingly colored striped Bourbons.

'Honorine de Brabant' keeps its foliage for us even in the summer. It tolerates neglect and irregular watering and blooms more than any Bourbon except 'Souvenir de la Malmaison'. Its flowers are at their best in the fall, but it is rare to pass the plant at any time without finding a few blooms.

'Honorine de Brabant' is quite flexible in the garden. In spite of the bicolored flowers, it has an overall soft look that blends easily into most settings. It is one of the few Bourbons that will make an attractive bush when grown freestanding, so it can be incorporated into the middle or back of a mixed border or be planted alone as a specimen. With a little selective pruning of side branches, the canes can be trained around a pillar or perhaps an ornamental lamppost. 'Honorine de Brabant' can also be used quite effectively as a pegged rose, accenting the unusual style of training with its unusual flowers.

Zone 6 / 5 ft. to 7 ft. high / 3 ft. to 5 ft. wide / very fragrant / pink blend / remontant

"Maggie"

"Maggie" is a found rose, but it has been registered with the American Rose Society under its study name because there is little likelihood of determining its original identity any time in the near future. This registry means that "Maggie" can be exhibited competitively at official American Rose Society shows, and it also increases the probability that all the nurseries that carry this variety will distribute it under this single, agreed-upon name instead of confusing local variations.

Our original plant of this variety was collected by Dr. William C. Welch, Extension Landscape Specialist at Texas A & M University. He found it in the garden of a Louisiana plantation that his wife's grandmother (the Maggie for whom the rose is named) had purchased at the turn of the century.

Since we have been growing "Maggie", we have found many more bushes of it scattered

nameless through older gardens in Texas and Louisiana. It bears a strong resemblance to the popular old Bourbon 'Grüss an Teplitz', but has a few distinct differences. It bears an even closer resemblance to the less well-known variety 'Eugène E. Marlitt', but here, too, there is a stumbling block. Experienced rosarians have researched the background of both varieties and suggest that whatever it really is, "Maggie" was sent out by nurseries as a substitute to meet the excessive demand for the extremely popular and well-publicized 'Grüss an Teplitz'. Since 'Eugène E. Marlitt' was not listed in southern nursery catalogs of the period, there is a reasonable suspicion that "Maggie" is merely a look-alike of that variety. We must admit that we won't mind if "Maggie" is never identified — the sweet, old-fashioned name it now bears is so much more appealing than any of the alternatives.

The plant is extremely vigorous, throwing out long canes to the height of about 6 ft. or 7 ft. when left unpruned, though it will make a large, well-branched, self-supporting bush after it has been cut back a few times — as were the

three specimens in the photo above. The foliage is healthy and generous, very similar to that of the commonly grown, large-flowered climber 'Blaze', which is probably a near relative. The flowers are double, occasionally imbricated, of a rich carmine-rose that darkens to crimson in cool weather. "Maggie" blooms very freely, answering the need for red roses throughout the growing season both in the garden and in a vase. The perfume is the spicy rose scent of the true Bourbon, and very powerful — especially in a closed room.

"Maggie" can be trained as a pillar rose if the canes are not shortened, and we have seen beautiful specimens nearly covering a 6-ft. tall trellis with foliage and flowers. Our only caution with this rose is that the richer the soil, the larger it gets, so if you treat it well, don't be surprised if you have an 8-ft. or 9-ft. bush on your hands.

**Zone 6 / 6 ft. to 8 ft. high /
3 ft. to 5 ft. wide / very fragrant /
medium red / reliable repeat**

Hybrid Multiflora Roses

The various wild species of Multiflora are spread out across a large area of eastern Asia, including China and Japan. The first commercially distributed Multiflora was collected in China by Thomas Evans of the East India Company and introduced by him in 1804. This rose was *Rosa multiflora carnea*, which we have included under this class heading even though it is technically a hybrid species rose. The introduction of *R. multiflora carnea* was followed not long after by the introduction of another Chinese variety, the Hybrid Multiflora 'Seven Sisters', in 1817. It is quite possible that 'Russelliana', a Hybrid Multiflora of extremely mixed unknown parentage, is related to these double-flowered, pink and crimson Chinese varieties and that all of them can somehow be traced back to *R. multiflora cathayensis*, the wild single-flowered pink form from which *R. multiflora carnea* sported, that was not discovered and introduced until 1907.

It is not the handsome Chinese branch of this family, however, that has had the biggest effect on the rose world. Rather, the single-flowered white *R. multiflora*, described by Helen Van Pelt Wilson in *Climbing Roses* as "no more beautiful than a blossoming blackberry," has a toe in the door, genetically speaking, of at least three later classes of roses: the Polyanthas, the Hybrid Musks and the modern Floribundas. *R. multiflora* is also one of the most important and vigorous of understocks for roses grown in the colder zones of the northern United States.

R. multiflora is known as the Japanese Multiflora, though it is native also to Korea, China and Taiwan. It owes this designation to the fact that it was first described in 1784 by Swedish botanist Karl Peter Thunberg, who was employed as chief surgeon at a Dutch East India Company post in Japan. In *Old Garden Roses*, Edward Bunyard records having seen even earlier evidence of this rose's history in an exhibition of Chinese art. He identified as *R. multiflora* a rose that was shown in its wild state in the background of "one or two drawings" dated about A.D. 1200.

More recently *R. multiflora* has been used as an impenetrable stock fence (often described as "horse high, bull strong and goat tight") and as an embankment planting along highways to prevent erosion. In its natural state this rose grows in sandy and rocky places by streams, thriving in the poor soil, so it is not surprising that *R. multiflora* does well as an independent. It has escaped from gardens where it was originally kept in bondage as an understock and has now naturalized in the United States, especially in the Northeast. We have seen it scattered along the highways on Long Island, in New York, a blooming mass of white in early June, planted by no human hand but altogether giving the impression of a virtuous and valuable weed.

Plant Characteristics

All the wild forms of *R. multiflora* bloom in large clusters, and all the hybrid garden varieties with which we're familiar also show this cluster-flowering trait. Canon Ellacombe, a 19th-century British cleric and rose lover quoted in H.L.V. Fletcher's *Rose Anthology,* recorded that he had once counted more than 600 scented white flowers on a single truss of *R. multiflora.* None of our selections is quite that floriferous, but the class as a whole calls to mind the phrase "dripping with flowers." The individual flowers tend to be on the small side, but the overall display during the spring blooming season is so overwhelming that it justifies the existence of these roses for the rest of the year. Of the varieties described under this heading, only 'Trier' is truly remontant, with 'Veilchenblau' making a small effort to repeat in the fall; the other varieties bloom only once a year.

Members of this class are all scented, but there is no characteristic fragrance—they are all quite interestingly different. Because the Hybrid Multifloras are members of the Synstylae group (distinguished by the styles in the center of the flower being fused into one column), they give off most of their scent from the styles rather than the petals, and the fragrance seems to last longer and carry more freely in the air. (The 'Musk Rose', *R. moschata,* and 'Prairie Rose', *R. setigera,* are also members of this group.)

Culture

Species in the Synstylae group are known for their resistance to blackspot and other fungal diseases, and the Hybrid Multifloras are no exception. We avoid spraying them—they don't need it, and their foliage can be damaged by the stronger sprays. With their tolerance for poor soils, their willingness to cope with drought and even partial shade and their ability to withstand both heat and cold, Hybrid Multifloras are among the easiest of roses to grow.

Hybrid Multifloras are known primarily as climbers, with long vigorous canes and healthy, matte-green leaves that are often slightly downy on the underside. Prickles vary by variety from the dangerously armed 'Trier' to the almost smooth 'Veilchenblau', but on the whole, members of this class should be handled with reasonable caution at pruning time. Fortunately, they need only to have dead wood removed, and perhaps an occasional thinning if they are being grown in a controlled situation.

Landscape Uses

The roses in this class are mostly too vigorous for a small garden, unless there is room to let them expand vertically and perhaps cascade down from overhead. 'Russelliana' is the most compact and, with some thinning of the extra canes, can be grown as a pillar rose. All of these varieties, however, are at their best when given plenty of room to spread.

Hybrid Multifloras are superb roses for naturalizing, whether left to mound along a distant fence or encouraged to fling themselves up onto nearby trees. Their long, limber canes have a naturally flowing look that is particularly attractive when included in the landscape with a water feature such as a pond or stream. These roses are also good choices for dressing garden structures such as pergolas or gazebos. If Hybrid Multifloras are mixed with other varieties that are remontant (Noisettes, perhaps, or climbing Teas), there is never a reason to regret that they are once-blooming. Their single annual display becomes instead a prized event that is remembered and anticipated from year to year.

Selected Hybrid Multiflora Varieties

Rosa multiflora carnea
1804

R. multiflora carnea is actually a hybrid species rose, but it seems more natural to group it here with its close kin than to describe it in the species section of this book. It is a double-flowered form that evolved from the single-flowered *R. multiflora cathayensis*, a rose that is native to China only and is distinct from the more widespread *R. multiflora* in having rather flat corymbs of larger flowers, usually with a pink tinge. *R. multiflora carnea* follows the family tradition in producing strikingly large masses of flowers during its spring bloom, a quality that has made it of interest both in the landscape and for breeding purposes.

This rose was first introduced into England by Thomas Evans of the East India Company, but Empress Josephine soon collected it for her garden at La Malmaison, and it became popular with rose amateurs in France. *R. m. carnea* was well distributed throughout Europe in the early 1800s and made its way at about that time to the United States, where it still lingers in places where it has been left alone and not replaced by more fashionable plants. Multiflora roses, both hybrids and species, tend to be more shade tolerant than many other classes, and we have found them to be extremely self-reliant once they are established.

Of all the rambling Multifloras, *R. m. carnea* has the most liquid lines. The canes are long and

flexible (though they will stiffen into a trained posture with the thickening of age), and in the late spring the massed clusters of flowers are splashed along them like foam. Each flower opens from a tiny peach-pink bud into a neatly shaped reflexed pompom whose layers of cream-colored petals retain a pinkish tinge. The flowers have some fragrance, but it is not outstandingly strong—just enough to keep them from seeming barren. The leaves are a dull, dark green, with a hint of burgundy red in the new growth, and the prickles are sturdy but relatively few in number.

We have heard from other gardeners that *R. m. carnea* prefers a site with rich, well-prepared soil, but we haven't found this to be an absolute requirement. We transplanted one large specimen of *R. m. carnea* from an established bed to a spot out in a mowed field. Having given it this major shock, we promptly forgot all about it in the press of other business. The rose survived, with something of a struggle, on nothing but rainwater and the occasional lawn sprinkling, but a year later it had begun to forge ahead and show great promise.

Because of the long, graceful lines of its canes, *R. m. carnea* is particularly attractive when seen from a distance. It is vigorous enough to grow up quickly through the branches of a tree and healthy enough to be left alone to spill down a bank by a pond or stream where spraying would be an environmental hazard and pruning would be a struggle. This rose also responds well in a formal garden with a mixture of other climbing varieties that are either remontant or have a different season of bloom, and trained on structures such as pergolas and gazebos.

Zone 5 / 15 ft. or more / fragrant / light pink / once-blooming

'Seven Sisters'
1817

There is quite a serious controversy going on in old-rose circles about the identity of the "true" 'Seven Sisters', or more properly, about which of the many available roses labeled as 'Seven Sisters' are not. We are pleased to report that disputants from several sides of the issue have sanctioned the variety we grow as "quite probably the real thing." When the rose was first introduced, it was originally thought to be a species rose and given the Latin name of *R. multiflora platyphylla* or "broadleaf." Our 'Seven Sisters' is distinguished from the other contenders for the name by its very large, broad leaves and deeply serrated stipules.

Much of the reason for the confusion is that 'Seven Sisters' was an extremely popular rose when first introduced from China by Sir Charles Greville. It caught on quickly in France, where it was painted by Redouté, but it was also brought to the southern United States at a fairly early date. We know for certain that it was included as 'Grevillei' in Thomas Affleck's *Southern Nurseries Catalog for 1851 and 1852.*

'Seven Sisters' naturalizes well and we have seen surviving specimens in abandoned areas, but not many of the "true" variety in cultivated gardens. This is mainly the fault of nurserymen who, at least through the turn of the century, seem to have capitalized on the name and sold every cluster-flowered rose available to them as 'Seven Sisters'. As a result, most gardeners today who are familiar with the name from their grandmothers' gardens have differing memories of the rose's appearance.

For the record, 'Seven Sisters' is not a bush, it does not repeat its bloom and its flowers are neither red nor white. It is a vigorous, somewhat prickly climbing rose that bears clusters of small (2-in.), fragrant flowers. These are more interesting than beautiful, varying in number of petals from semidouble to double and in color from carmine through mauve, pink and cream as they fade. Since the buds in each cluster open at slightly staggered intervals, all the tones of color can be present at one time, with each flower a separate shade. It was this trait that led to the name of 'Seven Sisters', though there are rarely exactly seven flowers in any one cluster nor exactly seven different colors.

In the spring this rose is a show-stopper, so thickly covered with flower clusters that the large leaves are almost hidden. 'Seven Sisters' needs a fair amount of space to grow, but planting it at a distance from the house is no problem since it doesn't need a lot of care. It is a wonderful rose for naturalizing — if allowed to go its own way the plant will fill up a high fence corner and swing its long canes gracefully over the other side or scramble up onto nearby trees. We know one person with a small yard who simply cuts this rose down with a lawn mower once a year, after the bloom, to keep it at a reasonable size. We would rather see it used where such drastic measures are not needed, but the heavy pruning doesn't seem to bother this plant at all.

'Seven Sisters' is also a good rose to train up a pole and across a rope or chain to form swags. It is healthy and hardy enough to need no spraying or extra care, and the heavy extravagance of the spring bloom can change any structure into the semblance of a romantic Victorian postcard.

Zone 6 / 15 ft. or more / fragrant / pink blend / once-blooming

'Russelliana'
before 1837

'Russell's Cottage Rose' is the most familiar pseudonym for this variety, which suggests a history of garden friendliness that the correct (*Modern Roses 9*) name can't offer. Nothing is known of 'Russelliana's' origin or parentage, other than the obvious conclusion that it was somehow connected with a person by the name of Russell. Other names under which it can be found in the rose literature are 'Old Spanish Rose', 'Scarlet Grevillea' (from the relationship to 'Seven Sisters') and 'Souvenir de la

Bataille de Marengo', suggesting that it was fairly widely distributed across Europe.

Gwen Fagan, author of the marvelous book *Roses at the Cape of Good Hope*, attests to a broader distribution of 'Russelliana', reporting that it is "by far the most frequent red rose" in her part of Africa, and that remnants of hedges of this variety can be found in areas settled over 200 years ago by French colonists. Fagan speculates that 'Russelliana' was the source of scented petals for rose conserve

and salted roses, export items from South Africa even before the 19th century.

'Russelliana' would certainly be our pick of roses for standing up to heat, cold, drought, disease and neglect. Its dark green, rough, deeply nerved leaves have a bluish-purple bloom of good health. We have seen them turn a little yellow in very alkaline soil, but we have never seen any other symptoms of distress. This rose is considered to be disease free, and some of the wisest breeders of modern roses

are working to get 'Russelliana' characteristics back into the common gene pool.

The flowers are medium-sized (2½ in. to 3½ in. in diameter), flat and very double, and are produced in clusters that usually have three or four blossoms open at one time. They show the mixed heritage of this variety, with a Gallica trait of fading from magenta-crimson to a greyish-mauve color and a potent fragrance that is reminiscent of Damask roses. 'Russelliana' blooms fairly late in the spring, making a crimson spectacle of itself about the time that most other roses have

finished their first flush, so it gets a great deal of attention from visitors to our gardens.

With a little judicious pruning of low and extra-long canes (and removal of occasional suckers) we have succeeded in growing one plant of this rose as an arching bush, the centerpiece of a perennial bed. It remains handsome during all seasons, displaying flowers in the late spring and wonderful coarse foliage through the summer and fall. In winter the bare architectural lines are exposed to view and create an effective point of focus.

'Russelliana' can also be allowed to stretch itself as a climbing rose for a pillar or trellis, forming, as Philadelphia nurseryman Robert Buist wrote in *The Rose Manual*, "a mass of glowing beauty from pinnacle to base." In our garden, the canes have rarely exceeded 8 ft. in length, perfect for training as a restrained climber, though we understand that with time 'Russelliana' can reach a rampant 20 ft. and be sent up into trees.

Zone 6 / 5 ft. to 8 ft. high / 4 ft. to 7 ft. wide / fragrant / mauve / once-blooming

'Trier'
1904

Peter Lambert, the German breeder who created 'Trier', produced some of the most outstanding white roses in several different classes at the turn of the 20th century. The Hybrid Tea 'Kaiserin Auguste Viktoria' (1891), the Hybrid Perpetual 'Frau Karl Druschki' (1901) and the Polyantha 'Katharina Zeimet' (1901) all came from Lambert's nursery and were all important roses, though perhaps none had as much impact on the breeding of future generations as did 'Trier'.

A vigorous white rambler, 'Trier' was a seedling of 'Aglaia', which in turn was the product of a cross between *Rosa multiflora* and the Noisette 'Rêve d'Or'. 'Trier' was used extensively by the Reverend Joseph Pemberton in the development of the Hybrid Musk class and later by Wilhelm Kordes in the breeding of the Shrub rose class. The Lambert nursery did not survive World War II, but 'Trier' commemorates the town where it was located, and it continues to be used in breeding efforts by foresighted growers.

'Trier' looks like a wild rose, growing in a large tangle of canes that are well armed with sharp, curved prickles. The leaves are comprised of many small, blunt leaflets, and the flowers are also small (about 1½ in. in diameter). They are borne in clusters and open from pink-tinged buds into semidouble blossoms of pure white with a central tuft of gold stamens.

Both the fragrance and the fertility of this rose are immediately obvious. The strong musky scent carries in the air quite a distance from the plant, and each cluster of white flowers develops into a cluster of small, bright reddish-orange hips. Since 'Trier' repeat-blooms on a regular basis, displaying a flush of snowy flowers five or six times over the course of the growing season, blossoms and hips will be on the plant at the same time. The hips linger well into the winter and can be used in late-season flower arrangements for a touch of bright color.

There is no need to warn gardeners not to deadhead the spent blossoms on this rose — it would be much too great an undertaking to dream of attempting (and would remove the developing hips as well). 'Trier' tends to grow into a foothill, if not a small mountain of a rosebush, building up 6 ft. to 8 ft. in all directions. With thinning and trimming, it can be trained as a climber in a controlled garden setting, but it is an ideal rose for naturalizing at the boundary of garden and woods or along a pasture fence. The canes will show some dieback at the ends that should be trimmed off after the winter, but 'Trier' is really quite cold hardy and, for us, rarely gets damaged significantly by either frost or disease.

A nice compromise between limited garden space and a desire to grow this large, musky and enthusiastic variety would be a planting of 'Trier' by an unattractive shed or small outbuilding. In three or four years the shed would become a mound of rose with a door pruned into it, full of birds' nests and visually at one with an informal garden environment.

Zone 5 / 8 ft. to 12 ft. high / 6 ft. to 8 ft. wide / fragrant / white / remontant

'Veilchenblau'
1909

'Veilchenblau' translates from the German as "violet blue," and this rose has also been known as the 'Blue Rambler' in both England and America — possibly because it was the closest thing to that color available in a climbing rose. 'Veilchenblau' is not really blue at all, but that crimson-mauve shade that was so popular in the Old Garden Roses and then fell out of favor with the development of the orange-red Hybrid Teas. This rose comes by its intense coloring naturally, as the product of a cross between the Hybrid Multiflora 'Crimson Rambler', which had been collected in Japan in 1893, and the Hybrid Setigera 'Souvenir de Brod', from 1886, whose flowers were a blend of crimson, cerise and purple.

Interestingly, from the time 'Veilchenblau' was introduced by the Schmidt nursery up until the middle of this century, and perhaps even later, it was described in rose books with an apology for its blue tint. The very thing that made the variety special also made it unfashionable. 'Veilchenblau' can be found in old gardens from Texas to Australia, but mainly because it was used as an understock for a while and it is quite vigorous enough to outlast any graft.

We have grown very fond of 'Veilchenblau', but that is only to be expected given our style of gardening with a combination of roses and perennials. The long, rather stiff canes need almost no pruning and are virtually thornless. The foliage is bright green, healthy and neatly pointed, and the clusters of small, crimson-purple flowers blend nicely with the other colors in our gardens and do so much better than any garish orange-red rose could hope to do. Each flower in a cluster is slightly different, for the flowers not only open at staggered intervals so that each is at a different stage of fading to a lovely violet-blue, but they also display irregular streaks of white on just a few of their petals. All the flowers have the same white center and bright yellow stamens, and the distinctive sharp apple scent that is characteristic of this rose.

We have a plant of 'Veilchenblau' (shown in the photo at left) braided up a rough cedar pole that forms one of the supports for a long, rose-covered pergola. It is quite late-blooming, in May or even early June for us, so it helps to prolong the display as part of this planting of mixed climbing-rose varieties, some remontant and some not.

'Veilchenblau' is supposed to bloom only once, but we occasionally see some flowers on it in the fall. We have thought of twining it over an arch with a grapevine so that purple clusters of flowers would be followed by bunches of grapes in late summer and then by a few more purple flowers in the fall. With 'Veilchenblau's' apple scent, it would make a very fruity arrangement. 'Veilchenblau' also makes a good naturalized hedge, as shown in the photo on p. 42. Other gardeners have recommended combining 'Veilchenblau' with pale yellow or white varieties, such as the Noisettes 'Jeanne d'Arc' or 'Alister Stella Gray', or even with the late-blooming species rose *Rosa moschata*.

Zone 5 / 12 ft. or more / slight fragrance / mauve blend / once-blooming

Tea Roses

In *The Southern Nurseries Catalog for 1851 and 1852*, Thomas Affleck wrote of Tea roses that "They are looked upon by lady amateurs as the most perfect of all—and deservedly so." "These are really the cream of the Rose world—they are the nobility, the upper ten…," observed Duncan Gilmour in his 1887 book *Rose Growing*. Such polished compliments tend to make it sound as though Tea roses are too sophisticated to grow in just any old garden, but they are actually among the least demanding of plants.

Tea roses take their name not from high teas with dainty cups, lace gloves and lightly buttered scones but from the days of the opium trade with China when everyone was familiar with bulk amounts of aromatic, loose, dried tea. The original name, Tea-scented roses, was shortened over time, but even today some controversy remains about the unique and allegedly tea-like perfume of these roses. As John Fisher explains in *The Companion to Roses:* "Opinions are divided as to whether it recalls that of fresh tea, the cases in which tea leaves have been packed, or the dried leaves themselves; indeed, some experts claim not to have detected any resemblance in the scent of these roses to tea of any form."

Students of the chemical nature of fragrant oils put Tea roses in the orris category. (Orris is the iris root that is ground and used as a fixative for potpourri.) However you name it, the scent of Tea roses is memorable—dry and cool rather than sweet; rich without being cloying.

Both the fragrance and the large petals characteristic of most Tea roses are inherited from their ancestor *Rosa gigantea*, the wild Tea rose. Native to southwestern China and Burma in the foothills of the Himalayas, this species lives up to both its name and its surroundings by climbing to heights of 30 ft. to 50 ft. and producing huge, five-petaled, creamy-white flowers of blowsy beauty along its well-armed canes. The pastel coloring and the broad prickles were also passed on from this side of the family, but the Tea roses' most important trait, remontancy, was the gift of their other parent, the ubiquitous *Rosa chinensis*.

The first cross of these two species to turn up in the West was 'Hume's Blush Tea-Scented China'. Apparently, this rose was sent to Sir Abraham Hume in 1809 by his cousin Alexander, who was the head of the East India Company's tea factory in Canton, China. The second such cross to move west was 'Parks' Yellow Tea-Scented China'. It was collected for the Royal Horticultural Society by John Damper Parks, who shipped it from China in 1824. These two varieties are the stud roses of the Tea class, just as 'Old Blush' and 'Slater's Crimson China' are the studs for the Chinas.

Unfortunately, these Tea parents, especially 'Hume's Blush', are now so rare as to be almost extinct. If they are still growing anywhere, it seems most likely to be in Bermuda, which was well provided with roses by its English settlers. Bermuda's climate allows for no dormancy period, and it is primarily the heat-loving Teas, Chinas and Noisettes that have survived there. Bermuda is far ahead of most countries in paying attention to its foundling roses and has led the way worldwide in reregistering some of these orphaned plants under the quaint and informative common names by which they are known to the islanders, while continuing to research the roses' original identities. 'Hume's Blush' and 'Parks' Yellow' have been identified tentatively among the numerous old Teas that are still thriving in the nooks and crannies of the island's gardens.

Plant Characteristics

Tea roses as a class are well suited to any southern climate (roughly Zones 7 through 10) and can be found in warm areas around the rose-growing world—especially in countries colonized by the English during the 19th century. They bloom in cycles, producing flowers on new growth at about six-week intervals throughout the growing season. Teas do not require dormancy at all, so it is no hardship for them to perform for a nine- or ten-month growing season (or year-round, as in Bermuda). Near the colder edges of Zone 7, some Teas can occasionally be damaged or even frozen to the ground by an unusually severe winter cold snap (temperatures below 10°F for more than a day or two), but if they are established own-root plants they will almost always return vigorously from the root. In Zone 6, Teas can be grown in the garden in carefully sheltered areas, perhaps near a south-facing wall, and with some winter protection.

In defense of the cold hardiness of Tea roses, Elizabeth von Arnim wrote in 1898: "There is not a German gardening book that does not relegate all Teas to the hothouse. I rushed in where Teutonic angels fear to tread, and made my Teas face a northern winter. They did face it, however, under fir branches and leaves, and today are looking as happy and determined to enjoy life as any roses, I'm sure, in Europe." (From *Elizabeth and Her German Garden*, quoted in Anne Scott-James's *The Language of the Garden*.) For gardeners who yearn for Teas in the colder areas of the North, they can be grown in containers (large ones, for these are large bushes) and brought into shelter for the winter, or they can be encouraged to bloom year-round in a greenhouse.

The new foliage of Tea roses is beautiful, displaying various shades of dark, bronzy red—a trait that is shared with some varieties of China roses. The prickles of Tea roses can be quite attractive, too, especially the broad red "thorns" along the new growth. Not all Teas are heavily armed, but a number of them have enough of these sturdy prickles to inspire caution when handling.

Unlike the China roses, which seem to grow at a steady and even pace, new plants of Tea roses, though willing to bloom often, have a habit of seeming to squat and wait for the first year they're in the garden before putting on a major flush of growth. Presumably, though one doesn't like to disturb them by digging down to look, the Teas spend this time putting down a solid root system. After two years, they will be quite as large as if they had grown in a more balanced fashion, and from this point on they maintain a fairly stable rate of growth.

There seem to be two different shapes among Tea rose bushes, especially noticeable when the plants are very young, that might be attributable to separate breeding influences. One group, including such roses as 'Safrano' and 'Maman Cochet', grows in a spreading, side-to-side pattern at first. The other shape, typified by 'Monsieur Tillier', is more erect and stocky. By the time the bushes are mature, the differences in form are so slight as to be unnoticeable, but it is helpful for beginners to know that their "uniform" hedge of Tea roses might look as if it contains specimens from two different classes for a while.

Culture

The culture of the Tea class is simplicity itself. Tea roses enjoy a good, richly organic, well-drained soil, but they won't fuss too much if it is heavy in clay. (Clay holds nutrients, which they like, whereas sandy soil does not.) They are remarkably free of disease if they get a good amount of sun (six to eight hours at least) and plenty of free air movement. We have a large bed of Tea varieties exposed to the full heat of the Texas sun on a fairly breezy hill, and they give one of the best, most trouble-free performances in our gardens.

Though many other writers have already said the same thing, it is worth noting again that Tea roses do not like hard pruning. A little trimming is good, as is cleaning out awkward branches and dead wood, but if a Tea rose gets cut back by much more than one-third, it will go into a serious sulk and not bloom heavily again until it has gotten over it. (One friend of ours records a 'Duchesse de Brabant' that stayed angry with her, she says, for three years.) Teas have a wonderful natural form, full and broad and well branched, so there is no hardship in letting them reach their potential. They make good large bushes, almost as wide as they are tall, and cover themselves with a garden's worth of flowers. A few varieties with very double flowers will tend to ball in high humidity, but most open cleanly.

Landscape Uses

Tea roses mix well in beds with other roses and perennials, and they also make outstanding specimen bushes when placed alone in the landscape. They can be grown as an informal hedge or trimmed into a constantly blooming foundation planting around a house, deck or porch. All of the Teas hold their own as cut flowers, lending themselves to soft, voluptuous arrangements like those in old paintings. And all of the varieties we describe are scented, though to differing degrees.

Selected Tea Varieties

'Bon Silène'
before 1837

The breeder of 'Bon Silène', J.A. Hardy, was not a professional nurseryman but the curator of the Luxembourg Gardens in Paris. He must have been an amateur in the true French sense of the word, a lover of roses, for he bred several varieties and he is noted for the particularly interesting cross of a species rose and a near relative of the rose, *Hulthemia persica*. The resultant plant, *x Hulthemia hardii*, is beautiful but difficult to grow. 'Bon Silène', which was also an adventurous experiment at the time Hardy created it, is beautiful and easy to grow. It must have been one of the earliest Tea rose hybrids, for the original Tea parents, 'Hume's Blush' (1809) and 'Parks' Yellow' (1824), had been available for only a few years before the new variety, 'Bon Silène', came on the market. It is the oldest Tea variety that we have grown, and one of the most classic in form and behavior.

The flowers of 'Bon Silène' show the influence of *Rosa gigantea* in their long, shapely buds of a deep rose color. The open petals reflex and twist, and their effect is showy even when the sun has had a chance to fade them a little. The effect of a bush of this variety in full bloom is quite as striking as anything the modern rose world has to offer. An interesting point to note is that the rosy petals are veined with a slightly darker pink, as are those of the China rose 'Old Blush'. The parents of 'Bon Silène' are not recorded, but it seems quite possible that 'Old Blush' was somehow included in the mix. 'Bon Silène' has been an active and productive rose parent itself, and the well-liked Tea rose 'Papa Gontier' is credited to its line.

We find 'Bon Silène' fairly often in cemeteries in many different parts of the South. It is always a big, healthy bush with plenty of good-sized, double, deep pink flowers. It is obviously hardy under conditions of neglect and varying climate, and we have never seen any disease problems in either cultivated or independent plants. The Tea scent is not overpowering, but it is definitely present, just as the flowers themselves, although not perfect, seem to be always present throughout the growing season.

'Bon Silène' is a natural to stand alone as a specimen plant, for it can be seen and enjoyed from a distance as well as close up. In our garden it took a year or two to get established, but the amount of time can vary. A correspondent in Florida wrote to tell us that her plant had been christened "the rose that ate the garden," because it had grown to 6 ft. high by 4 ft. wide in less than a year.

Zone 7 / 4 ft. to 6 ft. high / 3 ft. to 4 ft. wide / fragrant / deep pink / reliable repeat

'Safrano'
1839

Though its parents are unknown, 'Safrano' is recorded by Roy Shepherd in *The History of the Rose* as "the result of that first successful attempt to control parentage by hand pollination." In other words, the pollen of one rose was dusted by human effort onto the stigmas of another rose, and the breeding parts were covered so that nature (in the form of breezes and insects) could not interfere with the result. Previously, most crosses, even those such as 'Champneys' Pink Cluster' with known parents, were assumed to be the result of placing the desired bushes near each other and letting nature handle the pollination.

'Safrano' is probably the best known of the older Teas. It can be found in many old southern gardens and on many old graves. The specimen in the photo above is at least 100 years old and probably receives little care. 'Safrano' is also found throughout Australia, New Zealand, South Africa and Bermuda—anywhere that a warm climate will support its constant bloom. It is tough, disease resistant (though there are some reports of mildew on 'Safrano' on the foggy

West Coast) and handsome, and requires little care to bloom throughout the season. The flowers are only really beautiful in the fall and spring, when the long, shapely fawn-colored buds open into semidouble blossoms of buff apricot. (The summer sun fades this delicate color to a rather dull beige.) The pale, tawny flowers show up perfectly against a background of dark green foliage with plum-red new growth.

'Safrano' is an excellent rose for the landscape because of its large, full, bushy shape and elegant coloring. Many lovers of old roses who first bought this rose for its history have since discarded it for varieties that are prettier up close, but nothing can improve upon a bush of 'Safrano' seen at the proper perspective of a slight distance.

'Safrano' looks good against any dark background, from shrubbery to black wrought-iron fences to brick walls. We planted it on either side of the entrance to the public library in nearby Navasota, Texas, and in spite of scanty maintenance and heavy traffic, the bushes are

developing into an attractive feature that repeats the mixed buff and brick red of the building and softens the stiff architectural outline. 'Safrano' responds well to the very lightest of pruning and shaping—"tidying" would be a better term for the minimal clipping it prefers—and gets better with each year's growth.

There is a good sport of 'Safrano' called 'Isabella Sprunt', named after the daughter of Reverend James Sprunt of Kenansville, North Carolina, who introduced the rose in 1855. 'Isabella Sprunt' is equal to 'Safrano' in every feature except that the flowers are sulfur yellow instead of buff apricot. Its effect in the landscape is both lighter and brighter than the more quietly colored original. Both roses have a pleasant Tea scent.

Zone 6 / 4 ft. to 6 ft. high / 3 ft. to 4 ft. wide / fragrant / apricot blend / reliable repeat

Glen Austin

'Sombreuil'
1850

Unlike most climbing Tea roses, 'Sombreuil' is not a sport from a bush form. It seems to have developed as a complete entity rather than as the alternative form of another rose. Of course, this observation is true only if we can be sure that the 'Sombreuil' in commerce at present is the same plant that Monsieur Robert introduced in 1850.

In *Old Roses* Ethelyn Keays describes the 'Sombreuil' that she collected as "blooming in large clusters on a very sturdy bush." Half a century later, we are growing a variety that goes under the same name but never has more than three buds in a group, more often single blooms, and grows vigorously to 10 ft. or 12 ft. Mrs. Keays' description of the individual flowers, however, matches our bush quite well: "full, fragrant bloom...a fine expanded form...strongly textured petals stand in excellent order." There is nothing quite like 'Sombreuil', so it is hard to believe anyone would confuse it with another rose or, worse still, forget it entirely and reintroduce a different plant under this name.

The word *sombreuil* means "darkness" in French, but this rose has flowers that are discs of light. Large, white and flat (the size and shape of moon pies, for an analogy from the South), the flowers are full of petals that overlap neatly into sections and curve like the feathers on the neck of a dove. Their fragrance is potent, very Tea, rich and dry, and the stems are long enough to make 'Sombreuil' a good cut flower.

'Sombreuil' is a good rose for a pillar—the sturdy canes are just the right length for braiding to the top of a 6-ft. or 8-ft. post, and the broad, dark green leaves make a dramatic backdrop for the large, white flowers with a pale cream tint at the heart. Be warned, however, that 'Sombreuil' is well armed with a full set of wide, sturdy prickles down the length of each cane. This is a rose that is best trained with gloves on both hands. We grow 'Sombreuil' not only as a pillar, but also in a more relaxed style, fanned out and woven casually through the picket fence surrounding a cottage garden.

'Sombreuil' doesn't require spraying (it never seems to catch any fungal diseases, though it does occasionally shed its foliage under heat stress), so it can be planted in the back or middle of a bed without worry. It needs no pruning, except to remove any dead or unwanted canes. And 'Sombreuil' has the unique quality of looking beautifully old-fashioned set amongst old-fashioned flowers or very highbred amongst Hybrid Teas—a useful and versatile rose.

Zone 7 / 10 ft. or more / very fragrant / white / reliable repeat

'Duchesse de Brabant'
1857

If you live in a warm climate and can have only one rose, it had better be this one. 'Duchesse de Brabant' is a classic. Even the alternate names of 'Comtesse de Labarthe' and 'Comtesse Ouwaroff' (from later introductions of the same rose) acknowledge its right to high title. This rose was introduced to our collection some years ago as "Adella," a foundling propagated from the garden of a woman of that name. But 'Duchesse de Brabant' is so distinctive a rose that it was one of the very first to be identified under its true name by visiting rosarians.

One of the best-known legends about 'Duchesse de Brabant' is that it was the favorite flower of President Teddy Roosevelt. In 1920 J. Horace McFarland (editor and rosarian) wrote to Roosevelt's widow, Edith, asking for details. He printed her reply in *The American Rose Annual* that year: "My husband's favorite rose was a very old-fashioned one, which I have found it impossible to get of late —

the Duchesse de Brabant her name is. He associated it with his mother's garden and mine. In White House days he usually wore one in the buttonhole of his grey coat — as DeCamp painted him. In the portrait, a blue bowl of the same rose is on the table."

Fortunately, most growers of old roses now carry 'Duchesse de Brabant', and the rose is easy to obtain. It is a fairly typical Tea in its vase-shaped habit of growth, but the apple-green foliage is slightly wavy, giving a soft look to the full, healthy bush. This is the perfect background for the cupped flowers of soft pink that have a cabbage-like roundness to them, as if they were picked straight out of one of those luscious old rose paintings. In bloom nearly continuously, the flowers can be counted on for a rich whiff of fragrance at any time of the day, even under the hot Texas sun. 'Duchesse de Brabant' has to be one of the most fragrant roses available, brimming with the rich, cool scent so typical of the Teas. It

is an excellent cut flower and looks even prettier when fully open than it does as a bud.

In the landscape, 'Duchesse de Brabant' is the perfect specimen plant, attractive from a distance as well as close up, and more resistant to disease and cold than almost any other member of its class. It displays the classic Tea form shown by 'Monsieur Tillier' (see p. 200) and 'Rosette Delizy' (p. 206).

There is a sport of 'Duchesse de Brabant', a variety called 'Madame Joseph Schwartz', that was introduced in 1880 and is cream white with just the faintest wash of apricot pink. It is equally as tough and as beautiful as the original variety, and the two types are lovely together in both the garden and the vase.

Zone 6 / 4 ft. to 6 ft. high / 3 ft. to 4 ft. wide / very fragrant / light pink / reliable repeat

'Marie van Houtte'
1871

We can't help visualizing the unknown lady for whom this rose is named as a most formidable woman. 'Marie van Houtte' is still to be found in a number of old gardens, and we have never seen a weak-looking specimen. There are almost as many unidentified yellow Teas with pink edges as there are unidentified red China seedlings, but if a particular yellow and pink Tea is so vigorous that it makes us a little nervous, we find that there is a good possibility it will turn out to be 'Marie van Houtte'.

'Marie van Houtte' is theoretically a bush rose, and it can be grown easily that way with a little selective pruning. It has an interesting tendency, however, to throw out occasional 6-ft. long canes, and if these are not pruned off, it can be trained as a bushy, healthy pillar.

The flowers are large, double, straw yellow or cream with darker yellow centers and a lilac-pink wash around the edges. True to their class, the flowers of this rose will gradually blush to an all-over pink in the hot sun. (A mark of China blood?) The foliage is healthy and dark olive-green, shows no tendency to disease and covers the bush nearly to the ground.

'Marie van Houtte' makes a handsome and low-maintenance specimen plant and would also do well as a hedge. It is a little too vigorous to recommend as a container plant, but there is a very similar rose that grows on a more restrained scale and is thornless to boot. This rose is 'Mrs. Dudley Cross', introduced in 1907. 'Mrs. Dudley Cross' averages 4 ft. in height and width compared to the 6-ft. dimensions of a well-grown 'Marie van Houtte'. The flowers of 'Marie van Houtte' are a little larger and, in our garden, seem to have a few more petals, but both varieties have the pink edges and the cool scent of Tea and both make excellent cut flowers.

'Mrs. Dudley Cross' looks very pretty in a large container, and we have seen it used to great effect as a softening touch by the front door of a slate-blue clapboard farmhouse. It blends well with other roses and perennials in a mixed bed, especially in a smaller yard. 'Marie van Houtte', on the other hand, has never looked better (to our eyes) than it does as a huge bush spilling over the white board fence by the entryway to our office. It is part of a mixed planting of once-blooming species roses and a few remontant types. The result is an incredible all-over spring flush with continued summer and fall bloom at irregular intervals along the entire fence line.

Zone 7 / 5 ft. to 7 ft. high / 4 ft. to 5 ft. wide / fragrant / pink blend / reliable repeat

'Perle des Jardins'
1874

Yellow roses have a reputation for weakness, disease problems and lack of fragrance. They didn't get this reputation from the yellow Teas but from the modern crosses that have the bright yellow color and blackspot susceptibility of their odd-smelling parent, *Rosa foetida*. The yellow Teas are not cold hardy, but apart from that they are as tough and highly fragrant as any gardener could desire. 'Perle des Jardins' was, in fact, once the most popular of all yellow roses, grown in mass quantity in greenhouses to meet commercial demand.

Here in the deep South, 'Perle des Jardins' belongs out in the garden rather than under glass. It can be hurt by an unexpected freeze, but it always seems to come back vigorously from its diminished state.

As proof of general hardiness, we have found this rose (or seedlings of it) in many locations throughout Texas. At one point we had four different foundlings, all yellow Teas and all nearly identical: "Ode Yellow" and "Jessie Mae" (named for the gardeners) "Seguin Yellow Tea" (named for the city), and "November Surprise" (named for the amazing display of yellow roses that caught the attention of a rustler in late November). 'Perle des Jardins' was sold so widely in the late 19th century that it would be no surprise if some nurseryman had run out of stock and substituted the most similar roses he had. If these foundlings are different varieties, however, the only clue is that some seem to have more prickles and some have fewer.

'Perle des Jardins' has fat, very double flowers that are nicely shaped as buds and often quartered when fully open. The color is a dark canary yellow in cool weather, pale straw under the sun's heat, and the Tea scent is quite strong when the flowers are first open. The foliage is thick and dark green and, with the encouragement of very light pruning, covers the plant almost to the base. The flowers are so large and noticeable that some gardeners will want to deadhead the spent blooms—the petals tend to cling and they turn brown as they fade. Also, because the flowers are so double, they may ball in damp conditions. Fortunately, the rose blooms so regularly that a few spoiled flowers are no great loss.

'Perle des Jardins' is well named "pearl of the gardens," because it makes a charming and distinctive specimen plant whether in the landscape or in a container. It displays the classic Tea form shown by 'Monsieur Tillier' (see p. 200) and 'Rosette Delizy' (p. 206). A well-grown bush will provide all the yellow roses any one person, even a Texan, could want and will do so throughout the growing season. Best of all, there is a climbing sport of 'Perle des Jardins' that bears the same name and the same fat, fragrant flowers. The climber is hardier than the bush and makes a very satisfactory substitute for that sometimes finicky favorite, 'Maréchal Niel'.

Zone 7 / 3 ft. to 5 ft. high / 2 ft. to 3 ft. wide / fragrant / medium yellow / reliable repeat

'Souvenir de Thérèse Lovet'
1886

A classic, old-style Tea rose with a more modern color, 'Souvenir de Thérèse Lovet' resembles 'Bon Silène' repainted red. This rose is a crucial link in a long and distinguished line of great Tea roses that began with the first variety to be created outside China. That first Western Tea rose was named 'Adam', not because its breeder was gifted with the foresight to predict a whole new race of roses but because that was his own name. 'Souvenir de Thérèse Lovet' was a seedling of this 'Adam' and a parent of the handsome rose 'Général Galliéni', which was, in turn, a parent of vivid little 'Rosette Delizy'. As genealogists admit, blood will tell.

'Thérèse' (no disrespect to the wife of breeder Lovet, but the name is too long for familiarity) has good-sized flowers that are quite double but open like those of 'Bon Silène' to show the central stamens as the petals reflex and twist. When the flowers are freshly open, the color is that of dark, ripe cherries, lightening by only a shade or two in the full sun. This is a rose that will satisfy any craving for red, but with a soft, rich look instead of a harsh color. Foliage is plentiful, and the bush has the classic full, shapely form of the sturdiest Teas.

'Thérèse' is not a rose that is easy to find in American nurseries. We got our start from budwood sent to Louisiana rosarian Cleo Barnwell through the director of the National Garden in Sweden, who probably collected it at the Sangerhausen Rosarium in what was then East Germany. Our experience is that 'Thérèse' makes a very good-looking pot plant for several years but grows too big to stay in a container forever. We have planted it in several places, but our favorite bush is the focal point in a fence-line garden that gets little care. We often forget to water it, but it rarely lets us down. Its landscape form closely resembles 'Bon Silène' (see the photo on p. 192).

'Thérèse' blooms quite often throughout the growing season and has never shown any trace of disease or freeze damage. This is the sort of plant for which the Heritage Roses nursery in California has coined the term "an independent rose." Once established, 'Souvenir de Thérèse Lovet' acts as though it needs nothing more from humans than their appreciation.

Zone 7 / 4 ft. to 6 ft. high / 3 ft. to 4 ft. wide / fragrant / deep red / reliable repeat

'Madame Antoine Rebe'
1890

We got our start for 'Madame Antoine Rebe' from the same source as our 'Souvenir de Thérèse Lovet'—from the Sangerhausen Rosarium in East Germany by way of Cleo Barnwell and the director of the National Garden in Sweden. It is exciting to think that after 40-odd years of restriction, a rose garden of this importance (the Sangerhausen Rosarium is the largest rose collection in the world) is once again accessible to rosarians from all over the world. If 'Madame Antoine Rebe' and 'Souvenir de Thérèse Lovet' are examples of the treasures laid up there, the gene pool of good roses available for improving the breed will be valuably increased.

'Madame Antoine Rebe' is not to be found anywhere in the South—in fact, we think that Cleo Barnwell, in her life-long habit of searching for and rescuing good roses, is responsible for its first introduction into the United States. We have been unable to find any references to this rose in English-language rose books or catalogs, so it seems quite likely that our grandparents were deprived of its beauty.

The buds of 'Madame Antoine Rebe' can be strikingly perfect, fat and high-centered. As they open, the deception is revealed—there are only about eight or ten petals, but they are artistically positioned, slightly separated and shaped like the curved ends of the handles of silver spoons. The color is a rich scarlet with a bloom on it like good silk, so that the flowers can appear dark pink when seen from one angle and crimson from another.

The bush is strong, angular and rugged with plenty of foliage to back up the heavy flushes of very lightly scented flowers in spring and fall. 'Madame Antoine Rebe' is an outstanding specimen plant, very undemanding in its requirements for care and with a presence that manages to be intense and subtle at the same time.

Its landscape form is the classic Tea shape of 'Monsieur Tillier' (see p. 200) and 'Rosette Delizy' (p. 206). 'Madame Antoine Rebe' is a rose that will not appear to its best advantage next to other roses, because the flowers require more than a quick glance to reveal their unique beauty. We prefer to see it used as an accent, the way the French used the beauty spot, to draw the eye to a certain part of the garden or a particularly handsome line of fence that might otherwise go unnoticed. It's a good rose to plant by a garden pond, too, where its simplicity will quietly accent the peaceful feeling of the water.

Zone 7 / 4 ft. to 6 ft. high / 3 ft. to 4 ft. wide / fragrant / red blend / reliable repeat

'Monsieur Tillier'
1891

'Monsieur Tillier' is one of a pair of roses that are inextricably connected. The other half of the pair is 'Général Schablikine', another good Tea that was brought out by the well-known French nursery of Nabonnand just one year after Bernaix, the most important commercial growers of Lyon, introduced 'Monsieur Tillier'.

The two roses do not look exactly alike, and anyone who is familiar with both can easily tell them apart. The rose we call 'Monsieur Tillier' has flowers with more shades of color in them and a very double, rather flat shape when fully opened. The rose we call 'Général Schablikine', on the other hand, has flowers with fewer but more shapely petals that stay in the purple/pink range, lacking the strong hint of copper that characterizes our 'Monsieur Tillier'.

The difficulty in identifying these two roses is that on our side of the Atlantic they are sold one way, and on the European side their names are reversed. As to who is right, well, neither side knows. It is remotely possible, though we hate to admit this, that since they had the roses first, the Europeans may have them the right way around. But it is much too late to change what everyone is used to, so be aware of which side of the Atlantic you are ordering from when you purchase either of these roses.

'Monsieur Tillier' has been a stalwart performer in our garden and has long held a secure position both as a specimen rose and as a member of a softly multicolored bed of Tea roses (it's the only bed at the display gardens designed to have nothing in it but roses). Its distinctive flowers are only of medium size, but they seem to be always present on the neat, sturdy bush. They are very double, with petals that are crowded together in a pattern that is not quartered but imbricated, or overlapping. The color can include shades of salmon and rose, sometimes darkening to purple or fading to coppery pink, and the typical cool Tea scent is present as the flowers first open.

The effect of the bush in full bloom is bold and strongly defined, so it contrasts well with "softer" looking roses like 'Duchesse de Brabant' and 'Perle des Jardins'. 'Monsieur Tillier' will always stop the eye in any garden setting. It can be used equally well close to a house as a foundation planting or at some distance, either to disguise an unattractive necessity like a propane tank or to break up and enhance a plain building.

Zone 7 / 4 ft. to 6 ft. high / 3 ft. to 4 ft. wide / fragrant / pink blend / reliable repeat

'Maman Cochet'
1893

It is impossible to read the names of old roses and not get interested in their human connections. In the case of 'Maman Cochet', the name is a guarantee of quality, because Mother Cochet was the matriarch of the famous family of French rose breeders that spanned several generations and introduced some of the finest roses of the 19th century. Breeders seem to save their best roses to name after royalty or their own family members, and there are several roses with the Cochet name, but 'Maman Cochet' is the most beautiful.

'Maman Cochet' is the result of a cross between the vigorous 'Marie van Houtte' and shapely, pink 'Madame Lombard'. We had heard that 'Maman Cochet' was not as strong as other Teas, so we experimented by planting the tiniest rooted slip we had, about the size of a pencil, in a bed with established Tea roses 3 ft. to 4 ft. high to see how it would fare. It got neither more nor less care than the established plants and had to fend off the same grasshoppers and other plagues that sweep through our pasture-bounded gardens.

After one year the slip had formed a very small bush, less than 12 in. in height, and produced one flower. The second year it shot up 18 in. and increased considerably in width, growing in the open, side-to-side fashion typical of certain Teas. We dared to prune the bush lightly at that time, just for shaping, and from that second year it has pulled its weight with the other roses in the bed.

Joyce Demits

'Maman Cochet' blooms as often as the other Teas, but it doesn't have quite as many flowers. No doubt this is because each of its flowers is a work of art and requires more energy to produce. The buds of this rose are beautiful. Large, high-centered and pale porcelain-pink, they satisfy lovers of the Hybrid Tea as much as they do old-rose aficionados. The slowly opening, orris-scented flower keeps its shapely form as it exposes a center of slightly deeper pink. The very base of each petal is lemon yellow, but the flowers are very double, so it is rare to see into them that far. The dull, dark green foliage contributes to the matte beauty of the flowers, so that the whole bush looks like a fine piece of painted but unglazed china.

The specimen in the photo above has reached 'Maman Cochet's' maximum height of just over 5 ft. Our plants of this rose rarely reach more than 3 ft. in height and make a good Tea for container gardening even in the warm South. One bush artistically placed on a flagstone patio (perhaps in an unglazed pot of cream-white clay) would make the difference between blandness and elegance.

A note of caution: Old roses with very double flowers are susceptible to balling in conditions of high humidity, and 'Maman Cochet', with its many delicate petals, is no exception. This rose may not be the perfect choice for gardens on the coast.

Zone 7 / 3 ft. to 5 ft. high / 3 ft. to 4 ft. wide / very fragrant / pink blend / reliable repeat

'Madame Berkeley'
1899

We know very little about the history of 'Madame Berkeley', only that it was introduced by the Bernaix nursery in 1899. There seems to be no record of its breeding or use in gardens or even of the lady for whom it was named. We are quite sure, however, that of all the apricot Teas 'Madame Berkeley' is our favorite.

For some reason of genetics, Teas are the only Old Garden Roses to bear apricot-colored flowers. Pink and white, China crimson and Gallica purple, even yellow, if you count a few Persian roses, can be found in the other Old Garden Rose classes, but not the tawny shades of buff and apricot. Perhaps this elegant coloring contributed to the extreme popularity of Tea roses as much as did their long-budded, graceful flowers.

'Madame Berkeley' has both lovely color and handsome shape. The lightly scented flowers are very double, long in the bud and attractively irregular upon opening fully. The petal arrangement is not exactly quartered but somewhere between quartered and the high-centered form of a Hybrid Tea. The color is apricot with a warmer salmon in the center and a touch of gold at the very base of each petal. The summer flowers are not as good as those of spring and fall — smaller and pinker and not as distinctive — but 'Madame Berkeley' can be forgiven since it is so perfect during cooler weather.

It takes a year or two for this rose to develop a good bush. 'Madame Berkeley' belongs to the spreading, slightly angular and open group of Teas, but once established and lightly shaped with the pruning shears, it will make a full and handsome plant that flowers very freely. In garden form 'Madame Berkeley' will resemble the 'Bon Silène' shown in the bottom photo on p. 192, though it is somewhat smaller.

The reason we prefer 'Madam Berkeley' to more upright and sturdy apricot varieties such as 'Mademoiselle Franziska Krüger' is hard to pinpoint exactly. It seems to be a question of balance and proportion. Their flowers are nearly identical for us, but they look more lovely on the slender stems of 'Madame Berkeley' than on the stiffer, thicker stems of the other rose. Also, 'Madame Berkeley' looks wonderful growing in a soft mound in a bed spilling over with old-fashioned perennials — and there are no hard edges to disturb the overall feeling of lushness.

One of the most attractive ways to use this rose, and apricot Teas in general, is in contrast with dark red roses. The two colors are elegant together, whether in a vase or in the garden. A few bushes each of 'Madame Berkeley' and 'Cramoisi Supérieur' arranged in a bed or alternated irregularly along a wrought-iron fence ought to improve property values in the neighborhood. The same handsome effect can be achieved by growing both varieties in half barrels.

Zone 7 / 3 ft. to 5 ft. high / 3 ft. to 4 ft. wide / fragrant / apricot blend / reliable repeat

The flowers are in balance with the size of the bush — big fat cabbages of silvery rose that darken to cerise in the heat of the summer sun and hide a touch of buff at the base of the petals. They are enormous in spring and fall, very double and cupped and full of the refreshingly cool scent of Tea. 'Mrs. B.R. Cant' can make a great difference in the landscape and should have a place of honor either alone or in the center of a bed. This is the sort of plant that will make the neighbors think of you as someone who grows roses, even if you have only one bush in the yard.

'Mrs. B.R. Cant'
1901

We hear this rose called 'Mrs. R.B. Cant' more often than not, even when the name is being read directly from the label. Since we have been practicing on it for many years, we never get it wrong (any more), but it may help others to keep it straight if they know that Mrs. Cant was the wife of Benjamin R. Cant, owner of one of England's greatest rose nurseries. Cant's of Colchester has bred and sold roses since 1765, and Benjamin R. was responsible for most of the firm's achievements during the 19th century, including a silver cup at the very first National Rose Show in 1858. The rose named for his wife was introduced just five years before Cant's death, and perhaps it took him that long to create just the right one. At any rate, he chose well, because the rose is unforgettable, and the lady's name will always be remembered (more or less accurately) because of it.

'Mrs. B.R. Cant' is not suitable for a small garden. This rose makes such a large plant that it's almost a whole garden by itself. For the first two years it will seem out of balance, too open and leggy; but once it reaches 6 ft. in every direction, the proportions come together as they should. Since 'Mrs. B.R. Cant' is a Tea, there is no point trying to prune it back hard to keep it under control, because it will just sulk and refuse to bloom well. With a light shearing once or twice a year, it can be kept at 5 ft. or 6 ft., but if room is available 'Mrs. B.R. Cant' will be happy to grow to 8 ft. up and sideways and bloom in an equally expansive style. It's clearly not a container plant.

'Mrs. B.R. Cant' is very healthy and vigorous, but it can be damaged by unexpected freezes if caught in full bloom, and the petal-packed flowers will often ball in extreme humidity. It needs plenty of sun and space to grow and to show what it can really do. Most years, 'Mrs. B.R. Cant' is the first, or among the first, of our roses to bloom, presenting us with a flower or two right after St. Valentine's Day.

Zone 7 / 6 ft. to 8 ft. high / 5 ft. to 7 ft. wide / very fragrant / medium pink / reliable repeat

'Lady Hillingdon'
1910

'Lady Hillingdon' is the result of a cross between 'Papa Gontier' and 'Madame Hoste', which makes it a granddaughter of 'Bon Silène' and an aristocrat in lineage as well as in name. This rose has remained fairly popular ever since its introduction by the British nursery of Lowe and Shawyer in 1910. It is one of the few old roses that can be found included in gardens of modern roses, usually in its climbing form.

Whether grown as a bush or a climber, 'Lady Hillingdon' is a memorable and distinctive rose. The flowers have long buds and are a vivid apricot, almost orange, when they first open. The color fades to a less-striking creamy white under the full brunt of the sun, so this is a rose that will be better appreciated if it gets some shade in the afternoon. The flowers are semidouble, varying in the number of petals according to the season and the local microclimate. They stay cupped rather than opening fully and have the advantage of rarely balling in humid weather.

There are two things about 'Lady Hillingdon' that are particularly noteworthy, even though they are characteristic of the Tea class as a whole to a lesser degree. One of these qualities is the fragrance. It is the dry, cool Tea scent carried to its most intense peak. Reactions from people who smell it vary. Some are enchanted, some are oppressed. We have heard it compared to everything from ambrosia to airplane glue. The other interesting characteristic of 'Lady Hillingdon' is that the bronze-green foliage produces lush new growth of dark plum purple. The color combination of apricot, bronze and plum is gorgeous and would make this rose a favorite even without the distinctive fragrance.

We have found 'Lady Hillingdon' to be a little slow growing but very healthy, and it is slightly more cold hardy than some of the other Teas. The bush form (which resembles the 'Monsieur Tillier' pictured on p. 200) works well either as a specimen by itself, say at the corner of a house or beside a brick chimney, or in a bed with other roses and perennials. Because of its unusual color, 'Lady Hillingdon' looks best with flowers of blue, crimson and white—yellows and pinks don't quite blend if they are too close to this rose. The climbing sport, introduced in 1917 and shown in the photo below, is very easy to train and presents a stunning picture as an untidy pillar or spilling over a fence—preferably near a garden pond.

Zone 7 / 4 ft. to 6 ft. high / 3 ft. to 4 ft. wide / climber to 15 ft. / very fragrant / yellow blend / reliable repeat

'Rosette Delizy'
1922

Created during the transition from old roses to modern roses, 'Rosette Delizy' is a little of both. The color is more startling, the flower more high-centered than in most of the old Teas, but the bush is full and healthy and gives credit to a lineage that can be traced back through 'Souvenir de Thérèse Lovet' to 'Adam', the first European addition to the Chinese Tea-scented roses.

Rosette is a French word meaning "little rose," and 'Rosette Delizy' is the smallest of Tea bushes, rarely reaching more than 3 ft. in height. The flowers are full-sized, however, and very double and shapely. This rose takes the traditional soft yellow and pink Tea to a new level — the yellow is a heavy ocher and the pink wash a distinct brick red on the petal tips. It is an attractive combination in its way, but one that

takes a little time to assimilate as belonging to an Old Garden Rose. People who are used to Hybrid Teas take to it immediately, whereas those who have been growing pastel old roses sometimes do not like it.

'Rosette Delizy' is a very good plant for a gardener who is thinking of adding old roses to her garden but is not sure about giving up the vivid, high-centered flowers of the labor-intensive Moderns. For one thing, 'Rosette Delizy' is an excellent size for growing in a large container, so if it doesn't fit with the other roses in the garden, it doesn't matter — it can be enjoyed apart.

The large flowers, unusual coloring and good Tea scent make this little rose a natural conversation piece whether it is positioned by the front door or in pots on a patio. 'Rosette Delizy' is one of the few nonwhite roses that looks good in an ordinary orange clay pot, and it would not be out of place in a tile and adobe

home with Mexican decor. Planted out in the garden, 'Rosette Delizy' will draw the eye quickly, and it functions best if it is the focal point of a small bed rather than an unblending intruder in a larger mix of roses and perennials.

We have heard that 'Rosette Delizy' is tender, even for a Tea, but it has so far stood up to even the most unexpected hard freezes in our garden, so we are reserving judgment on its alleged tenderness. We do know that the heavy flowers ball and refuse to open if they get rained on or are subjected to extreme humidity, so consider your climate carefully or be prepared to forgive this unique little rose for its faults before you decide to grow it.

Zone 7 / 3 ft. to 5 ft. high / 3 ft. to 4 ft. wide / fragrant / yellow blend / reliable repeat

Hybrid Perpetual Roses

Hybrid Perpetual roses are a product of jealousy, pure and simple. By the end of the 1830s, Europeans had grown accustomed to the wonderful repeat-blooming roses recently introduced from China, but they were frustrated by the lack of cold tolerance in those varieties. The new Noisette and Bourbon classes had been created from crosses between the China roses and the only remontant old European roses, *Rosa moschata* and the 'Autumn Damask', respectively. Noisettes and Bourbons were also limited in hardiness, however, and couldn't tolerate winters much colder than Zones 7 and 6. It must have been very trying for northern gardeners to see that those in warmer climates had yards full of roses blooming throughout the entire growing season, whereas the cold-hardy roses, lovely as they were, bloomed but once.

Crosses were made between China roses and the old European Gallicas and Damasks, but remontancy is a recessive genetic trait and must be present in both parents to manifest in their seedlings. A large group of Hybrid China roses was created, but these roses also bloomed only once. Breeders in England and especially in France began crossing Hybrid Chinas (particularly 'Gloire des Rosomanes', a Bourbon-China cross, and 'Malton'—both scarlet roses) back with Chinas for more remontant genes, and with Bourbons, Damasks and just about anything else that would hold still, and soon the bloodlines became a wonderful tangle. The breeders did achieve their goal, however, and the Hybrid Perpetual class became a distinguishable group of large-flowered roses with the fragrance and color of the European varieties and at least some ability to flower more than once.

From fewer than 50 varieties in 1843, the class had increased to 150 by 1853 and to more than 800 by 1884. When French entrepreneur and rose lover Jules Gravereaux assembled his renowned garden at l'Hay les Roses in the first few years of the 20th century, he is thought to have included some 1,700 varieties. Hybrid Perpetuals had completely taken over the tastes of the rose-growing world, though there were a number of dissenters in the ranks of rose aficionados. Shirley Hibberd, editor of *The Gardener's Magazine* from 1861 to 1890, wrote in his 1864 work, *The Rose Book:* "This class is like Moses' serpent, it swallows up all the rest; or rather it would do so, were there not always a few resolute rosarians blessed with large and eclectic tastes to save the others from the total eclipse that constantly threatens them. Of their pedigree, who shall tell?"

Hibberd spoke from the position of a man who had Hybrid Perpetuals to waste, whereas the true goal of the breeders who developed the class had been expressed some years earlier by Philadelphia nurseryman Robert Buist. In his 1844 book *The Rose Manual*, Buist explains: "This is a new tribe, that has originated within a few years, between the Perpetual and Bourbon roses, possessing the beauty and fragrance of the former with the growth and foliage of the latter; they produce an abundance of flowers from June to November; they open a field of pleasure to the northern grower and amateur, which had hitherto been reserved only to the fanciers of more favored climes."

Buist was expecting a bit much, both in terms of simple bloodlines and of a long, abundant flowering season, but he pinpointed the once-blooming vs. remontant jealousy issue with no problem at all. It is marvelous what humans can accomplish given the right amount of motivation.

Plant Characteristics

The best feature of a Hybrid Perpetual rose is its flowers. Their bushes tend to be stiff and rather awkward, much taller than they are wide, and are clothed with leaves only about one-half to two-thirds of the way down from the top. Hard pruning—for us this means cutting back at least one-half of the bush in the early spring (mid-February here)—will help the bushes to grow thicker and to produce more flowers, but Hybrid Perpetuals rarely achieve a very graceful form. If we were not so attracted to their flowers, we might well have written them off long ago as not much more garden worthy than the equally awkward Hybrid Teas. The flowers really are glorious, though; large and full and very fragrant, with the rich, subtle colorings that make old roses both so distinctive and so easy to blend into a garden setting.

Culture

With the exception of 'Frau Karl Druschki' and 'Paul Neyron', we have found very few Hybrid Perpetuals lingering in gardens in the deep South. They tend to blackspot more than most varieties of Old Garden Roses, and they can get sickly in the relentless heat of summer. Once established, however, they are remarkably tough, and we know of specimens of 'Frau Karl Druschki' and 'Paul Neyron' that are at least 30 or 40 years old.

The best treatment we have found for Hybrid Perpetuals is to mulch them thickly, water them well and plant them where they will get good morning sun and some afternoon shade. The goal is to keep their roots as cool as possible, with enough sun so that the plant stays healthy but not so much that the flowers burn. Whether or not to spray these roses for blackspot is a choice best left to the individual gardener. An established Hybrid Perpetual is not likely to be destroyed by any fungal disease, but it will definitely look more attractive with its leaves on than off. A light spray of mixed baking soda and water, now available commercially, applied when signs of blackspot first appear, may be all that's required to keep these roses looking their best.

In the northern Zones, Hybrid Perpetual roses have fewer problems. In fact, they are almost the best Old Garden Roses for cold climates. Where they can have an adequate period of dormancy without the stress of trying to bloom for a nine-month season in melting sun, they perform like the champions they were planned to be.

Landscape Uses

We have found two ways to grow Hybrid Perpetuals that satisfy us. The first is to include them in a mixed bed of roses and perennials. The perennials cover up the bare bottoms of the Hybrid Perpetuals, and the changing picture of bloom as each type of plant has its flowering season takes the performance pressure off this class of roses so that their beautiful spring flush and light fall display are enough. The other way to grow some Hybrid Perpetuals is as pegged roses, trained out horizontally over the ground. This lateral positioning of the canes encourages leaves and flowers to be produced at every bud instead of just at the top, and the result can be truly spectacular. We have noticed that if the ends of the canes are in contact with the moist ground, some Hybrid Perpetuals die back at the tips, so we have learned to peg them a few inches above the soil instead.

Selected Hybrid Perpetual Varieties

'Marquise Boccella'
1842

Thanks to the perseverance of the Heritage Rose Foundation, the earliest name of this rose is now documented fairly well as 'Marchesa Boccella'. But this is not the name you will find in most of the rose literature. It wasn't even 10 years after its introduction in France by amateur rose breeder Romain Desprez that the name was corrupted to 'Marquise Boçella', perhaps because there are so few Italian rose names and so many French ones that the original seemed wrong to those who heard it and recorded it. Even in *Modern Roses 9*, published in 1986, research had taken the name back only as far as 'Marquise Boccella', with two "c"s. 'Marchesa Boccella' may be the name that will be found in *Modern Roses 10,* barring further revelations. Also, the rose currently being sold as 'Jacques Cartier' is thought to be identical to 'Marquise Boccella', another source of confusion.

'Marquise Boccella' has survived in a number of gardens in the North (it is quite cold hardy) as well as in the South. Thomas Affleck lists it along with 25 other Hybrid Perpetuals in his *Southern Nurseries Catalog for 1851 and 1852.* He describes it simply as "cupped, pale blush, dwarf, beautiful."

'Marquise Boccella' is distinct among the surviving Hybrid Perpetuals for a number of reasons. One distinguishing feature is the dwarf size that Affleck notes. We rarely see a bush above 4 ft. in height. Whereas many Hybrid Perpetuals tend to be a little leggy and uncouth in their growth habits and need harder pruning than any other of the Old Garden Roses, 'Marquise Boccella' is tidy and compact. Its slender, erect, bristly canes need only to be groomed for dead or weak sections, with a light overall trim in the spring or fall to encourage foliage and bloom.

Another interesting feature of 'Marquise Boccella' is what Graham Stuart Thomas, writing in *Shrub Roses of Today,* calls its "high-shouldered habit." The serrated, slightly wavy, jade-green leaves grow almost up to the base of the calyx, leaving no stem and giving the impression that the flowers have been balanced carefully on the top of each cane like dinner plates on a juggler's poles. The flowers themselves usually come in clusters of one to three and are reminiscent of Damask roses in form, color and scent. Medium-pink buds open to pale pink, cupped and then flat flowers that are a little smaller (2 in. or 3 in. across) than other Hybrid Perpetuals but with an amazing number of narrow petals. The final stage of the flower is almost globular, as the pale petals reflex back to expose a central knot

Malcolm Manners

around a green button eye. The wonderful lemon-and-spice fragrance fades with exposure, so the flowers should be cut for vases just as they are unfolding.

Its compact size makes 'Marquise Boccella' a perfect addition to any small garden or even to a patio container garden. This rose is worthy of inclusion in a fragrance garden as one of the first choices. Our plants show no disease problems if given adequate air and sun, though they sometimes show a dislike of alkaline soil by producing yellowed leaves. Proper organic soil preparation takes care of this simple problem and allows 'Marquise Boccella' to become a very handsome bush.

Zone 4 / 3 ft. to 4 ft. high / 2 ft. to 3 ft. wide / very fragrant / light pink / reliable repeat

'Baronne Prévost'
1842

Introduced in the same year and by the same breeder, Romain Desprez, as 'Marquise Boccella', 'Baronne Prévost' is a testament to the serious nature of amateur hybridization that was popular in 19th-century France. Desprez is also known for the Noisette climber 'Jaune Desprez', but it was his contribution to the class of Hybrid Perpetuals, especially 'Baronne Prévost', that made a place for him in rose history equal to that of some of the famous breeders of the day.

'Baronne Prévost' was the perfect prototype for a class that was just beginning to emerge as separate from the roses then available. It is a vigorous plant with something of the look of old European roses in its coarse foliage, leggy habit and stiff canes arrayed with narrow prickles. 'Baronne Prévost' is a better garden subject than many of the later Hybrid Perpetuals. Though no less susceptible to blackspot and other fungal diseases than most of its kin, the bush tends to be thicker — almost chunky — and well-covered with foliage most of the time.

'Baronne Prévost' was developed before the high-centered flower of the Tea roses had really begun to gain popularity, so the flowers of this variety are the charming old rose style. Each flower is wide (about 4 in. across) and shallowly cupped, almost flat, with a multitude of rose-pink petals arranged in swirls or quarters around a knot at the center. The petals often show a lighter shading of lilac pink that gives the flower more depth and a richer appearance than a solid color alone could achieve. The fragrance is very good, still close to that of Damask roses and not as heavily sweet as that of the later Hybrid Perpetual varieties, which have more Tea and Bourbon influence.

Hybrid Perpetuals in general require more attention than do most classes of Old Garden Roses, and 'Baronne Prévost' will respond beautifully to proper care. If it is given a rich, well-drained soil, six to eight hours of sun a day, plenty of manure tea, a thorough pruning in the spring and the occasional treatment for leaf problems as they occur, we are quite willing to agree with Graham Stuart Thomas (writing in *Shrub Roses of Today*) that there is "no reason why it should not go on for another hundred years."

'Baronne Prévost' has a very definite place in a mixed border of roses and other old-fashioned flowers. It is reasonably free-blooming and will cover itself with scented flowers quite heavily in the spring and fall, with a few blossoms produced at intervals in between. This rose is a little too short and chunky for classic pegging, but the plant shown in the photo above left has been "semi-pegged" by pulling the canes to the side, though not clear to the ground, and securing them at that angle. 'Baronne Prévost' also makes a good specimen plant in its natural shrub form, which is much like that of the 'American Beauty' pictured on p. 212.

'Baronne Prévost' is the ideal Hybrid Perpetual to practice on if you are unsure whether to include members of this class in a collection of Old Garden Roses. Though far from perfect in the landscape, it is one of the best and toughest of its class — a real survivor.

Zone 4 / 4 ft. to 5 ft. high / 2 ft. to 4 ft. wide / very fragrant / medium pink / remontant

'Paul Neyron'
1869

'Paul Neyron', introduced by the French nursery of A. Levet, is the best-known variety of Hybrid Perpetual available today, and it is a good example of the mixed heritage that produced this class. Its immediate forebears are both famous Hybrid Perpetuals ('Victor Verdier' and 'Anna de Diesbach'), but the next generation back includes the important early Tea rose 'Safrano'.

At 7 in. in diameter, the flowers of 'Paul Neyron' are larger than those of any Hybrid Perpetual, perhaps of any rose. 'Paul Neyron' is the one rose most likely to be familiar to gardeners as 'Grandma's Cabbage Rose'. Here in the United States we don't think of the cabbage for its neatly layered, imbricated form that gave a name to the old European *Rosa centifolia* varieties—the official 'Cabbage Rose' of antiquity. Instead, we think of it as a big, fat, impressive vegetable and freely identify it with our biggest, fattest rose flowers. The fact that 'Paul Neyron' is not a Centifolia and therefore not a true Cabbage rose matters not at all. It is enormous, it is heavy, it performs best in cool weather—it has the aura of a cabbage right down to the thick, somewhat coarse petals.

The canes of 'Paul Neyron' are stiff and erect, reaching 4 ft. to 5 ft. in our garden and up to 6 ft. in cooler Zones. Foliage is thick, at least for the top two-thirds of the bush, and the individual leaves are medium green in color and large enough to balance the great flowers. 'Paul Neyron' is often listed as a "thornless" rose, but we've found this to be a relative term. Our plants almost always have a few prickles of good size scattered here and there along the canes, though

rarely on any of the flower stems. This variety is susceptible to blackspot in our garden and will occasionally drop all its leaves as a result. Sometimes we spray it, sometimes we don't. Even if the blackspot is ignored, 'Paul Neyron' will flush with healthy new leaves in its own time.

The large flowers are very double and impressive, and in actual form they resemble tangled peonies more than tidy cabbages. Their color is a rich dark pink so distinctive that the term "Neyron pink" is sometimes used to describe the flowers of other varieties. We find the flowers quite rewardingly fragrant, though to some noses they are just lightly scented. 'Paul Neyron' blooms heavily in the spring, surprises us now and then with a repeat performance in the summer, and saves its largest and most handsome flowers for fall.

Because of its coarse, leggy appearance, 'Paul Neyron' is not a perfect rose in the landscape, but mixed into a perennial border it will be a focus of attention when in bloom and not too noticeable when resting. It can be used effectively as a specimen plant, pegged, or trained on a low trellis or fence by gardeners who are willing to make a special effort to fuss over it, prune it hard, give it extra fertilize and spray it with something now and then—in other words, treat it almost like a modern Hybrid Tea.

Zone 4 / 4 ft. to 6 ft. high / 2 ft. to 3 ft. wide / fragrant / medium pink / remontant

'American Beauty'
1875

We are not certain whether we actually have this rose in our display gardens. Several different varieties of 'American Beauty' are currently in commerce, and the controversy rages hot and heavy about which, if any, is the true historic 'American Beauty'. The original was introduced in France in 1875 by the Lédéchaux nursery as 'Madame Ferdinand Jamain', and was then reintroduced in the United States in 1886 by Bancroft and Field Brothers as 'American Beauty'. In 1925 it was named the official rose of the United States, and nurserymen and florists were apparently unable to resist attaching the highly marketable name to whichever varieties were close enough to pass for 'American Beauty' with a trusting public. We have often heard visitors to our gardens ask to see "that old red

rose, 'American Beauty'," when in fact the rose is and always has been a startlingly intense dark pink.

Our plant of this rose matches the old descriptions very closely. Better yet, in flower at least, it matches the variety called 'American Beauty, Climbing'. (The climbing form is not a sport of the bush — it has different parents entirely — but it does seem logical that the flowers must have been a very close match for the name to have been given to an unrelated variety.) Also, a number of erudite rosarians have looked at our plant and have neither denied that it is 'American Beauty' nor suggested that it is something else.

Our 'American Beauty' is a fine, handsome plant with a stiff, erect bush that fills out over time until it is 4 ft. to 5 ft. tall and 2 ft. or 3 ft. across. The large leaves are rich green, and the canes have only a light scattering of prickles. The flowers are deep, glowing pink — almost cerise — and quite large. They are cupped, very double (about 50 petals per flower) and extremely fragrant. It is easy to see why this rose was such a famous cut variety.

We have heard that 'American Beauty' is difficult to grow and that it is not cold hardy, but we have not had any significant problems with

our variety. It has been sent north as far as Zone 4 with no complaints sent back, and we have found it to be one of the more garden-worthy Hybrid Perpetuals. We cut the plant back by about one-half in early spring (mid-February for us) and give it another, much lighter trimming in early fall (about the end of August). The result is a thick, healthy bush with a decorative load of large flowers that are good in the spring and even better in the fall (though it does not always repeat for us with a full-blown fall show). Summer flowers are a little sparse, as is summer foliage, but on the whole 'American Beauty' is a very rewarding rose to grow. The key with this rose, as with many Hybrid Perpetuals, is to give it a few years to root out solidly and get established before expecting a great performance in the garden.

'American Beauty' does well in a mixed border or as a specimen plant to accent some garden feature. The flowers are striking in arrangements: One of the most vivid antique rose combinations is this rose with 'Frau Karl Druschki', which is sometimes called 'White American Beauty'.

**Zone 4 / 4 ft. to 6 ft. high /
2 ft. to 3 ft. wide / very fragrant /
deep pink / remontant**

'Baron Girod de l'Ain'
1897

The blood of the crimson China roses flows through one branch of the Hybrid Perpetual class, showing up not only in the color but also in the brighter green, smoother and more pointed foliage. 'Baron Girod de l'Ain', introduced by Reverchon in 1897, is one of these China-influenced varieties. It comes by its red blood honestly, if distantly, as a sport of 'Eugène Fürst' which can be traced back through 'Baron de Bonstetten' to 'Général Jacqueminot' and thus to the China 'Gloire des Rosomanes'.

The most interesting feature of 'Baron Girod de l'Ain', however, is not the vivid crimson color but the thin white edges that distinguish the petals. Since the old crimson China varieties often had an irregular streak of white on odd petals here and there, it seems possible that the gene for this trait may have shown up, slightly mutated, in this Hybrid Perpetual. 'Roger Lambelin', another Hybrid Perpetual variety with almost the same genealogy, shows white markings even more strongly than 'Baron Girod de l'Ain', but is a little more difficult to grow.

We acquired 'Baron Girod de l'Ain' as a curiosity, not really expecting this lesser-known member of a rather fussy class to do very well under our laissez-faire system of gardening, but we have been pleasantly surprised. In a few years' time it has developed into a full, compact bush that varies between 3 ft. and 4 ft. in height, depending on how hard we prune it. It has the same erect, stiff canes as other Hybrid Perpetuals, adequately armed with prickles and covered with shapely, bright green leaves.

In the landscape 'Baron Girod de l'Ain' resembles the bush of 'Paul Neyron' pictured on p. 211. 'Baron Girod de l'Ain' does drop foliage from blackspot in the heat of summer, but it recovers quite well and is always well clothed during the spring and fall bloom seasons.

The flowers are borne in compact clusters of three or four, and they are large and very cupped with slightly wavy petals of distinctive crimson-red and an irregular white edging. They are quite charming either on the bush or in a flower arrangement, and they have a good measure of rich sweet fragrance. There is something satisfying about a really red rose (no other flower strikes quite the same emotional chord), and 'Baron Girod de l'Ain' is just the right color both to meet the desire for red and to blend gracefully with other flowers in the garden — something the harsh orange-red modern roses cannot do.

We have this rose planted as a specimen at the edge of a casually landscaped area that has a pond as the focus. We planted it there so that we could pull it out easily when it failed, but since it has surprised us by thriving, we have learned to enjoy its unexpected qualities. 'Baron Girod de l'Ain' would look at home in a formal border, but its simple flower shape and clean rich color are very compatible with the wildflowers, native trees and five-petaled rose varieties that are its near neighbors in the pond area. We are now wondering if, with proper care, this rose might not make a really handsome container specimen, perhaps with white sweet alyssum or silver thyme to fill in at the plant's bare base and trail gracefully over the sides of the pot.

Zone 4 / 3 ft. to 5 ft. high / 2 ft. to 3 ft. wide / very fragrant / red blend / slightly remontant

'Ards Rover'
1898

Ward or *vard* is the Arabic word for rose, and *ard* is a variant that is used in some related Semitic languages. Knowing this, it would be hard to believe that the breeder, Alexander Dickson II, wasn't making a play on words when he named it. He may also have been making a reference to the Old Testament story of Joseph of the many-colored coat. After this biblical hero was reunited with his 11 brothers, they spent time catching up on family news, and the King James Version records that the youngest son of the youngest brother (Benjamin) was named Ard.

Dr. Ruth Borchard (*Oh My Own Rose*) has found an even more detailed version of the story, in which Benjamin tells Joseph of his children, saying, "and the last is called Ard because he is as beautiful as the rose." As recently as 1986, Patrick Dickson, the grandson of Alexander Dickson II, introduced a Gold Medal-winning Floribunda named 'Ards Beauty', so perhaps our idea of the connection in meaning isn't too far-fetched.

'Ards Rover' is one of the very few genuine climbing roses we have encountered in the Hybrid Perpetual class. Its parentage is unrecorded, but it is a variety all of its own and not a sport of any other plant. In our garden, this rose has been surprisingly vigorous, becoming established quickly and

putting on several feet of growth each spring and each fall until it reached 10 ft. or 12 ft. It needs no pruning, except to remove any dead wood, and it is not subject to any severe disease problems, at least in our experience. The large, slightly coarse leaves are rather sparse in summer, but that isn't atypical for any rose in our Zone 8 climate.

The flowers of 'Ards Rover' are almost the most handsome we have ever seen on a red climbing rose. They will satisfy any Hybrid Tea enthusiast with their large size and shapely, high-centered form, and they are a color to please lovers of Old Garden Roses — a rich blush-crimson with a shading of maroon. The fragrance is excellent, rich and dark like the rose itself. Once established, a process that usually

takes about three years for a climbing rose, 'Ards Rover' manages several flushes of bloom in the spring, scattered flowers that show some sun damage in the summer and a restrained (and, for us, not always reliable) but very lovely display in the fall.

We have used this rose as a specimen, braiding it up one of a short row of pillars that accents a gravel path (shown in the photo above). 'Ards Rover' would also look good trained in a fan shape against a tawny stone wall or woven up each corner of a white latticework gazebo in a formal garden.

Zone 4 / 12 ft. or more / very fragrant / deep red / slightly remontant

'Frau Karl Druschki' is a healthy rose for the most part, though it can suffer from an occasional attack of mildew if weather and temperature conditions are right. A light spray of baking soda and water will usually correct this problem, and planting the rose in good, fertile, well-drained soil in a sunny location will help prevent mildew.

Like other Hybrid Perpetuals, 'Frau Karl Druschki' will benefit from a fairly hard pruning in the spring (removing up to about one-half the bush) if it is to be grown as a shrub. The climbing form needs only to be groomed for removal of dead wood, and the shrub form can be allowed to grow out and be trained as a pillar or pegged rose. Many Hybrid Perpetuals, including 'Frau Karl Druschki' make excellent pegged roses, but the canes should be fixed a little way off the ground to prevent dieback at the tips from contact with the moist soil.

Zone 4 / 6 ft. to 8 ft. high / 5 ft. to 7 ft. wide / slight fragrance / white / remontant

'Frau Karl Druschki'
1901

After failing to win a contest for breeder Peter Lambert as the best unnamed rose of German origin at the Frankfurt Fair in 1900 (acquiring the name 'Count Otto von Bismarck' was part of the prize), this perfect white rose was given the name 'Frau Karl Druschki' in compliment to the wife of the President of the *Verein Deutscher Rosenfreunde,* the Association of German Friends of Roses. 'Frau Karl Druschki' became a favorite rose of Edward VII (great-grandfather of Queen Elizabeth II) and was spread widely among growers in Europe and America under its own name and several alternates. "Reine des Neiges" (or "Snow Queen") is the most common listing. This was Lambert's earliest choice and was easier to market than the German name as World War I loomed. In the United States it was also sold as "White American Beauty", and we have seen it hiding behind this name in a group of cheap waxed and burlapped Hybrid Teas at a chain store.

There are two forms of 'Frau Karl Druschki' — the original shrub and a climbing sport introduced in 1906. Both varieties can in fact be trained as climbers, it's just a question of the degree of height desired. The shrub has leggy, moderately prickly and vigorous canes that will easily reach 6 ft. or 7 ft. if allowed to grow to their limit. The coarse, light-green leaves are thick at the top of the plant, though a little sparse near the bottom. This is one of those "bare-shinned" roses that looks more balanced with a bushy underplanting of salvia or rosemary.

The flowers are very shapely, unfurling from carmine-tinged buds in a classic Hybrid Tea, high-centered fashion. Fully open, they are pure white, double (about 35 petals per flower) and quite large, making 'Frau Karl Druschki' a perfect rose for cutting. The flowers last well both on the bush and off, and their only real flaw is the absence of fragrance. It is a comment on their beauty that the flowers of this rose have managed to be so greatly admired when they lack what to us is the most important quality of roses.

"Granny Grimmett's" reintroduced in the 1970s

"Granny Grimmett's" has an unknown past but an interesting recent history. We acquired our start from Siegfried Hahn, an artist and rosarian living in Santa Fe, New Mexico, who was able to get it from Valdemar Petersen's nursery in Denmark in 1977 just before that admirable nursery closed down. The variety seems to be listed nowhere else at all, so we feel very fortunate to be one of the nurseries enlisted by Mr. Hahn to propagate a valuable rose that might otherwise have vanished entirely.

It is quite possible that "Granny Grimmett's" is not the original name of this rose. Not only is it a very homey sort of a name to take its place amongst the "Madames," "Duchesses" and "Générals," but it sounds suspiciously like the tag we ourselves would assign as a study name to an old rose found in Granny Grimmett's garden. If this is the case, there is little hope of ever knowing anything about this variety except that Petersen placed it — quite rightly, we think — with the Hybrid Perpetual class.

"Granny Grimmett's" is a tough, compact bush with very prickly canes and slightly rough, deep green leaves. It is not as lanky as many Hybrid Perpetuals, so it is easier to use in the garden. After "Granny Grimmett's" has had a year to two to get established in good soil, it shows a great resistance to any attacks of disease or insects. It doesn't require a hard pruning, just tidying up now and then, but it will not sulk if clipped back to fit into a chosen niche.

Joyce Demits

The flower color is, to quote the artist donor, "deep, luscious, rich crimson-madder-amaranthe as if straight from the palette of Titian." The flowers are quite double, with a cupped, cabbage-like form reminiscent of the old European roses. The golden stamens are often visible in the center, as is an occasional streak of white on one or more of the velvety petals (signs of crimson China heritage), and the fragrance is wonderful, almost pure Damask in its spicy tang. One of the nicest qualities of this rose is that its flowers hold their color even in the fiercest sun. There may be fewer petals in the blossoms of midsummer, but the dark crimson-red never burns or fades.

"Granny Grimmett's" blooms quite reliably throughout the growing season, though it doesn't always put on a big fall show for us, and its color and fragrance make it eligible for a number of garden uses. In form it is much like the 'American Beauty' bush pictured on p. 212, but more compact. We have grown "Granny Grimmett's" as a container specimen with great success and also as an accent at the corner of a small weathered shed that had no other flowers around. Because of its compact size, this rose would be a good choice for inclusion in a small garden where the emphasis is on fragrance. "Granny Grimmett's" would also look attractive as the centerpiece of a planting of grey or silvery-green herbs.

Zone 4 / 3 ft. to 5 ft. high / 3 ft. to 4 ft. wide / very fragrant / deep red / remontant

Sources for Antique Roses

Antique Rose Emporium
Route 5, Box 143
Brenham, TX 77833
(409) 836-9051

Container-grown own-root roses and companion perennials available by mail order or at the Retail Center/Display Gardens in Independence, Texas. Catalog is $5.

Country Bloomers Nursery
RR 2,
Udall, KS 67146
(316) 986-5518

Mostly own-root roses, some grafted, available by mail order or retail. Send legal-size SASE for rose list.

Forest Farm
990 Tetherow Road
Williams, OR 97544
(503) 846-6965

Species roses grown from seed or propagated from plants grown from seed. Catalog is $3.

Greenmantle Nursery
3010 Ettersburg Road
Garberville, CA 95440
(707) 986-7504

Primarily own-root roses and historic fruit trees. Some varieties budded on virus-free *Rosa multiflora* rootstock. Send legal-size SASE for mail-order rose list of 250 varieties.

Heirloom Old Garden Roses
24062 Riverside Drive NE
St. Paul, OR 97137
(503) 538-1576

Own-root roses and miniatures, primarily by mail order. A good source of David Austin's English roses (see p. 219). Breeding new varieties from Old Garden Roses. Catalog is free.

Heritage Rose Gardens
16831 Mitchell Creek Drive
Fort Bragg, CA 95437
(707) 964-3748

Own-root, field-grown two-year-old roses by mail order. Catalog is $1.

High Country Rosarium
1717 Downing at Park Avenue
Denver, CO 80218
(303) 832-4026

Own-root roses grown from tissue culture and cuttings. Primarily mail order. Catalog is $1.

Historical Roses
1657 West Jackson Street
Painesville, OH 44077
(216) 357-7270

Budded roses on stock selected to be virus free. Send legal-size SASE for mail-order rose list.

Hortico, Inc.
723 Robson Road
RR 1
Waterdown, Ontario L0R 2H0
Canada
(416) 689-6984

Budded roses on clean *Rosa multiflora* rootstock grown from seed. Some own-root roses. Primarily mail-order with retail facilities at above address. Catalog is $2. No import permit required.

Lowe's Own Root Roses
6 Sheffield Road
Nashua, NH 03062
(603) 888-2214

Own-root roses by mail. Order before May 1 for pickup or shipping 18 months later. Catalog is $2.

Pickering Nurseries, Inc.
670 Kingston Road
Highway 2
Pickering, Ontario L1V 1A6
Canada
(416) 839-2111

Grafted roses on clean rootstock available by mail order or at the retail center at above address. No import permit is required, but nursery cannot accept orders from U.S. customers for patented varieties. Catalog is $3.

Rose Acres
6641 Crystal Boulevard
Diamond Springs, CA 95619
(916) 626-1722

Own-root roses available by mail order or at the retail center at above address. Send legal-size SASE for rose list.

Ordering roses from overseas nurseries requires a permit form obtainable from:

Permit Unit
United States Department of Agriculture
PPQ
Federal Building, Room 638
Hyattsville, MD 20782

Imported roses must be quarantined for two years. Roses cannot currently be imported into the U.S. from Italy, Australia, New Zealand or South Africa.

Despite the inconvenience of the quarantine, we recommend two nurseries in England. Their catalogs are fascinating, and they sell varieties not available in the U.S.

David Austin Roses
Bowling Green Lane
Albrighton
Wolverhampton, WV7 3HB
England

Some of David Austin's roses are now available through nurseries in the U.S. Minimum order from the nursery in England is £75.

Peter Beales Roses
London Road
Attleborough
Norfolk, NR17 1AY
England

Minimum order is £50.

Many other excellent sources for Old Garden Roses can be found in the *Combined Rose List* compiled by Beverly R. Dobson and Peter Schneider. Updated annually, the rose list costs $15 and is available from:

Peter Schneider
P.O. Box 16035
Rocky River, OH 44116

Rose Associations

North Texas

The Dallas Area Historical Rose Group is associated with the Dallas Rose Society. Members meet monthly to discuss the collection, preservation and identification of old roses. Membership is $15 per year per family (U.S. and Canada) and includes a monthly newsletter, "The Yellow Rose." Contact:

> Joe M. Woodard
> 8636 Sans Souci Drive
> Dallas, TX 75238

Central Texas and Houston

The Texas Rose Rustlers is the affiliated group for this area. They and the Dallas group pool forces for at least one major rose rustle every year to collect cuttings in different areas. Membership is $7 per year and includes four issues of the newsletter, "The Old Texas Rose." Contact:

> Margaret Sharpe
> 9426 Kerrwood
> Houston, TX 77055

National

The Heritage Roses Group, founded in 1975, is the national organization for the study of old roses. The H.R.G. publishes the "Heritage Roses Letter" on a quarterly basis. Membership is $5 a year and includes the newsletter. For information, contact the regional coordinator in your area:

Northeast:

> Lily Shohan
> RD 1, Box 199
> Clinton Corners, NY 12514

Northcentral:

> Henry Najat
> 6365 Wald Road
> Monroe, WI 53566

Northwest:

> Judy Dexter
> 23665 41st Street S.
> Kent, WA 98032

Southeast:

> Dr. Noel R. Lykins
> 1407 Metcalf Road
> Shelby, NC 28150

Southcentral:

> Karen Walbrun
> Route 2, Box 6661
> Pipe Creek, TX 78063

Southwest:

> Betty L. Cooper
> 925 King Drive
> El Cerrito, CA 94530

> Marlea A. Graham
> 100 Bear Oaks Drive
> Martinez, CA 94553

> Frances Grate
> 472 Gibson Avenue
> Pacific Grove, CA 93950

The **Heritage Rose Foundation,** established in 1986, is the first nonprofit corporation devoted exclusively to the preservation and study of heritage roses. There are plans to establish several test gardens in the near future. Annual membership is $10, which includes a quarterly newsletter. Contact:

Charles A. Walker, Jr., President
1512 Gorman Street
Raleigh, NC 27606

The **American Rose Society** maintains a garden of old roses at their national headquarters, though their primary interest is modern roses. Membership is $25 per year, which includes a monthly magazine and an annual. They also publish *Modern Roses 9.* Contact:

American Rose Society
Box 30,000
Shreveport, LA 71130

Canada

The Canadian Rose Society includes members who are interested in old roses. Membership dues are $18 per person or $20 per family and include the quarterly journal and an annual. Contact:

Dianne D. Lask
686 Pharmacy Avenue
Scarborough, Ontario M1L 3H8
Canada

England

The Royal National Rose Society in England is an excellent source of information with many old-rose experts among its members and a new subsidiary group that specializes in old roses. Membership dues fluctuate with the pound and are now about $17. Dues include a quarterly magazine. Contact:

Royal National Rose Society
Bone Hill, Chiswell Green Lane
St. Albans, Hertfordshire AL2 3NR
England

Australia

Australia's climate allows gardeners there to grow the same varieties of old roses that we do in Zones 7 to 10 in the United States, and they have a very active heritage roses group (Heritage Roses in Australia). Annual dues are $10 (Australian) and include a newsletter. Contact:

Robert Peace
5 Bon Street
Alexandra, Victoria 3714
Australia

New Zealand

New Zealand's climate is also amenable to many of the same roses we grow. Heritage Roses – New Zealand is the group active in that country. Annual dues are $25 (New Zealand) and include a quarterly newsletter. Contact:

Elaine Petrie
Swannanoa Lea, RD1
Rangiora, New Canterbury
New Zealand

Books for Rosarians

Contemporary Books on Roses

It can be difficult to find information about antique roses, especially as many of the classic works such as those by Graham Stuart Thomas and Gertrude Jekyll are now out of print. We have included in the following list some of our favorite books that are currently available.

American Rose Society (Peter A. Haring, ed.). *Modern Roses 9.* Shreveport, Louisiana: The American Rose Society, 1986.

Compiled by the American Rose Society, this "International Checklist of Roses in Cultivation or of Historical or Botanical Importance" has been thoroughly updated. In consultation with heritage rosarians, the A.R.S. has corrected errors that have been around for 50 years. This book is a must for anyone who wants to be accurate about rose nomenclature. Hardcover, 402 pages.

Austin, David. *The Rose.* Woodbridge, Suffolk: Antique Collectors' Club, revised ed. 1990.

A review of 950 varieties of roses by one of the world's leading rosarians. An English nurseryman and breeder who specializes in Old Garden Roses and the new "English" roses, David Austin has put together a thoroughly enjoyable reference work including advice on cultivation and landscaping. Hardcover, 440 pages, over 340 color photographs.

Beales, Peter. *Classic Roses.* New York: Henry Holt & Co., 1985.

Classic roses that have stood the test of time are the focus of this comprehensive book by one of Britain's foremost growers of Old Garden Roses. An insightful text, including rose history, cultivation and landscaping suggestions as well as variety descriptions. One of our favorite reference books. Hardcover, 384 pages, 513 color photographs.

Beales, Peter. *Twentieth-Century Roses.* New York: Harper and Row, 1989.

This is the ideal companion volume to *Classic Roses.* It brings the reader up to date on the best roses introduced since 1985, with a good section on shrub roses. Cultivation and landscape uses are covered in detail. Beales' love of roses shows throughout the book. Hardcover, 320 pages, more than 400 color photographs.

Christopher, Thomas. *In Search of Lost Roses.* New York: Summit Books, 1989.

Horticulturist, adventurer and master rose raconteur Thomas Christopher has researched the renaissance of old roses in modern gardens after they had been nearly lost. This book has great historical importance and is highly readable. Hardcover, 240 pages, no photographs.

Fisher, John. *The Companion to Roses.* Topsfield, Massachusetts: Salem House, 1987.

A fascinating encyclopedia-style book of information on rose-related topics from A to Z. Whether you want to know about rose perfume, the "Yellow Rose of Texas" or how to graft a rose tree, the information is here. Hardcover, 224 pages, many black-and-white illustrations and 24 color plates.

LeRougetel, Hazel. *A Heritage of Roses.* Owings Mills, Maryland: Stemmer House, 1988.

Part of the fascination of old roses is the long trail of history that stretches behind them. This book, the result of 15 years of travel and research, should answer many questions on the "where did it come from, how did it get here" list. It is also excellent on the subject of garden use of old roses, though the information is directed at English gardeners. Hardcover, 176 pages, 50 photographs.

Phillips, Roger and Rix, Martyn. *Roses.* New York: Random House, 1988.

This book features precise information on more than 1,400 varieties of roses, all of them illustrated in breathtaking photos. The virtue of this book is that the roses are photographed in groups, so their relative sizes, shapes and colors are easily understood. Photos of species roses in the wild are another plus. A glossy, coffee-table-size paperback, 224 pages, color photographs throughout.

Scanniello, Stephen and Bayard, Tania. *Roses of America.* New York: Henry Holt & Co., 1990.

The focus on American roses gives this work great interest, especially as it is based on Scanniello's experience as rosarian at the Brooklyn Botanic Garden's Cranford collection. It contains a history of the rose in America, photos and brief descriptions of old and modern roses, an introduction to landscape use and detailed information on pruning and training. Hardcover, 224 pages, over 300 color photographs.

Reprints of Classics in Rose Literature

All these reprints are the work of one small publishing firm, Earl M. Coleman of Stanfordville, New York. We list only a selection of the works Coleman has reprinted.

Ellwanger, Henry B. *The Rose.* 1882. Reprint, 1978.

A man of strong opinion and authority, the author left nothing to chance in his "Treatise on the Cultivation, History, Family Characteristics…of the Various Groups of Roses." Ellwanger remains the authority on Hybrid Perpetuals and his "technical terms" chapter is of value to both novice and veteran growers. Hardcover, 306 pages.

Keays, Ethelyn Emery. *Old Roses.* 1935. Reprint, 1978.

A book of great nostalgic appeal recording the research of a devoted rose lover into the old roses to be found in American private gardens in 1935. Good chapters on early Noisettes, Hybrid Perpetuals and Teas. Hardcover, 280 pages, 29 photographs.

Parsons, Samuel. *Parsons on the Rose.* 1888. Reprint, 1979.

Subtitled "A Treatise on the Propagation, Culture and History of the Rose," this 1888 guide was the most popular book on roses in circulation for over 50 years. The information on cultivation is written from Parsons' own experience and is still valuable. Hardcover, 224 pages.

Paul, William. *The Rose Garden.* 1848. Reprint, 1978.

Lavishly produced in 1848, this volume contains descriptions of over 2,000 rose varieties in addition to information on history and cultivation. Hardcover, 388 pages, 15 color plates.

Shepherd, Roy E. *History of the Rose.* 1954. Reprint 1978.

The original edition of this classic has been out of print for 20 years, but it remains one of the most thorough, informative and readable explanations of the development of the rose. Hardcover, 296 pages, 26 photographs.

Other Gardening Books of Interest

Although not specifically about gardening with old roses, these books are of particular interest because each does an excellent job of expanding on topics we cover in this book.

Boisset, Caroline. *Vertical Gardening.* New York: Weidenfield & Nicolson, 1988.

Climbing roses are prominently featured in Boisset's book, along with some 200 other plants suitable for the vertical garden. Design ideas are enhanced by information on plant cultivation requirements. Hardcover, 144 pages, many color photographs.

Verey, Rosemary. *The Scented Garden.* New York: Random House, 1989.

An informative work with a good section on roses that ties in the history of the rose with the actual plants. Subtitled "Choosing, growing and using the plants that bring fragrance to your life, home and table," this book is wonderfully encyclopedic on the whole question of scent. Hardcover, 167 pages, lavishly illustrated.

Welch, William C. *Perennial Garden Color for Texas and the South.* Dallas: Taylor, 1989.

Dr. Welch brings his many years of experience in landscape design to this valuable and informative reference work that features cottage gardens, old roses and companion plants. An excellent book on perennials. Hardcover, 304 pages, nearly 500 color photographs.

Bibliography

Affleck, Thomas. *Affleck's Southern Rural Almanac and Plantation and Garden Calendar for 1860.* Reprint. Brenham, Tex.: The New Year's Creek Settlers Association, 1986.

————. *The Southern Nurseries Catalog for 1851 and 1852.*

American Rose Society. *The American Rose Annual.* Vol. 38, 1953 and Vol. 68, 1983. Shreveport, La.

————. (Haring, P. A., ed.). *Modern Roses 9.* Shreveport, La.: American Rose Society, 1986.

Beales, Peter. *Classic Roses.* New York: Holt, Rinehart & Winston, 1987.

Borchard, Ruth. *Oh My Own Rose.* Self-published, 1982.

Buist, Robert. *The Rose Manual.* 1844. Reprint. New York: Earl M. Coleman, 1978.

Bunyard, Edward. *Old Garden Roses.* 1936. Reprint. New York: Earl M. Coleman, 1978.

Capek, Karel. *The Gardener's Year.* London: Allen and Unwin, 1931.

Christopher, Thomas. *In Search of Lost Roses.* New York: Summit Books, 1989.

Curtis, Henry. *Beauties of the Rose.* 1850-1853. Reprint. Palo Alto, Calif.: Sweetbriar, 1981.

Dobson, Beverly. *Combined Rose List 1991.* Irvington, N. Y.: Self-published, 1991.

Earle, Alice Morse. *Old Time Gardens.* 1901. Reprint. Detroit: Omni Graphics, 1990.

Ellwanger, H. B., *The Rose.* 1882. Reprint. New York: Earl M. Coleman, 1978.

Fagan, Gwen. *Roses at the Cape of Good Hope.* Capetown: Breestraat-Publikasies, 1988.

Fisher, John. *The Companion to Roses.* Topsfield, Mass.: Salem House, 1987.

Fletcher, H.L.V. *The Rose Anthology.* London: Newnes, 1963.

Fruitland Nurseries Catalog. Augusta, Ga., 1913-1914.

Gilmour, Duncan. *Rose Growing.* London, 1887.

Gordon, Lesley. *Old Roses.* New York: Beaufort Books, 1983.

Hibberd, Shirley. *The Rose Book.* London: Groomsbridge, 1864.

Hole, S. Reynolds. *A Book about Roses.* London: Edward Arnold, 1896.

Jekyll, Gertrude and Edward Mawley. *Roses for English Gardens.* 1902. Reprint. Woodbridge, Suffolk: Antique Collectors' Club, 1982.

Keays, Ethelyn Emery. *Old Roses.* 1935. Reprint. New York: Earl M. Coleman, 1978.

Krüssman, Gerd. *The Complete Book of Roses.* Portland, Ore.: Timber Press, 1981.

Milman, Helen. *My Roses and How I Grew Them.* London and New York: John Lane. 1900.

Nelson, Robert. *The American Cotton Planter.* Montgomery, Ala. 1855.

Parsons, Samuel B. *The Rose: Its History, Poetry, Culture and Classification.* New York: John Wiley, 1860.

————. *Parsons on the Rose.* New York: Orange Judd Co., 1888.

Porter, Katherine Anne. *The Days Before.* New York: Harcourt Brace, 1952.

Prince, William Robert. *Prince's Manual of Roses.* 1846. Reprint. New York: Earl M. Coleman, 1978.

Rivers, Thomas. *The Rose Amateur's Guide.* 1837. Reprint. New York: Earl M. Coleman, 1978.

Scott-James, Anne. *The Language of the Garden.* London: Viking, 1984.

Shepherd, Roy E. *The History of the Rose.* New York: Macmillan, 1954.

Slosson, Elvinia. *Pioneer American Gardening.* New York: Coward-McCann, 1951.

Stevens, G.A. *Climbing Roses.* New York: Macmillan, 1933.

Thomas, Graham Stuart. *Climbing Roses Old and New.* London: J.M. Dent, 1965.

————. *Shrub Roses of Today.* London: J.M. Dent, 1962.

Thomas, Graham Stuart and C.C. Hurst. *The Old Shrub Roses.* London: J.M Dent, revised ed., 1979.

Willmott, Ellen. *The Genus Rosa.* 2 vols. London: John Murray, 1914.

Wilson, Helen Van Pelt. *Climbing Roses.* New York: M. Barrows, 1955.

Index

Editor: Jill Hannum
Designer: Deborah Fillion
Layout artist: Robert Olah
Photographs, except where noted: G. Michael Shoup
Copy/production editor: Peter Chapman
Illustrator: Steve Buchanan

Typeface: New Caledonia
Paper: Influence soft-gloss matte, 70 lb., neutral pH
Printer and binder: Ringier America, New Berlin, Wisconsin